WORKING O

WORKING ON BOUNDARIES

Gunnar Hjelholt and applied social psychology

Edited by Benedicte Madsen and Søren Willert

AARHUS UNIVERSITY PRESS

© Copyright: The Authors and Aarhus University Press, 2006
Printed in Denmark by Narayana Press

Cover design: Jørgen Sparre
Cover illustration: Section of Berit Hjelholt's woollen tapestry
»Spænd over os dit himmelsejl« (2005) photographed by Poul Pedersen
Back cover: Berit Hjelholt's drawing of a young Gunnar Hjelholt (1953)

ISBN 87 7934 255 8

AARHUS UNIVERSITY PRESS
Langelandsgade 177
8200 Aarhus N
Denmark
Fax (+45) 8942 5380

White Cross Mills,
Hightown
Lascaster, LA1 4XS
United Kingdom
Fax: 01524 63232

P.O. Box 511
Oakville, CT 06779
USA
Fax: 860-945 9468

www.unipress.dk

FOREWORD

In his own country, Denmark, and perhaps even more so internationally, applied social psychologist Gunnar Hjelholt was renowned in circles professionally engaged in group dynamics and consultancy work within a Lewinian or Tavistock oriented framework.

In December 2002 this pioneer of applied social psychology died at the age of 82. A memorial conference was held in Aarhus (Denmark) in August 2003 under the auspices of the Centre for Systems Development at the Institute of Psychology, University of Aarhus. With the title *Homage to Gunnar Hjelholt: Working on Boundaries*, the conference was planned and chaired by the two editors of the present book.

The plan and original outline of the book took shape in the context of the memorial conference. Of its three parts, Part One is based on biographical material, collected and presented by the two editors. Part Two includes seven essays written by friends and colleagues of Gunnar Hjelholt, who live in six different countries: Austria, Belgium, Denmark, France, India and Sweden. Most of the manuscripts in Part Two are based on oral presentations given at the conference. Part Three brings seven articles or chapters written by Hjelholt himself during the period 1960-1995. Two of them were originally written in Danish and have been translated as part of the editorial work.

We would like to express our sincere gratitude to the authors of the manuscripts in Part Two, and to the author of the Epilogue, who all consented to invest the necessary time and energy to make this book possible.

We also wish to thank Annie Dolmer Kristensen, our competent secretary at the Institute of Psychology, University of Aarhus, who has given invaluable assistance in the areas of translation and linguistic clarification, and Mary Lund of Aarhus University Press who has been our untiring English language consultant.

The generous financial support of Aarhus University Research Foundation has made the publication of this book possible, and is much appreciated.

Benedicte Madsen & Søren Willert
Aarhus, September 2006

TABLE OF CONTENTS

Homage to Gunnar Hjelholt: Working on Boundaries

In August 2003 a memorial conference was held with the title "Homage to Gunnar Hjelholt: Working on Boundaries". In her introduction, Benedicte Madsen probed into the ways in which Hjelholt had used the boundary concept. A revised version of her script is presented in this prologue.

The quotations, all of them addressing the boundary theme, are obtained from two sources. One is Hjelholt's own article, "Europe is different" from a 1976-anthology edited by Hofstede & Kassem and brought as Chapter 14 below. The other source is an interview book from 1996 (written by the editors of the present book), *Survival in the organization. Gunnar Hjelholt Looks Back at the Concentration Camp from an Organizational Perspective* (Madsen & Willert, 1996 – referred to in several of the following chapters). In the prologue, references to the two sources are made by way of publication year, 1976 and 1996 respectively. Italics are added.

PROLOGUE

The boundary notion

By choosing the title "Europe is different" for his 1976-essay, Gunnar Hjelholt wanted to point out that in Europe – its multitude of geographical, national and institutional boundaries taken into consideration – it is easier for social scientists to "recognize our identity as 'searchers' trying to formulate important questions" (1976:242). He warned against expanding social and organizational research too far into the world of business, thereby obscuring the difference between research and profit seeking. The subtitle of the essay is "Boundaries and identity as key concepts". Identity presupposes boundaries, social as well as psychological demarcations. Man needs to be able to distinguish himself and his group from the rest of the world. Hjelholt's reflections on boundaries in terms of differences and demarcations were quite prophetic:

> You can guess my attitude toward the predominantly American organization theories advocating the organization structure as matrix organizations or temporary systems. I think that all the theories which *try to get away with or loosen boundaries* are attacking the group identities, and in this way, while temporarily ensuing flexibility inside the organization, they export problems to the outside, where we get a society of alienated, rootless individuals (1976:241-2).

If we go on looking at social boundaries, including inter-group relations, the limited access to scarce goods such as status and power creates other sorts of boundaries:

Here we come to one of the *most fundamental boundaries between groups*: on the one side those who have, on the other side those who have not; those with power and those without (1976:242).

Although he often criticized what he understood to be an exaggerated concern with individual growth and development, Gunnar Hjelholt was well aware of man's need to guard his personal boundaries. When interviewed about the aftermaths of the concentration camp, he noted:

If you really share such experiences with someone else, then a strong intimacy results … the full disclosure implies a *transgression of personal boundaries* (1996:77).

Boundaries are related to structure, and structure is a necessity. But there is always the question of balancing the extremes:

There is a balance. I know that you cannot live without structure. *Boundlessness is not good* – what is good is to *overstep the boundaries* (1996:86).

Every boundary has a distinct quality: clear or obscure, open or closed, more or less solid or permeable, etc. Gunnar Hjelholt called for open boundaries and he was rather taken by open systems theory. As we have seen, he emphasized the need for boundaries that could secure the identity of the people involved. However, the same boundaries should allow for movement. He saw an optimal illustration in his own Hammerfest study involving fishing trawlers:

We found a smooth, well-functioning crew where *no boundaries hindered the work* (1976:239).

Contrarily, he despised the old institutions – and scores of new ones, as well – that shut themselves off in relation to users, clients and the surrounding society. Turning inward into self-sufficiency implies a disregard of one's primary task and mission.

One can 'work on' boundaries in a number of ways. For one, the members of a group may work on their own boundaries in terms of managing or changing them. In this sense, a boundary is more than a demarcation line, it is a borderline across which people, responsibilities, tasks, commodities and other entities of negative or positive importance to the group may be transmitted or exchanged. Gunnar Hjelholt touched upon this type of boundary by referring to his experience with the tanker fleet. In the early 1960s he acted as a consultant for "a progressive Danish shipping company", as he put it, and made the following observation:

> The responsibility for the system and the *handling of boundary problems* was placed inside the system, with the members (1976:238).

Incidentally, this achievement was a result of his own interventions. In other words, the consultant can work with boundaries by helping the members of the client systems manage the boundaries themselves.

In Gunnar Hjelholt's case, perhaps the phrase 'working on boundaries' could also be interpreted as working with groups on the outskirts of society. His sympathies and his hopes for the future lay here. A marginal group sees the system more clearly than a majority group and has a greater potential for movement, he claimed.

In yet another denotation, 'working on boundaries' means studying and reflecting on the boundary phenomenon as such. Gunnar Hjelholt did this quite a lot. The following chapters show how well aware he was of the need to establish a certain distance in order to understand a system. One logical conclusion of this conviction is that the consultant must place himself on the boundary of the group, working from there. This position prevents the consultant from being enmeshed. He was preoccupied with the danger of being swallowed by the system. The boundary position makes it possible to take in the system as a whole, from the outsider's perspective. Real understanding requires distance or, rather, a subtle balance between membership and engagement on the one hand, distance and dis-interest on the other.

When placed on the boundary the consultant may be able to guard it so that the client system can concentrate on solving its task. Relating to the shipping case, Gunnar Hjelholt states his view of the consultant's prime function as a boundary keeper:

> The crew was given the full authority to *plan inside their boundary*, the ship, and my role was to be the *boundary keeper* and see to it that the company's directors did not interfere in the process (1976:237).

As it were, being on the boundary was a general pattern in his life. A mind set, an overall life choice, perhaps a character trait or even a destiny. From early childhood, he placed himself in this position – "on the fence":

(As a young boy) I spent a lot of time with our neighbour's sons. They were full of energy. One day we were playing in the yard and mother told the boys' father that I wasn't really in on the fun, but sitting passively *on the fence* watching. The father corrected her by pointing out that I was participating by provoking the boys with remarks and commentary (1996:18).

Gunnar Hjelholt did not exactly sit on the fence while confined in a concentration camp during World War II. Here, he was forced to participate and struggle for survival. But even under these extreme conditions he felt a difference in the way he related to his fellow prisoners:

Some of my fellow prisoners had much stronger bonds than I did ... Creating 'distance' was the only way I could manage (1996:75).

Even after his death, Gunnar Hjelholt stays alive on the boundary – on the intangible fringe areas of the group of people who worked with him, got inspired by him and loved him. His spirit survives.

INTRODUCTION

Background and contents

By Søren Willert & Benedicte Madsen

This book is about a professional person, his life and his work. It is also about the social and professional environment that lent him inspiration and that, in turn, he inspired. The person is applied social psychologist Gunnar Hjelholt (1920-2002). Due to its person-centered approach the book may be read as a piece of professional biography. At the same time it is a historically oriented case study in professional culture and culture construction. The culture in question is a particular brand of Lewin-inspired social psychology that Gunnar and the authors of part II have spent their lives developing: group dynamics and organizational consultancy.

The first four sections of the present introduction paint a picture of Gunnar Hjelholt from a professional and personal perspective, presenting basic information about his life and career. The two following sections tell the story of a professional collaboration project involving Hjelholt and the editors – a project that ultimately resulted in the present book. The final section contains summary presentations of the 16 chapters and the epilogue.

The apprentice years

"Working on Boundaries" is the title we chose for this book. In the prologue we already stated our reasons for doing so. Subsequent chapters will present numerous examples of the particular relevance of the boundary theme to Gunnar Hjelholt – as a person and as an applied social psychologist.

Placing yourself *on the boundary*, tends to make you a person who, from a social point of view, is neither a complete insider, nor a complete outsider. You may very well be recognized and accepted as a member of the community, but your membership role implies a certain ambiguity. Are you on your way in or on your way out? Are you coming or going? Or is the boundary line simply your preferred place to stay? As we see it, 'the boundary' is a useful concept for putting the personal-professional history and identity of our main character into perspective. In addition, it is a theme of general interest and relevance.

Sociologically speaking, Gunnar's roots were in the middle class intelligentsia. The atmosphere of his family-of-origin he described as a mixture between intellectual absorption and reform-oriented activism. "I have always found myself suspended between two poles. My father was a researcher, the one who observed and reflected. My mother was the reformer and missionary. But there was also a little bit of missionary in my father."[1] Gunnar was born 1920 in Copenhagen, on the boundary line between a middle class and a working class neighbourhood. During the turbulent thirties, characterized by economic depression, massive unemployment, increasing polarization between political right wingers (Fascism, Nazism) and left wingers (socialism, communism), Gunnar's sympathies unquestionably belonged to the left, while, at the same time, he was hesitant to join the ranks of a political organization.

> I must have been involved in political activities in one way or another through-
> out the entire period until the war broke out. My circle of acquaintances
> included numerous political activists. But I never really *belonged*. I have never
> been a member of any party either, I was always on the edge of the labour
> movement.[2]

Rather than expressing themselves through organizational membership, Gunnar's political sympathies inspired him to set up individual projects. Some time during 1936 or 1937 he went on a bicycle trip to the Harz Mountains, Germany, at the same time acting as a courier committed to bringing clandestine letters to a group of Social Democrats in Braunschweig.

> In Braunschweig the police picked me up while I was bicycling around in the
> middle of the town. At that point, I no longer had the letters – one of the
> many times that I got lucky. But, because I said "Grüss Gott" instead of "Heil
> Hitler", I got my ears boxed. ... I was arrested and released because they did
> not have anything on me. But this event did not make my attitude towards
> Nazism any more positive.[3]

---

1   Madsen & Willert, 1996, p. 16.
2   Ibid., p. 20.
3   Ibid., p.19.

Some few years later, he envisaged himself as a possible future war reporter.

> At the end of October 1939, Russia put pressure on the Finns to surrender parts of their country. I called a provincial newspaper ... and asked if they would like to have a correspondent in Helsinki. They promised to pay me, and I flew to Helsinki as the youngest journalist of all those who flocked there to cover the events.[4]

And yet, during the five year-long German occupation of Denmark, Gunnar gradually made a change from his preferred position as a free, i.e. self-governing political agent into that of organized resistance fighter.

> *When did you decide to become active in the resistance movement?*

> That is a two-sided story: I did not want to become attached to any movement, and at the same time I wanted to be an active participant. That is the way it has always been with me; what you call 'Gunnar on the edge'. The question is: When do you make the decision? It probably starts with some suggestion or other: Can you distribute newspapers? So it is a question of several small steps, and then you eventually belong to "them".

As it happened, for Gunnar there was a price to be paid for his organized involvement in the Danish resistance movement. In the summer of 1944, the last of the "five cursed years" of World War II, he got arrested and was later sent to Porta Westphalica, a German concentration camp where he was interned for nine months, from September 1944 to April 1945.

For many, death was the outcome of internment in a Nazi-German concentration labour camp. For the survivors, the internment inevitably led to a radical change of the personal life perspective. Gunnar talked metaphorically about camp life pushing you to such extremes that, in the end, you were prepared to make *deals with the Devil*. "You want to appear as a good person in relation to the ones closest to you; as someone of high principles who has certain values. But in the concentration camp, we certainly did things to our friends and to our fellow men which do not fit that dream image (...). We made deals with the Devil, you see. You want to close off large parts of your life because you were dealing with the Devil, and you would prefer not to share that with your loved ones."[5] Engaging oneself in this kind of extreme bargaining puts an enormous strain on a human being.

---

4   Ibid., p. 21.
5   Ibid., p. 77f.

However, the very extremity of the event may also lead to extraordinary insights about the human condition – insofar as one manages to stay alive, that is.

In the subsequent Chapter 1, more can be read about ways in which Gunnar's internment became an important life event. The chapter also tells about how, in 1948 after a three-year convalescent period, he was enrolled at the Psychological Laboratory, University of Copenhagen. On the face of it, his enrolment might be seen as a sign that his life had now taken a turn back to normality. Such a notion is not entirely justified. The university student Gunnar Hjelholt had strong reservations concerning the intellectual nourishment he was offered at his study place. During his university years his quest for learning was primarily satisfied when, on his own initiative, he stepped outside the formal boundary line defined by classroom and curriculum, using society 'out there' as his dialogue partner. In this way he gathered for himself the kind of knowledge he considered useful, and at the same time got a chance to submitt whatever academic knowledge he had acquired to the acid test of relevance and practicability.

In 1951, Gunnar graduated after three years of study. In Denmark at that time, university-trained psychologists were few in number, but society moved towards an increasing demand for the kind of professional services they offered. During his first seven years as titled psychologist, he was employed in a number of organizations and institutions, jointly characterized by their contribution to the social reorganization which, during the post-war years, consolidated the Danish welfare state. From a sociological viewpoint, it once again seems that Gunnar's position had become perfectly normal and suitable for a newly graduated psychologist at this point of Danish history. And yet, as a wage earner Gunnar experienced considerable difficulties subordinating to the standards of normality. On several occasions he got himself involved in morally tinged value conflicts with his organizational environments. The wage earner position left him no opportunity for choosing the boundary position, i.e. no possibility to arrive at a compromise between the insider and outsider perspectives. On more than one occasion he ended up resigning from his job.

His last job as salaried psychologist was at the Danish Technological Institute in Copenhagen. Traditionally, this organization had been engaged in delivering technological assistance to small and medium-sized enterprises. Gunnar was recruited as part of a planned strategy aiming at extending the Institute's range of customers, namely through the inclusion of management-technology as a supplementary business area. Not only was he headhunted for this particular purpose. The Institute further decided to invest in Gunnar's post-doc training in the United States. The training took place in Delaware, but also allowed him, during the summer of 1958, to visit the international centre for group dynamics and organization development: The National Training Laboratories (NTL) in Bethel, Maine. Altogether, Gunnar stayed as consultancy trainee in the United States for eight months. Chapter 2 is a thorough account of his stay and the way it gave direction to his future career.

Shaping European group dynamics and organizational consultancy

Gunnar Hjelholt's return to Denmark in 1958 marked the end of what might be called his professional apprentice years. He was now 38 years old. Before going to America he had been searching for 'something' that might serve him as a lasting vocation, but had not found it. He had made use of opportunities that came his way. He had gained valuable experience – some of which could only be attained at a personal price. He had not yet taken the steps that were to become vital for forming his personal career. Gunnar's return from the United States marked a turning point in his professional biography, making him shift from a predominantly reactive to a far more proactive mode of being, thereby also allowing his surroundings to get a much clearer picture of his special talents and propensities.

On his return, Gunnar was still earning his salary at the Danish Technological Institute. His postgraduate training had been paid for by his workplace as a strategic, future-oriented investment. Gunnar acknowledged their generosity by taking on the position as head of a department formed to build up management consultancy as a new line of business. In 1960, however, he left the place – thereby quitting, for good, the life of the salaried employee. He became a self-employed consultant, established his own non-profit firm and called it *Applied Social Psychology*. For the remainder of his professional life, he was working on the boundary of organizations, i.e. in the position that, obviously, not only suited him best, but also seemed to make the most of his special talents.

We have already learned that Gunnar's preferred position was on the boundary line. Individuals on the boundary line link up with the community, but in their own peculiar manner. They may bring value to the community, and the community may be valuable to them, but they never merge completely with any particular grouping. This is a valid description of Gunnar's professional career as it unfolded after his return from the States, i.e. for the last 45 years of his life.

The post-war development in society produced a general demand for formally qualified psychologists. Within this setting, special demands would arise for Gunnar's personal way of managing and developing his qualifications – both in a national and an international context. His experiences from NTL, coupled with a talent for systems development on a large-scale, made him a central figure in the shaping of a European variety of organizational consultancy and group dynamics. His important role in European applied social psychology will become clear from the chapters in part II of this book, written by psychologists from six different countries. Further, his influence on the development of Danish applied psychology can hardly be overestimated. During the 1960s and 70s and beyond, his natural talent for facilitating other people's learning processes, interactions and joint decision making, in combination with a personal liking for the teacher role, made him a professional mentor, not only for the first generation of Danish organization consultants but also for many clinical psychologists. In 2001, in view of his all-round importance as coach, supervisor and provocateur for Danish psychologists in the 60s and onwards, Gunnar Hjelholt was made honorary member of the Danish Psychologists' Association.

The farm house in Vust

Gunnar Hjelholt was born on April 30th, 1920. He had two younger sisters, Ingrid and Karin. His parents were Elsa and Holger Hjelholt. The father held a doctoral degree in history. The mother, who was of Swedish descent, was a person of great moral strength. All through life, Gunnar felt himself suspended between the two parent poles: reflection vs. action, observation vs. participation.

In 1946, Gunnar travelled to Stockholm to resume close friendships from the pre-war years. He also attended a summer school in the Swedish skerries. Here he fell in love with Berit Erikson (born on September 21st, 1920), a young textile designer from Finland. In 1947 and 1948 he taught in the said summer school and visited Berit's home in a Finnish-Swedish fishing village in the Gulf of Bothnia. They were married in Finland in January 1949 and settled down in Copenhagen. Their two sons Lars and Anders were born in 1950 and 1953, respectively.

Around 1970, Gunnar along with Berit and their two sons moved to a farm house in Vust. Vust is a small locality in the North-Western part of Denmark, somewhere between Thisted and Fjerritslev.[6] They acquired a flock of sheep so that Berit could secure her own wool for weaving. The large barn gave her plenty of room for the many looms. Part of the two-winged cottage was fitted with guest rooms and group rooms suitable for Gunnar's legendary workshops. Vust also provided the setting for numerous visits by friends and colleagues from Denmark and the rest of the world, as is testified in many of the subsequent chapters.

After the move to Vust, Berit proved to be an outstanding textile artist.[7] People in Denmark know at least one of her works, namely the large woollen tapestry behind the speaker's rostrum in the Danish Parliament, completed in 1987.[8] Gunnar acknowledged that she had made some severe sacrifices when they married and he sincerely respected her talents: "When we got married, she was considered one of the promising designers, and for her the marriage meant giving up her career. Professionally, she made a personal sacrifice to my advantage. But all that changed when we moved to Vust".[9]

For 33 years, Berit and Gunnar lived together in Vust. On the morning of December 27th, 2002 Gunnar died peacefully in the low-ceiling cottage. He had been quite ill during the previous six months, confined to his bed and his oxygen apparatus. His lungs had given in. Before Christmas he seemed to have recovered slightly, and he enjoyed professional conversations with colleagues who travelled to Vust, and engaged himself in their projects. During his last few days, however, he began to weaken gradually. Gunnar spent quite some time reflecting on the various ways in which the two hospitals he frequented, as well as the municipal care system, functioned. Some of the systems became targets of his anger and scorn, whilst in other situations he acknowledged the kindness of the doctors and nurses.

---

6   As early as the autumn of 1969, they moved to a rented house in the area and subsequently bought the small farm in Vust in the spring of 1970. Incidentally, Gunnar reported that the Beatle, John Lennon, and his wife, Yoko Ono, had stayed for a short time in their house during the winter of 1969/70. Berit adds that Lennon had his hair cut on the very same kitchen bench as many of the contributors to the present book have sat on. The farm was sold in October 2005 as Berit moved to a small house in Fjerritslev.

7   See Pedersen 1990 and 2005, two books on Berit Hjelholt's tapestries.

8   With reference to a patriotic song written by the Danish poet Helge Rode, the tapestry is called "Som en rejselysten flåde" ["Like a fleet bound for journey"]; music by Carl Nielsen.

9   As for the origin of this citation and other biographical data, see the subsequent section of the present introduction.

On January 2nd, 2003 he was buried in the churchyard in Vust, next to his youngest son, who died at the age of 38.

Applied social psychologist

If someone asked Gunnar Hjelholt to define his professional work area he would name it 'applied social psychology'. According to Gunnar, he was the first Danish psychologist to use the title 'applied social psychologist' as a professional self-characterization. The expression tells about a dream he had, and one that he wanted to realize professionally. Professional practice should make contributions to our general understanding of reality – or at least, that was how things *ought* to be in the best of all worlds. 'Applied social psychology' reflects his wish to establish mutually enriching exchanges between consultancy work with its commitment to the client, research work with its commitment to scientific standards, and a general engagement in social affairs. Doing applied social psychology was for Gunnar a means towards inspiring and extending the boundaries of social psychology as an academic field of knowledge.

Judging from the way he managed himself professionally, Gunnar stayed true to his dream. He was knowledgeable and inquisitive with regard to large-scale matters: world affairs in general, as well as small-scale matters: the immediate situation here and now. Throughout life he nourished his inquiring mind by extensive reading in psychology, sociology, politology, philosophy and litera-ture. When in his professional capacity, the state of the client system became his object of study. One got the impression that, above everything else, his working style and intervention methods rested on an untameable urge to *arrive at a thorough understanding of what was going on* – in the client system, in himself, in the relation between the client system and himself, not forgetting the interaction with the environment that served as context for whatever was going on.[10] Within the dictates of decency, broadly conceived, he did not shy away from satisfying this inclination. One of Gunnar's very special talents consisted in offering hypotheses or action proposals which sounded so vague or ambiguous, but nevertheless enticing, that representatives from the client system would put lots of energy into finding out what was *actually* meant, thereby enlightening, not only themselves, but Gunnar as well: "What the devil is he talking about? What could it mean? What does he want us to do? – *We'll show him, yes, indeed we will!*" In our experience, Gunnar's success with such interventions rested not least on the fact that behind their seemingly vague

---

10 Action research, that is – according to one conception of this kind of investigation, cf. Chapter 2 and several of the contributions in Part II.

or puzzling qualities, one experienced a *genuine will to understand*. Gunnar was not putting on an act. However cryptic his interventions might appear, they were solidly and unquestionably rooted in his whole being, body and soul. One other reason why his interventions – be they cryptic or not –carried such an impact, was that they often seemed inspired by a considerable amount of good old-fashioned wisdom.

Gunnar was unquestionably a wise man. As a consultant, one of his special strengths was an ability to utilize his perceptiveness and sensitivity in ways that would seem to play games with 'normality'. He had an eye for the oblique angle. Frequently, he would make situational comments by focussing on something that until that point had not been in focus for other actors in the field: either because it was too obvious and simple – "something anybody could see", and therefore not worth paying attention to, or because it was too strange, bizarre, enigmatic and therefore close to the outermost boundary line of what could or ought to be commented on *at all*.

Gunnar telling stories about his life: a collaboration project

Gunnar Hjelholt's extensive network, resulting from the kind of activities mentioned above, forms an important background for the publication of this book, but another background derives from a collaboration project between Gunnar and the two editors which evolved during the last 20 years of his life.

This book's editorial team did *not* receive their basic training from Gunnar. Our collaboration with him developed within the framework of our university-based teaching and research activities. In 1985, as colleagues at the Department of Psychology at the University of Aarhus, we had started a project group called *Systems Development and Systems Evaluation*. Supervised by us, psychology students were given a chance to gain practical, real-world experience as consultancy trainees or apprentices. The project enriched our jobs as university teachers, while at the same time it gave us a platform for studying and developing consultancy methods. We understood ourselves as action researchers. The consultation jobs we engaged in served as a cumulative data-base illustrating organizational worlds and the handling of professional contact with such worlds. In 1988, our experiences with these activities led to a formalization and expansion through the establishment of the *Centre for Systems Development* (CfS), a small sub-unit at the Department of Psychology at the University of Aarhus.[11] When presenting the professional aims of this unit to outsiders, we would emphasize our inspirational debt to Kurt Lewin who was cherished by Gunnar as well, and whose writings formed the theoretical basis for the professional tradition Gunnar had met at NTL.

Gunnar was not directly involved in this course of events, but we knew him and at times we met and exchanged views. In direct as well as indirect ways he showed his appreciation for our professional initiatives. In view of his experiences as a psychology student, detailed in Chapter 1, this appreciation is easy to understand. Gunnar did not think highly of his own study place, the Psychological Laboratory in Copenhagen in the late 1940s. According to him, the Laboratory had neither lived up to its responsibilities as an educational institution nor as a research institution. Basically, as a student and later as a professional, Gunnar viewed the classroom teaching offered in his student days as meaningless: 'academic' in the worst sense of the term. He had been forced to search outside the Laboratory to acquire the kind of learning experiences we now offered our students. CfS was only a *small* unit of the *large* Department of Psychology in Aarhus. But at least *it existed,* and as Centre managers we *made an effort* to deliver to our students some of the material they could rightfully demand from their place of study.

We valued Gunnar's appreciation – and in due course we reciprocated. The more our contact with the Danish consultancy profession widened, the more we realized how important Gunnar had been as an inspirational source for this professional field – the field he had once termed 'applied social psychology'. Gradually we started to perceive CfS as a university-based unit responsible – among other things – for carrying on and further developing the professional tradition that Gunnar had kick-started in the early 1960s. At times we used Gunnar as a consultant for various purposes at the Centre and as a coach for our students. On such occasions Gunnar sometimes told stories. He himself *was* history. Seen in retrospect, our exchanges with him contributed greatly to extending and clarifying our professional self-understanding. Then, in 1991, we asked him if he might be interested in committing himself, in a more serious fashion, to the role of informant for a personal-professional biography edited by us. He agreed. The original working title for the project was 'Gunnar on the Edge'. For everyday purposes, we simply called it the Collaboration Project.

---

11   By the end of 2005, we regrettably had to close down CfS, due to lack of support from the University.

The Collaboration Project was intended as a reconstruction of the Danish history of applied social psychology. Practically speaking the project evolved through day-long interviews with Gunnar in his home in Vust. One of us had the role of interviewer – keeping Gunnar's narrative rolling through countless questions while the other served as note-taking secretary. The idea was to transfer Gunnar's long-term memory onto paper. After each meeting we put together a full written account of the interview proceedings, including lists of any loose ends that remained – things not understood, questions set aside for future interviews. Gunnar read and commented on these statements, and took it upon himself to produce various working papers for the project.

In a struggle against time, the Collaboration Project ran its course. Gunnar was 71 years old when the interviewing started. His body showed marked signs, not only of old age but also of the after-effects of the tuberculosis he had contracted during his concentration camp internment. His lung capacity was seriously reduced. "Half of my left lung and three quarters of my right lung are useless".[12] He was a heavy smoker and workwise he did not spare himself – former CfS-students, who regularly consulted Gunnar as their supervisor, told about the continued professional vigour and mental flexibility of 'the old man'. But then with increasing frequency all through the Collaboration Project we were informed that his body temporarily gave in, and that he was bedridden. For someone with considerably less than half the normal lung capacity, catching pneumonia must have been somewhat disturbing!

On April 30th, 1995, Gunnar turned 75. The day became the occasion for our publishing the first and, until now, the only product[13] emanating from the Collaboration Project. The publication, based on the edited interview text, contains Gunnar's retrospective narrative on his experiences as a concentration camp inmate. We presented the book at his birthday reception where some of his contacts from the Danish Resistance Movement were among the guests.[14] Shortly after the reception, the three of us met in Vust for the purpose of drawing up guidelines for future phases of the project. In an early part of

---

12 Madsen & Willert, 1996, p. 64.

13 Except for Madsen, Willert & Hjelholt, 1994 – a small article on the mini-society design.

14 At the reception, we presented a Danish mimeo version of the publication entitled *Overlevelse i organisationen*. (Madsen & Willert, 1995). At the suggestion of and with economic support from the EIT (The European Institute for Trans-National Studies in Group and Organizational Development) and its General Secretary Veronika Dalheimer (cf. Chapter 4 in the present publication), the book was later translated into English (Madsen & Willert, 1996). For further information about Gunnar's influence in EIT, see Chapter 2 in particular.

the interview we asked Gunnar for his evaluation of our collaboration so far. The following dialogue ensued:

What has participation in this project meant to you personally?

I guess it helped me to get a better hold on history. Get a clearer view.

Are you referring to large-scale history: Danish or World history, so to speak, or to your own history?

Well, to both, as a matter of fact. Or, rather, to the relation between the two, the relation between the inner, personal perspective, and the outer. When trying to understand certain events, you may ask questions about what happened in the outer world at the time. Another kind of question deals with what happened to the persons involved and inside these persons. The two sets of events are part of the same story – which implies that a third type of question may be asked, namely about the *relation* between the two kinds of events. That's the type of questions I have been asking myself. The project has made me become more aware.

In itself, the concentration camp is nothing special. At a certain point in time, it just happened. As for myself, I'm nothing special, either. I'm just one person among a huge number of persons. But the two are connected, and my very attempts at understanding that connection suddenly make both become interesting.

The project has made me more inquisitive concerning the way things are connected. It has also influenced my way of listening to other people or reading what they have written. I start wondering about the connections between what they say or write, and 'all the rest'. Take, for instance, the relation between a researcher writing at a certain time, and then all sorts of external events that are part of the story too; all the things happening in the world simultaneously that have influenced his thoughts.

Our immediate reaction is that your answer strikes us as kind of surprising! If anything, our collaboration project so far has had you as its stable centre. At some point we actually got a bit worried, or even anxious, when you told us that old nightmares from the years following your internment had started to pop up again – seemingly as a side-effect of our success in gradually squeezing more and more old memory stuff out of you. Naturally, it hasn't been without personal costs for you to have us coming here all the time, just squeezing and squeezing. At times you must have felt like a tube of toothpaste. Still, your

INTRODUCTION

answer seems almost completely devoid of reference to your personal life-sphere, or to pos-
sible personal costs derived from your participation. Instead you talk in the most general
terms about 'interesting relations between inner and outer' and about the way in which
research comes about.

I believe there's a very good reason for my answering that way. The one aspect about our project that still makes me extremely uncomfortable is the aspect related to my *being its main character.* The role as protagonist is something that scares me. My discomfort not only stems from the fact that, often, I don't know *how to behave* in that position. That only worries me a bit, right then and there when it happens – but it doesn't *scare* me. What scares me is a certain danger attached to the position as main character. When you accept that role there are things you much too easily avoid, leave alone, leave out. But they are things that *must necessarily be attended to.*

In my experience, a lot of professional work has floundered exactly because of this main character stuff.

Within ordinary clinical work, the professional is simply the person whose job it is to keep the dialogue on track – keep it flowing – so that the *task,* that's at the centre of everything, can be taken care of. But then, sometimes, all of a sudden *the professional* becomes the important one, becomes the main character. Maybe that's how he sees himself, maybe others see him like that. 'Oh my God – the big-man therapist, the guru!' *Everyone* has to listen to his extremely deep and important statements. Who cares about whatever the client might have to say?

The same thing may happen to the consultant. When *you start to enjoy it yourself,* start enjoying your position as main protagonist, then the work you were meant to do is doomed to collapse. And the same thing may happen in organizational life – in the building of organizations: once the boss becomes the prime protagonist, the task of creating a viable work community is forgotten.

Experiences like these worry me a lot and make me sense the potential danger in our collaboration project too. What we do together is fine as long as it nourishes my professional reflections. Makes me aware of new connections. Brings this and that into a clearer perspective …

What exactly might make the process a bad one?

That I should start to enjoy it. 'Wow, look – there he is – the Great Man – role model and hero of social psychology!'

Moving from collaboration project to the present book

What happened to the project from then on, that is, after 1995? Following the three-party meeting in Vust we simply decided to move on from where we left off. The Collaboration Project was meant as a historical account of applied social psychology in Denmark with Gunnar's personal and professional biography as its vantage point – the camera angle determining the way 'everything else' would be seen. In the then recently published manuscript, we had explicated how Gunnar, in retrospect, was able to conceive of the concentration camp as an organizational prototype and relate these qualities to his own role as organizational survivor in the camp setting. Main character or not, with this manuscript we had presented but an initial sketch of Gunnar Hjelholt, the applied social psychologist.

The project stayed in our minds ever since the reported meeting in Vust. From time to time we put some practical energy into it as well, by doing new interviews, editing existing text and developing plans for the composition of the planned publication. However, in spite of such efforts, the project remained unfinished. The division of labour agreed upon between the three of us was unequivocal. To the extent that we asked him to do so, Gunnar would offer his personal recollections as well as any relevant documentary material in his possession. The responsibility for making something out of the material and taking initiatives lay with us. In practice, though, we neglected the project. In our work schedule we did not give it sufficient priority to ensure its continued progression. From being an activity fuelled by joyous commitment on our part, it increasingly turned into a tedious burden which took up space in our bad conscience. *We wanted to finish the project*, but our good intentions remained frustrated, and it was nobody's fault but our own. Some years later, when we had asked Gunnar how important it was *for him* to still be alive on the day when the next book was on the street, he had put his finger on the bad conscience-component which weighed so heavily *on us*:

Oh, I did find it amusing to be there for the publication of the first small book – and afterwards to hear the comments from others. Otherwise, I haven't really been thinking a lot about what you ask me. On the other hand, it must be kind of embarrassing for you to have the project dragging on like this – one year after another. One year after another your annual report states that you are *working* on this project. Well, what about it? – Are you getting anywhere?

As already stated, Gunnar died on December 27th, 2002. Ultimately, his death was what pushed us into revitalizing the Collaboration Project, albeit in a changed form. An obituary written by one of us drew many reactions from Gunnar's old friends and colleagues, reactions that led to the decision to arrange a memorial conference. The conference was held in August 2003 under the heading *Homage to Gunnar Hjelholt: Working on Boundaries.* Keynote speakers and participants agreed that the publication of a book like the present one would be fitting.

Summaries

The book is divided into three parts. Part One, containing Chapters 1 and 2, is based on the material that, for so many years, had burdened our conscience. Chapter 1, **Exploring organizational life from within – Gunnar Hjelholt in search of a professional platform,** illustrates, and puts into perspective, Hjelholt's life and professional experiences during the ten-year period from 1948-1958, i.e. between his return to Denmark from the concentration camp and his post-graduate studies in the United States. The first section of Chapter 2, **The boundary keeper – Gunnar Hjelholt on group dynamics and consultant roles,** is the story about Hjelholt's stay in the United States and the intellectual commotion brought about by his encounter with Lewinian group dynamics. The last part of the chapter deals with the pioneer years, roughly 1958-1970, when he became part of the group that established a European tradition for group dynamics and consultancy work.

Part Two of the book includes seven essays written by people from six countries and two continents. The chapters deal with Gunnar Hjelholt as an applied social psychologist and with matters to which he was dedicated. The authors are consultants, typically engaged in organizational development as well as group training programmes; in addition, some of them hold, or used to hold, university positions. All of them contributed to the memorial conference in 2003, mentioned above.

"Hi, Gunnar! It is not easy to have a talk with you now that you have moved beyond the boundaries of time and space." This is how, using a letter to the deceased as his format, Leopold Vansina from Belgium tells about **Gunnar Hjelholt remembered as a rope dancer, a clown, a rebel and a critical thinker** in Chapter 3. It appears that Hjelholt kept tight ropes on his principles as the first Secretary General of the European organization EIT while reconciling opposing parties. In certain other contexts he was seen behaving like a clown or, rather, a jester. Furthermore, he seems to have been in never-ending rebellious fights for justice and the right of every human being to be free and to develop 'responsibility in freedom'. As for the critical thinker, we get a glimpse of long discussions between Hjelholt and Vansina concerning the situation after the breakdown of the Soviet Union, the relation between the USA and Europe and the human condition in general.

Chapter 4, **Seeing with the heart – Gunnar Hjelholt's influence on consultants in Europe** by Veronoka Dalheimer from Austria deals with a theme from *The Little Prince* by Antoine de Saint-Exupéry: what is essential is invisible to the eye. Dalheimer reflects on how she and her consultant colleagues learned from Hjelholt to use their own emotional reactions toward social systems. To *be in touch* seems to have been Hjelholt's personal touch, so to speak. Allowing oneself to feel the client system has for Dalheimer become a way of establishing ties with it.

In Chapter 5 on **Complexity, dynamics and the sense of meaning,** Jørgen Steen Christensen from Denmark takes his point of departure in a 1995 publication by Gunnar Hjelholt. On this basis, he presents and reflects on a case with Hjelholt in the role of process designer and implementing agent. Interpersonal, intragroup, and intergroup processes are complex dynamic phenomena. The consultant needs to simplify in order to intervene, but alas, when oversimplifying a problem, you falsify by ignoring *truly* complicating factors. Hjelholt is acknowledged for his ability to combine simplicity and clarity.

Chapter 6 by Ian Lauritzen from Sweden examines Gunnar Hjelholt's extension of the Lewinian laboratory method in an essay called **Minisociety – toward a psychology of society.** Not an arena for interpretations at an individual psychological level, it focuses upon learning about society as a system consisting of interdependent groups and sub-groups. Lauritzen details this very special design, its background, objectives and characteristics and he views it as an inspiring format for applied social psychologists striving to contribute to what Hjelholt called a psychology of society.

Chapter 7 by Swedish Harald Berg is titled **Gunnar Hjelholt – researcher and practitioner of applied social psychology.** Berg describes Hjelholt as a front figure in the European network of social psychologists, integrating different schools of thought and practice. In this endeavour he was positioned outside the academic society, creating his own arenas for discussing and developing ideas and serving as a mentor for young people.

In Chapter 8, Gouranga Chattopadhyay from India addresses **Unconscious transactions across boundaries**. From a politically engaged angle he offers two examples on the boundary phenomenon. In the first example, he agrees with Gunnar Hjelholt in the following argument: when the almost non-permeable boundary of the Iron Curtain, represented by the Berlin Wall, collapsed in 1989, the Western World's projections of its own dark sides boomeranged back into the societies from which they had sprung. In turn this led to America's anti-terror wars in Afghanistan and Iraq. Chattopadhyay's second illustration relates to the community of so-called untouchables in India, encompassing approximately 160 million citizens. As was the case with the Berlin Wall, this system has provided inter-caste boundaries that are rather impermeable.

The title of Chapter 9 is **Toward polyphony in human science – facing complexity**. Here, the French social psychologist Max Pagès describes how, from more traditional beginnings, he and various groups of collaborators moved toward a 'polyphonic position'. This stand may function as an antidote against the futile, power-infested search for absolute truths which is endemic to academic life in general. Using today's hypermodern multinational enterprises and political violence as examples, he elaborates on the implications that may follow from embracing such a polyphonic viewpoint, especially insofar as the intellectual and practical handling of complexity is concerned.

Part Three presents seven of Gunnars Hjelholt's own writings from the period 1960-1995. Chapter 10 is a translation of a journal article from 1960: **The small group as a factor in attitude changes**. It may be seen as an example of the kind of action research typical of the Lewinian tradition. Referring to research results from the field of group dynamics, the article reports on a number of experiments involving training groups carried out by Hjelholt and others during 1958 and 1959.

Mathew Miles from the USA, now deceased, was one of Hjelholt's close friends and collaborators. Together they tried out new ways in a Danish training laboratory in 1962 and documented the results in an article published in 1963. This paper, **Extending the conventional training laboratory design,** is presented as Chapter 11. The authors reason that by separating the various phases of a laboratory by periods 'back home' you allow for digestion and ensure the reality connection which otherwise has turned out to be a weak point.

Hjelholt used his consultation work with the Lauritzen Shipping Company as a case and presented the results in an essay called **Training for reality** (Chapter 12). As in Chapter 11, this paper provides evidence of his preoccupation with real-world matters at many levels. It also demonstrates that a spectacular success was closely related to the allocation of autonomy and responsibility to the crew as a whole.

As a further extension of the kind of training laboratory that Hjelholt and Miles had run in the early 1960s, Hjelholt invented his very own design and named it mini-society. His first publication displaying this new concept was an article from 1972, titled **Group training in understanding society: The mini-society**. This text is reproduced as Chapter 13.

"Characteristic of Europe is the presence of many borders and boundaries between groups of people". This is how Gunnar Hjelholt begins his paper **Europe is different – boundary and identity as key concepts**, originally published in 1976 and reproduced as Chapter 14. The paper addresses the ways groups of people live with the boundaries in the organizations to which they belong, and how important the identity of individuals, groups and organizations is. His illustrations are drawn from experiential organizations such as training laboratories; from mini-societies; from ships viewed as closed systems with visible boundaries and restricted territories; and from the Hammerfest case involving fishermen, a fishing plant and a town north of the Polar Circle.

A third anthology contribution, reproduced as Chapter 15, bears the title **North of the Polar Circle** from 1979 and tells the story of the said Hammerfest case.

The last text in Part Three, Chapter 16, is a translation of one of Hjelholt's last publications, from 1995: **Too strange – can we simplify our understanding of a complex and dynamic reality, and still avoid making it simplistic?** It is a system-theoretical text, probably a spin-off from a monograph he worked on but never finished. Hjelholt addresses fundamental questions pertaining to all kinds of social systems: structure and function, purpose and organization, boundary and environment.

In 2005, on Hjelholt's day of birth, April 30th, 'The Gunnar Hjelholt Prize' was awarded to Steen Visholm, a Danish scholar and consultant within the

psychodynamic tradition.[15] Visholm generously agreed to let us bring a translation of his speech as a final statement, that is, an **epilogue**. Visholm sees group
work as a mixed blessing and reminds us of how, in the years following 1968,
the trust in groups was exaggerated, to put it mildly. Nevertheless, he acknowledges Hjelholt's positive contributions. Further, and in line with several of the
authors in Part II of the book, Visholm is deeply concerned with the present
state of global affairs: "There is reason to fear that Bush and Blair, along with
forces in the Islamic world, are transforming the world society into a Sherif
& Sherif's summer camp experiment – but, alas, without a group of experimenters who can stop the process before it turns violent. A world order may
emerge where two fundamentalist religious groups oppose each other around
the theme of heroes against villains, including prohibitions against thinking
and telling the truth and an increased risk of violence and terror".

Before each chapter in Part Two and for the rest of the book we have placed a
preamble, giving a brief introduction to the chapter and connecting it to other
parts of the book. Moreover, the preambles contain data on the authors.

At the end of the book one will find a **Hjelholt Bibliography**, referring to
works from 1953 until 1997.

References

Madsen, B. & Willert, S. (1995). *Overlevelse i organisationen. Gunnar Hjelholt beretter med
koncentrationslejren som eksempel*. Psykologisk Instituts Center for Systemudvikling,
Aarhus Universitet (mimeo, later published in *Psykologisk Skriftserie Aarhus*, 1995 (3)).
Madsen, B. & Willert, S. (1996). *Survival in the Organization: Gunnar Hjelholt Looks Back at
the Concentration Camp from an Organizational Perspective*. Aarhus: Aarhus University
Press.
Madsen, B., Willert, S. & Hjelholt, G. (1994). Mini-samfundet plus minus 25 år [The
25th anniversary of the mini-society, looking back and ahead]. *Psykolog Nyt 3/94*,
90-92.
Pedersen, H. (ed.).(1990). *Billedvæveren Berit Hjelholt* [The textile artist Berit Hjelholt].
Udgivet af Hjørring Kunstmuseum.
Pedersen, H. (ed.). (2005). *Billedvæveren Berit Hjelholt II: Værker fra 1990 til 2005*. Udgivet
af kunstneren.

15　The prize was instituted in 2004 by the Danish NOJ-foundation. The original
Danish version of the speech was published i *Psykolog Nyt* 2005. The first year's prize
went to Jørgen Steen Christensen, the author of Chapter 5. The third year's prize
went to the editors of the present book. Information on the award winners as well as
the trust deed may be seen at www.krogager.com/hjelholt

PART ONE

BIOGRAPHICAL ACCOUNTS

1 EXPLORING ORGANIZATIONAL LIFE FROM WITHIN

Gunnar Hjelholt in search of a professional platform

By Søren Willert & Benedicte Madsen, Denmark

In May 1945, at the age of 25, Gunnar Hjelholt returned to Denmark and to his family after nine months internment in the concentration camp Porta Westphalica. This was a labour camp and the interned prisoners had to prepare the partial transfer of the Philips' production plant from the Netherlands to Germany. Such a transfer would enable the Germans to continue their production of war material, even if the Allies succeeded in recapturing the Netherlands. In order to secure the production plant against airborne bombing raids, it was to be built into a mountain.

About 50 years later, when we interviewed Gunnar about his experiences in, and reflections on, the concentration camp, he drew a picture of an organization characterized by ruthless, goal-directed rationality. One important difference between work systems in a 'normal' capitalist setting and Porta Westphalica was that for the latter the Nazi regime secured a continued supply of human labourers in the form of captured criminals, political opponents, Jews and others. In principle, any individual member of the camp labour force was dispensable. There were always plenty more where they came from. This gave rise to a peculiar production logic followed by the camp management team. In the name of profitability and with great consequence, they simply pushed members of their labour force to work themselves to death – knowing that each and every one could easily be replaced.

By controlling the production in the said manner – Gunnar further told to us – the production management team would even be in agreement with certain high-priority items within the national socio-political grand strategy of Hitler's Germany, i.e. its policy of systematic extinction of persons not wanted by the regime. Apart from yielding *economically profitable production*, the goal of *human extermination* was an organizational and political main objective for establishing and maintaining these camps.

The members of the production management team were camp prisoners themselves. They had been assigned to their function by the camp's topmost SS authorities. Looking back, Gunnar described the relation between SS authorities and production management as, in principle, analogous to the relation between a board of directors and executive management in normal capitalist work systems.

The introductory chapter has described how, in 1991, we started to interview the then 71-year-old Gunnar about his personal and professional life in general, including his nine months of forced labour in the concentration camp. Our book, *Survival in the Organization*,[1] is based on these interviews. On the one hand the book was written as one personal eyewitness report among many, telling about the extreme human conditions pertaining to camp life. At the same time, it was our aim to describe Gunnar's stay in the concentration camp as an organizational and professional learning experience. Our intention was to show how – as seen in a long biographical perspective – his personal experience as a camp inmate had contributed to shaping his professional profile as an applied social psychologist working in Danish and European contexts from the late 1950s.

To be sure, Gunnar could not have developed the organizational and professional insights that accompanied his description of camp life when he was still an inmate, nor, indeed, when he returned to Denmark as an ex-inmate at the age of 25. At this point, Gunnar was in miserable shape. He weighed 30 kilos. The tuberculosis he had contracted in the camp turned out to be extremely persistent, demanding several visits to a sanatorium and several operations. These operations cost him a lot of lung tissue. Towards the end of his stay in the concentration camp, Gunnar's one leg had been badly damaged in connection with a work-related accident. When in camp hospital, he had almost miraculously managed to avert amputation (to be performed by a dentist, himself a prisoner, using a handsaw!). Upon his return to Denmark it took a great amount of time and doctoring skills to make his leg function reasonably.

Altogether, Gunnar's convalescence lasted for three years, i.e. from 1945 to 1948. Healthwise, it was a period of ups and downs. For brief periods during 1946 and '47 he worked as a Folk High School teacher in Denmark and Sweden[2] – he also suffered frequent relapses and had to be re-hospitalized. During that same period he met Berit and married her.[3] Apart from income

---

1   Cf. Madsen & Willert, 1996.
2   Cf. Note 5 for information concerning the Danish folk high school.
3   See the introductory chapter.

from the teaching jobs, he received damages for his physical disabilities and a standard compensation allowance paid to victims of the war. These payments allowed him to buy a small terraced house for himself and his wife in Bagsværd, a suburb in the Copenhagen area. In autumn 1948, he was enrolled as a student of psychology at the University of Copenhagen and this enrolment formally placed him at the starting point of a career as an applied social psychologist – where the present chapter takes its point of departure.

The chapter is based on interview data collected for the Collaboration Project on which the authors and Gunnar cooperated during the 1990s (as described in the introductory chapter). It tells the story of a young man travelling in an organizational and societal landscape. The (implicit) purpose of his journey is to find *his proper place*, i.e. work setting, where he can settle down and use his talents in a personally meaningful way. The purpose was not easily achieved. More than once we find him packing his suitcase. "No, this is not where I'm supposed to stay, either!" The text is mainly constructed from Gunnar's personal-professional comments and reflections concerning the places he visited – made more than 40 years *post hoc* in response to the queries of two eager interviewers.

Catalogue of workplaces during 1948-58

In mundane language, the chapter contains a selective summary of Gunnar's recollections from six different workplaces he visited during the ten-year period between 1948 and 1958. One workplace, the Psychological Laboratory at the University of Copenhagen, was visited by him in the role of student. In all the others, his affiliation was employment-based. As text editors we have mainly focused on *the experiential learning* that he seemed to reap from these various workplace contacts. What did 'Gunnar learn about Gunnar' through his way of managing the organizational member role? What did Gunnar learn about organizational life and quality?[4]

4　In the context of the Collaboration Project described in the introductory chapter, we finished a draft text in 1998, representing a somewhat extended version of the present chapter. We sent the draft to Gunnar in Vust. At a later meeting, Gunnar returned the draft to us, having added several handwritten comments. Gunnar's comments were in part content corrections, in part supplementary information on themes covered. On a continuing basis, he also informed us whether he, as personal owner and source of the written narrative, would object to later publication of single passages. After the meeting in 1998, the basic outline of the project was revised, meaning that further editorial work on the 1998 draft was discontinued. The present Chapter 1 is an abbreviated, revised version of this draft where Gunnar's comments have been honoured.

Below follows a catalogue briefly presenting the six settings (institutions or organizations) in which Gunnar worked during the ten years – 1948 to 1958 – covered in the following pages. Taken together, the material can be read as a small-scale account of a large-scale societal development process, i.e. the establishment of the Danish welfare state. The historical starting point for this process goes back to the 1920s and 30s. Its high point is reached during the period covered by this chapter. The construction of the welfare state implied a radical change in many socially defined role patterns. In a Danish context the development of a professional identity for psychologists is closely bound to the emergence of the welfare state. This is evidenced in our presentation of Gunnar's study place, the Psychological Laboratory, and also by the fact that in all his *post*-university employments Gunnar was the first person to hold the job on the basis of a university degree in psychology. Gunnar: "In the early days of my career much of the work I did had previously been done by priests or school teachers".

The Psychological Laboratory, University of Copenhagen. 'Everybody knows' that by setting up the first psychological laboratory in the world in Leipzig in 1879 the German professor Wilhelm Wundt detached psychology from philosophy – thereby establishing it as an independent scientific academic discipline. What is not known by 'everybody' – outside a Danish context – is that the world's second experimental psychological laboratory was actually established in 1886 by Professor Alfred Lehmann in Copenhagen. For a long time the Laboratory only trained students aiming at a scientific career. In 1944, however, a curriculum including applied psychology was introduced. The study plan was primarily intended as a three-year supplementary course for school teachers enabling them to work as educational psychologists within the Danish public school system. 'Ordinary' students with an interest in the field were also welcomed as applicants. It took another nine years after Gunnar had passed his final exam before psychology, in 1960, became a 'normal' academic discipline that covered five-and-a-half years of study and offered supplementary specialization in clinical and occupational psychology.

Information – a Danish daily newspaper with a somewhat special history. *Information* was a child of the Danish resistance movement during the Second World War. It started as a medium for illegal transmission of information (hence the name) among resistance fighters and their supporters. After Denmark's liberation in 1945 it was transformed into a 'normal' newspaper, i.e. intended for the general market. The newspaper still exists. In its Danish context, it considers itself the equivalent to the French *Le Monde*, its slogan being 'the least lousy newspaper'. Gunnar's association (as a freelance journalist) with

Information started as early as in 1947 and came to an end in 1951 when he graduated with an MA in psychology.

Hindholm Occupational High School was located in the Zealand countryside. The school was a preparatory school for future child welfare service agents. Formally speaking, it enjoyed the status of a Folk High School, i.e. an autonomous teaching establishment having the individual pupil's spiritual enlightenment as an important educational goal.[5] Hindholm was Gunnar's first place of employment after graduation. As it turned out, it lasted only for a year (1951-1952). A few years later, Hindholm was transferred to the Ministry of Social Affairs. Gunnar's comment: "For many years, Hindholm had been a supplier of manpower to charity work based on private and religious initiative. Hindholm's transformation into a ministry supervised educational institution is an indication of the growing professionalization and nationalization of the Danish social sector that was part and parcel of the build-up of the Danish welfare state." At Hindholm Gunnar taught courses in psychology and theory of education. He took over from the school principal who had previously taught the two subjects without any formal educational background for doing so.

The Military Psychology Work Group was formed in 1952, Gunnar being one of its first four members. The Work Group was an institutional forerunner of what would later be known as the Institute of Military Psychology. According to Gunnar, soon after its inception the Work Group expanded, rapidly becoming the biggest Danish workplace for psychologists outside the public school system. Some members of the Work Group staff were permanent employees, while others had temporary and project-based contracts. Among the latter, many belonged to the research or teaching staff at the Psychological Laboratory. Thus, during those years, the armed forces became important institutional sponsors for the development of psychology in Denmark, also at university level. In Gunnar's words: "The university psychologists got themselves a lot of supplementary income by working for the army: all sorts of small- and large-scale projects, definitely of military application value, but also of a more general research value, boosted psychological science in Denmark. Also, many psychology students were hired as casual labour. A great number of psychologists from my generation received their first practical professional

---

5   For more than 150 years, the Folk High School movement has played an important and many-sided role in the development and modernization of the Danish society. Originally the Folk High School movement emerged as an emancipatory counterforce to the State educational system, derogatorily labelled as "the Black School". See, e.g., Borish 1991, for a combined historical and social-anthropological study of the phenomenon.

experiences in the army." On a small Danish scale, and with a certain delay, the process described above was a repetition of what had taken place in the United States during the Second World War, the armed forces becoming institutional sponsors for the general professional development of psychology. Gunnar's affiliation with the Military Psychology Work Group lasted for five years, from 1952-57. It represents his longest single salaried employment, not only during the period covered by the present chapter, but as such.

The National Council for the Unmarried Mother and her Child. As a social agency with auxiliary status, the National Council for the Unmarried Mother and her Child had been established in 1923 on private enterprise terms. In 1939, the agency had been given a statutory charter. Its history thus illustrates the same trend towards 'professionalization and nationalization' of social work in Denmark as was mentioned with reference to Hindholm Occupational High School. Gunnar's affiliation with the National Council was brief, lasting a year (1953-54) and being only a part-time job. "While working part-time for the Military Psychology Work Group, I added yet another part-time job – just one-and-a-half-days per week – with the National Council. I was their first psychologist. I wanted to find out whether this kind of work could possibly be my future professional field. I was far too inexperienced in clinical psychology. Would I be able to transform my knowledge into practice?" Gunnar's main function here was that of investigative caseworker in relation to women's abortion petitions, but he also did adoption casework. Within the agency's professional work team consisting of psychiatrists, social workers, and members of the legal profession, he represented the psychological perspective. As was usual then, Gunnar had not been recruited on the basis of a job advertisement formally addressed to psychologists, but rather as a result of hearsay within 'the network'. "During those years, psychologists found their way into many new positions in society. Advertisements were rare – except in the case of school psychologists".

The Danish Technological Institute. Ever since its founding in 1906, the main task of the Danish Technological Institute in Copenhagen had been to furnish small and medium business enterprises with state-subsidized development support (in the form of trade-specific technology research) and professional training courses. Originally founded by The Danish Federation of Small and Medium-Sized Enterprises, this organization was the Institute's permanent main sponsor. During the fifties, however, changes taking place in Danish society also led to shifts of balance in the Danish business sector, meaning that the Institute's traditional clients became less relevant in a future-oriented business perspective. These and other events led the Institute to plan for a partial business strategic reorientation. Hoping thereby to attract new dynamic clients, e.g., larger industrial production enterprises, a decision had been made to move into the fields of organization and management consultancy as new priority areas. As one step towards implementation of this strategy, Gunnar was recruited to the Danish Technological Institute in 1957. 'Somebody' in the Institute's management team had plans involving 'young Hjelholt' – who, at that time, happened to be one of the few Danish university-trained psychologists with organizational experience. However, as will appear later, the 'young Hjelholt' himself was not immediately involved in these plans!

A view of 'the fifties'

From this point onward, the chapter will primarily be based on Gunnar's recollections of what he encountered in his role as an informal participant observer placed inside the workplaces mentioned above – supplemented with his afterthoughts when, 40 years later, he looked back on this period of his life. Before moving fully into that area, however, we shall present his general notions concerning the historical epoch where these observations took place. To us – being about 25 years his junior – his notions were somewhat surprising as they did not, right away, match our ideas about which decade happened to be the most *interesting* in post-war Denmark ...

> *One generation separates us from you. When you entered the psychology course in 1948, at the age of 28, we had just turned five. As we see the world, the fifties was a period dominated by grey colour nuances. Not very exciting. If, as a decade, it had any merits at all, this was due to its paving the way for the sixties. The sixties was the period when things got started – politically, culturally ...*

I didn't experience the period that way at all. To me, 1948 and the following years are essentially *post*-war years. As long as the War had been in progress, it had dominated everything. Now the War was over. This meant there was lots of work to be done.

The Second World War had shaken us, made us all terrified. With one stroke it had made us realize how simple and easy, indeed, it is to threaten the established world order at the core. The humanist values and ideals – values we felt so sure of here in Europe, the old world, the fine, cultured world – had been turned upside down. Thought provoking, to say the least. We believed ourselves to be so utterly democratic. Nazism and Fascism told us a different story. If, in the future, we actually *wanted* democracy to function as system of governance, we jolly well had to make a determined effort to that effect. Education and re-education were necessary. Slogans like "Never another April the Ninth!"[6] were extremely important to us in the early post-war years including the fifties.

And not only that. The Second World War had also smashed up the material basis of existence for quite a lot of people – not *only* in Europe, but definitely *also* in Europe. A lot of reconstruction tasks needed our immediate attention. Just think of how the German infrastructure had been completely destroyed during the last war months. Similar problems, even if less dramatic, existed in many other places. To make the right choice among the many tasks that needed doing might appear difficult – because there were so many. But *to see the point and relevance of getting started* – doing at least something – was easy enough.

One further and final point is worth mentioning. Somehow the war experience had also prepared the ground for hope and optimism. Nazism had been a threat, but in the end it was defeated. The war demonstrated that determined humans can in fact accomplish what they strive for, if, jointly, they agree to put differences between them aside and submit to a common cause in spite of what sets them apart. The war had actually been won, Nazism overcome. Now was the time to move on.

Internationally speaking, during the post-war years the world opened up, became bigger. Contacts were established across old cultural and national borders. During those years we became aware that we all lived in one and the same world – that we were all dependent on each other.

During the thirties in the United States, Roosevelt had come forth as a progressive idealist by presenting his slogan about starting things anew: a New Deal, not only at a national, but also at an international level. In the European post-war context, this slogan was realized in the form of Marshall Aid. And it was effective! – in grim contrast to the development aid systems developed later.

In our Danish context, the fifties was the period when construction of the welfare state was the main point on the national agenda. Many problem areas which, till then, had been considered private or simply unavoidable parts of the natural order: poverty, illness, inequality and lack of opportunities ..., were redefined and became matters of joint concern calling for joint solutions. The

---

6   On April 9th, 1940, Germany invaded and occupied Denmark. Consequently the date has mythological status in a national Danish context. The expression "Never another April the Ninth!" became a kind of proverb during the post-war period and has in some measure kept that status.

war had also put a stop to the functioning of many public administrative 'systems'. Here and there in society, institutional lacunae were found; they must be filled. As an indirect result, the *post*-war years witnessed the emergence of many innovations and modifications of traditional social practice. A time for experimentation – inventing and discovering new ways of organizing society.

There was, of course, also another side of the coin. Society was in a state of constant change. That's why, for me personally, the decade was such an interesting period. However, changes also make people feel anxious and upset. Not everyone perceived the social experiments going on as interesting, nor felt that changes would be for the better. Institutions and individuals had to defend what they saw as their well-earned rights and privileges. Defend themselves against the new ways. Quite a few people saw their positions as threatened – in some instances for very good reasons! Looking back on my work experiences during the entire decade, it's easy to see the conflict between old and new, between forces pointing towards the future and those wanting to set the clocks back. In all corners of society, this conflict made its mark on institutional life.

Thinking about the fifties, one of the first things that comes to mind is that it was a period when the purpose or meaning of one's actions was fairly easy to grasp, for everyone to see. So many things needed doing; there was no need for a lot of vacillation. Everybody knew what he was for and what he was against.

Since then, in my opinion, it has become pretty hard to see the world – see your relationship to the world – that clearly. Back then, we didn't have to reflect so much on the *meaning of it all*. The meaning was right there, in front of us. Later, in the sixties for instance – the period which the two of you favour a lot more – much *thinking* was going on, often very varied and complex thinking, with the aim of deciphering or unravelling what the *overall* meaning could *really* be. Perhaps this is what made that period so interesting? I, for my part, feel that meaning has become increasingly hard to get at. In my opinion, much political and social activities from the sixties and onwards have been attempts at re-finding or re-establishing some sort of overall meaning or possible direction of it all. These various experiments have not succeeded in any very convincing way.

Now the road has been paved for Gunnar's own account of his various visits to organizations and institutions – in search of a professional platform.

Studying psychology

In 1948, Gunnar had enrolled as a psychology student at the University of Copenhagen – whereby he, formally speaking, took his first step towards what was to become his professional platform.

Gunnar's standard explanation[7] for his choice of study area went like this: before the war, in 1938, he had been admitted to the Department of Economics, but he never really got started. Returning to the study of economics would imply 5-5½ years before graduation. Among study programmes, psychology stood out because it could be completed in only three years. Why not try that? Gunnar was in a hurry. He had married, wanted to have a family, had already tried many things in life and was not interested in stretching his studies beyond what was strictly necessary. Internment in the concentration camp and subsequent rehabilitation had cost him four years. Right now, his main concerns about life were of a practical nature.

For these reasons, Gunnar ended up as a university trained psychologist, and without having wasted any time on the way. In 1951, i.e. after three years, equalling the official time-of-study, he got his much desired diploma. His contact with the academic discipline of psychology had thus started as a marriage of convenience rather than a romantic love affair. This impression was confirmed when we interviewed Gunnar about the ways in which his student years had been of inspirational value for his career.

Looking back, do you feel content with what you learned during your study years?

Well … – at least I'm pleased I completed the course within the official time frame. Now I had a university degree. That was definitely useful. And, well … I reckon I must have learned something … (pause)

Your answer doesn't come loud and clear!

No, and that's because your question is one I need to *ask myself*: what *did* I actually learn? – and how? Did my learning come from studying, or from the many small projects in which I engaged myself alongside the study as such? I contacted places and gave myself some tasks. The links to the psychology course were there – but for me, the most important things happened elsewhere.

---

7   Cf. Madsen & Willert, 1996.

For instance, I managed to get myself a month-long job at the Psychiatric Hospital in Middelfart. One ward psychiatrist hanged imself while I was there. Learning that the caretakers were just as insane as the officially insane, and equally hard-pressed, came as quite a shock to me. It taught me something about the professional caretaker role that textbooks could never have told me. I also found short-term employment at an observational summer camp – Fuglsø – for children with behavioural problems. There I learned a bit about sandplay observation. The camp principal was a psychologist; probably I'd met him as a guest lecturer at the University and he'd noticed my interest in the clinical field. Anyway, I contacted him and got permission to spend some time there.

The one practical activity from which I probably gained the most during my study years was a piece of classroom research I did with schoolchildren in Taastrup. As you know, politically I was a socialist even though my family background was middle-class. The children in Taastrup came from working-class families. I found it exciting to get an inside view of their culture and thinking style. During autumn and winter I collected a lot of data including essays and sociometric observations. In fact, at the Laboratory I had managed to strike a deal with the board of study to the effect that I could use my material for writing an essay replacing an exam in the discipline of the *Pathology of mathematics and writing*. But alas, when I handed in my report, they'd changed their minds and would no more accept this kind of essay. Thus, I had to sit for an exam which didn't make sense to me. I sulked – also because I was barred from making practical use of my data; to my mind, this small research piece contained valuable stuff. Later, I used the data for a couple of articles on how children experience punishment, and these I managed to sell a couple of times.

You must also have been obliged to look at a few books, eh…?

Well, I actually did. I did a lot of reading during those years. I didn't always find the formal study curricula terribly interesting, so my reading concentrated on fields not included in the curricula. A bit from here, a bit from there – in many ways fragmented. Still, I actually managed to collect for myself some kind of basic theoretical knowledge – something that served me well, later on. Many years later, when being trained by American psychologists in group dynamics, I saw them as lacking a proper theoretical foundation. They were brilliant practical and educational entrepreneurs, brilliant at combining research and applied work. In those fields, they could really teach me something. Yet, at times I somehow got the impression that they were almost *too* pragmatic and that, in comparison, I had an advantage in being theoretically more knowledgeable.

Your stories about your study years remind us, once more, of the theme of Gunnar being on the edge of things. On the one hand, you were an active university student – but only a part of you, not wholeheartedly. At the same time, you were doing your own thing, apparently guided by personal agendas. In many ways, the latter seemed to matter most. Is that a fair description?

Oh, sure. That's how it was.

Now, it's not our job to make you "confess" that, after all, you did learn a few things at university. Still, from an earlier interview, we remember you mentioning a certain kind of analytic or methodical rigour which you experienced as one of your strong points as an applied psychologist. Whatever else may be said about the Copenhagen psychology,[8] it was strongly oriented towards experimental work and empirical methods. As a student, you did practical laboratory exercises, wrote reports and the like …

Those laboratory exercises … oh, please no! If you ask me, most of them were a complete waste of time. They might deal with such things as sensory spots on the skin, some cold, some warm. How on earth did that connect with real life, with human beings? It would take a greater intellect than mine to make practical sense out of warm and cold spots – even admitting that in principle it's kind of interesting that 'the whole world' happens to be made up of that kind of spot feelings. Perhaps the teachings of the Laboratory were *correct*, whereas some of Freud's teachings may have been *incorrect*. But, at least, Freud did make a serious effort to reflect on things that were *important* for a psychologist to consider. Speaking generally, I didn't succeed in making out what could be important about those exercises. So I seriously doubt whether I learnt anything by doing them.

No, my father was probably the one who somehow taught me about the importance of keeping your thoughts straight, having an orderly method to go by when you investigate something. As you know, my father was a historian, in that profession it is of vital importance to keep records and data straight, to stick to your governing idea.

---

8   One of the authors – and interviewers – had been a student at the Copenhagen Psychological Laboratory and had thus, himself, been exposed to the experimental laboratory exercises mentioned below.

A university institute and a newspaper house compared

Between 1948 and 1951 Gunnar had two workplaces: he was matriculated as a student of psychology at the University of Copenhagen. Parallel to his studies, he worked as a 'culture vulture', i.e. freelance journalist, for the newspaper *Information*.

It was two completely different organizations with which he became acquainted.

Gunnar was affiliated to the Laboratory for the reason of learning something and becoming more knowledgeable. As we have seen, his respect for the Laboratory as a learning environment was not great. For this reason, he intentionally kept his formal study activities at the lowest possible level. He did what was required of him, no more. Speed, rather than quality, was what counted.

> Back then, the course programme in psychology was more or less structured like medicine, i.e. as one long string of isolated teaching subjects following the other. Each semester I had to make a decision concerning the number of subjects I could manage to lay behind me this time, so as to get my diploma and get out of there – the sooner the better ...

Gunnar's formal status at *Information* was that of an hourly-paid employee. He earned his salary by being productive, i.e. writing articles for the paper. The acquisition of significant personal enlightenment was nowhere mentioned in his contract with the newspaper house. Still, when looking back at his journalist years, he keeps returning to the personal development and important insight gained from that job. During interview sessions conducted more than 40 years later, his esteem for the newspaper house as a training experience for youngsters, like himself at the time, was undiminished.

> *Information* gave me a space where I could breathe – while, at the same time, I could earn some money. The latter was not unimportant. I was the breadwinner for a family – our oldest child was born in 1950. Furthermore – last, but definitely not least – it was a place where I felt I could learn something.

> *Whenever you speak of Information, there is a sparkle in your eyes. How come that workplace was so fantastic, seen in a learning perspective?*

> Everybody was taken seriously. At the editorial staff meetings, one of us might present an idea. If it had only a grain of interesting stuff in it, we would be

encouraged to take it further. Management showed confidence in each individual employee – believed in our power to create something of value. That confidence I could really use. I am a learning-by-doing person. At *Information* I was allowed to play around with my ideas in practice.

I suppose they didn't let you do just anything *at Information?*

Of course there were editorial as well as economic constraints. For instance, I once came up with a suggestion that we do an investigation of a small Danish community. American researchers had written books on the subject, I had read them and they inspired me a lot.[9] At first, the editorial board encouraged me to contact a sociology professor at the University for possible cooperation. Together with him I started to draft a questionnaire that was to form the basis for our investigation. But then, when I returned to the editorial meeting bringing along the final budget, they turned down their thumbs. Seidenfaden, one of the two chief editors, still supported my project in the light of my earlier successes with serial features – admittedly of a more modest size. But the other editor in chief, Outze, who was also responsible for the newspaper's economy, was not willing to give his support. So, in the end the project was turned down.[10]

In my personal perspective, it was rather a pity. Had the project been accepted, I would have had what corresponded to a small research grant at my disposal, to be spent on an investigation with obvious social-psychological relevance.

But – my personal interests apart: the actual procedure followed in dealing with my application lived up to the highest possible standards at a decent workplace. No one had issued any promises which, later, they dishonoured. The reasons given for turning down the project were fair. As a staff member, I was given full opportunity to present all my good arguments. I was listened to. In any organization it must be the task of top management to make decisions like the one Outze made, based on an overall judgment – and then to present the decision to the person in question.

---

9   West (1945) and Dollard (1949) are early classics within the field of community studies. In other interview sessions, Gunnar had commented upon the so-called Ecological Psychology tradition initiated by Barker, whose textbook (1968) summarizes research done since the late forties.

10 Børge Outze (1912-80) and Erik Seidenfaden (1910-90) are considered important figures in modern Danish press history.

          PART ONE

Good organizations, bad organizations

In Gunnar's world, *Information* became his best known example of *the good organization*. Among his workplaces during the period 1948-58, he explicitly singled the newspaper house out as *the* one organization where he never had any serious misgivings – neither about the place, nor its people. At the other end of his personal value scale, we have seen how the Psychological Laboratory served him as one prime example of a bad, or even very bad organization.

One key issue in his account of both organizations is his description of their respective ways of implementing their *primary tasks*. From a normative organizational perspective, the concept of task had acquired an almost sacred status for Gunnar. And, in that, he is not alone. Many theoretical traditions have put forth arguments stressing the importance of the task theme.[11] And yet, through our interviews and our encounter with his continuous and stubborn insistence on task as the core variable of any organizational analysis and evaluation, new facets and depth were added to our own understanding of primary task as a hub of organizational life.

To start with, let us introduce the reader to Gunnar's general evaluative reflections on his place-of-study, the Psychological Laboratory.

> Already during my study years I was confronted with the conflict between using the task as a guideline when managing organizational affairs, in contrast to letting yourself be governed by political ambitions or, indeed, a felt resistance to change.
>
> From society's point of view, the tasks that the universities are supposed to implement are of an indispensable nature. Universities serve a double purpose. On the one hand, there's the purpose of research: working to reach a valid understanding of the world – in the case of psychology such an understanding should be based on a human transactional perspective. Many people outside the University are engaged in that very same task. The University has a special commitment to deliver some kind of proof or documentation for their statements and knowledge claims, and to present them in a manner that may enable others to read and make use of the results of their work. Being society's public

---

11   Within the field of applied social psychology, the so-called Tavistock tradition is especially noted for the way it gives importance to the organization's *primary task* as a key concept in any qualified assessment of organizational quality or value. Chapter 2 contains material concerning Gunnar's contact to and thoughts about the Tavistock tradition.

research institution, the University has a special obligation to safeguard its research results and keep them available for the outside world.

On the other hand, there's the purpose of higher education: it is meant to serve as a meeting ground for citizens who share an interest in obtaining knowledge and skills within certain professional fields. The University is obliged to facilitate, in a well structured manner, this upgrading of skills – make sure that the proper professional expertise is available for guiding the students appropriately. Later on, the University must make itself available for providing a link between people who share the same kind of education, in case they might need to refresh or further develop their knowledge after having practiced in the outside world.

The importance of these two tasks is obvious. If universities have problems, those problems are *not* caused by a poor quality of their tasks as such. What infuriates me is that the University doesn't make a determined effort to manage its tasks properly – for, indeed, in many respects these tasks are definitely mismanaged. At least, that's what I've experienced time and again in my contact with the University. Far too great a share of what goes on at the University ends up in internal struggles – concerning power or influence or 'looking right', not sticking out. The system has developed a habit of avoiding risks at all costs. Likewise, the language used for communicating research results tends to become less and less transparent.

When I was a student, Danish psychology was united in a joint effort to develop a phenomenological or experientially based psychology.[12] My later work experiences as a psychologist have convinced me that this way of thinking has some very important professional merits. In my opinion, the focus on the individual person' unique experiential perspective counts as psychology's essential contribution to human and social development. More than anything else, it is the cultivation of this perspective that constitutes psychology as a basic science. Learning to deal with such a perspective and teaching it to others I see as our most important obligation as psychologists.

---

12   Gunnar refers to a research tradition called the Copenhagen School. Its key figure was Edgar Rubin (1886-1951). It was Rubin's ambition – an ambition he practised with great determination – that scientific psychology be founded on detailed descriptions of things and events reflecting the unitary way in which they appeared to the human observer.

Even so, what continually struck me during my years of study – well, and in all later years as well – was that *in practice* it turned out to be extremely difficult to develop these really quite simple ideas in reasonable ways. What made it difficult was that the work must be done in a university setting. The fear of *not being able to meet established scientific standards* got in the way. The institution got in the way of its own goal accomplishment! This is probably not the first time I quote the poem by Piet Hein saying that *humans are the only animals who risk stumbling over lines drawn by themselves.*[13]

During those years, more than anything else it was the natural sciences that scared the wits out of academic psychology: 'We must be able to quantify what we are doing, somehow our findings must be graphically represented!' Everybody was so intent on *being scientific* that the original ideas lying behind the whole enterprise were somehow forgotten. When reading the old Copenhagen School publications, what they were actually aiming at – those practical and theoretical issues that originally started them out – gets quickly blurred. What strikes you instead is the author's preoccupation with developing his own work into a self-sufficient discipline, building walls around it, criticizing other people's work. During those years, Rubin's safe deposit box was a well known and ill famed place for hiding various manuscripts – authored by his co-workers and colleagues – which had not been approved by His Highness the professor. Everybody was considering their reputation on the local scene, their respectability, trying to outmanoeuvre those who might endanger their own position. *The central tasks and issues* were forgotten on that score.

As regards teaching, it was the same old story. In principle, the teaching done was meant to benefit us, the younger generation, and make us wiser. In reality – with very few exceptions – what went on in the classrooms and lecture halls tended to be extremely uninteresting, with no bearing whatsoever on real life matters. The fact that my professional interests mainly centred on clinical and social psychology made me experience the curriculum taught as even more meaningless. During my years of study, those fields were practically banned, not spoken about.

Compared to his description of the Psychological Laboratory, Gunnar's account of the newspaper house *Information* as an organization and work place sounded refreshingly simple.

---

13   Piet Hein, Danish poet, 1905-96. See also chapters 13 and 16.

The primary task at *Information* was to get a newspaper published every day – well, and to make sure that the stuff written was worth reading: that the quality was as required.

All employees knew and let themselves be guided by this overall task; but the task wasn't talked about at lot. That was not necessary. All employees carried an implicit understanding of it in their heads.

Further evidence of the way things got regulated by a shared understanding was seen in the fact that only very few *stated* rules governed the way work was carried out on a day-to-day basis: division of labour, process control, etc. Somehow, it just happened. Everybody simply did what seemed to be the right thing to do. In that way problems sorted themselves out.

Information was a child of the Resistance Movement. A peculiar attitude, which also had been present in the Movement, somehow helped keep the newspaper house together as a workplace. In the Resistance Movement lots of similar stories had been told about the way in which individuals formed small col-laborational units and seemed able to use some kind of gut feeling that made them do the right things at the right moment, even though they were physically separated from one another, and with hardly any means for mutual communication. *Information* attracted people with just that talent. The goal of employees was not to push themselves forward, but to make the work community function. The amount of freedom delegated to each and everyone was incredible. Each individual employee used this freedom as a means towards the end of getting a high quality paper published on time.

Good and bad leaders

For Gunnar, talk about tasks and the handling of tasks will, with a high degree of probability, lead to talk about management and leadership. However many individuals have a share in management, it constitutes the organizational unit whose job it is never to lose sight of task and task performance – including a responsibility for allocating organizational resources in ways that may optimize task accomplishment.

During my time at *Information*, Børge Outze was its chief executive. Nobody had any doubts about that, his leadership was recognized throughout the organization. But I'm not at all sure Outze actually saw himself as the person whose job it was to 'manage the organization'. There wasn't much to worry about, things went quite smoothly. Everybody knew the basic idea: what their job was, what needed doing. That part of management which the textbooks describe as motivation, i.e. 'making the employees do this and that', didn't get much explicit focus at *Information*. Or you might say that the employees at *Information* were good at *self-management*, at least in a day-to-day perspective.

But then Outze happened to have one key qualification – one that I see as extremely important for the continued survival and development of the paper: he himself was tremendously skilled at putting words together on paper. He really gave us something to live up to. His professional standards were very high and this was a fact that influenced everybody else's way of thinking about his or her job. We weren't just supposed to make 'a newspaper'. It had to be a *quality paper*, and through his own writing he showed us how to go about it. On a daily basis his articles served as a professional challenge. In a long-term perspective they were an incitement for everybody to develop his skills. Still, he managed to uphold his own and everybody else's standard with *no authoritarian element* involved. From what I know or have heard of other newspaper houses this seems to have been quite an extraordinary feat of his.

From your account of Outze's way of administering his talents, he seems to have formed a sharp contrast to the persons you met at the University?

If Rubin, and his way of handling his role as chief executive, is used as a comparison, it's definitely true!

As a researcher and professional person, Rubin was exceptionally gifted. Probably, he might count as a genius. His quite brief doctoral thesis on figure and ground became the primary reason for his fame. This work secured him long term admission to each and every psychological textbook published for years to come. *Rubin's vase* remains a classic and, as such, is depicted in all sorts of contexts where the perspective of psychology is presented.[14]

He himself had this peculiar enthusiasm about 'messing around in a laboratory' – as he used to call it. He designed strange machinery to be used in the experimental testing of his ideas. But his 'messing around' helped him create results! Small monographs published in the international journals of the day,

---

14   To Edgar Rubin, the 'vase' was one example among many of the fact that people's general experiences (either "I see a vase" or "I see two profiles") are guided by a unitary perception of 'good form' rather than forms emanating from the way perceptual details were pieced together. Rubin's vase argument is connected with gestalt psychology, a theoretical approach that also inspired Lewin (cf. Chapter 2).

or feature articles for national newspapers – always phrased so that everyone could understand them. He kept insisting that articles be written so that "any maid or laundry woman would get the idea". When at his best, his own writings largely matched his ideals. Somehow hidden away in his articles, you would often come across formulations which served as genuine epistemological eye-openers and provided you with much food for thought.

Yes indeed, Rubin was a gifted man, a creative researcher, and – further – a man having ideas about the democratic reporting of research results with which I completely agree. All this makes it seem strange that his management style at the Laboratory was so utterly barren and, indeed, undemocratic to an extent I've hardly ever come across in any other place.

Rubin's barrenness as a leader was due to the fact that he made unyielding demands to any kind of research performed by his employees, i.e. research that the Laboratory and he himself would be formally responsible for. Somehow he must have thought that by making these demands he did what was required of him as chief executive of the Laboratory. What happened as an effect of this approach, however, was that Rubin's own talents – the things he was particularly good at – ended up having a negative impact on the institution. Instead of inspiring the employees: being a positive ideal and a professional challenge, his talents became a negative norm that would, in practice, prevent the employees from unfolding theirs.

The same kind of attitudes determined the Laboratory's stance on Freud and psychoanalysis. Personally, Rubin was of the opinion that Freud was wrong. Freud was an outsider, he came from the practical world, the world surrounding the University. Freud's ideas were based on qualitative arguments and individual cases, they were not experimentally supported. For these reasons, Rubin's rejection became the official doctrine concerning Freud. As such it was repeatedly promulgated in lecture halls and other academic settings.

The whole situation developed in a paradoxical manner. During those years, many among the teaching staff were in fact going through their individual psychoanalysis. At the same time, psychoanalysis was banned as a theoretical approach. Serious discussion about it was not allowed. It lacked in academic quality, it wasn't backed up by experiments. Such was the verdict of Professor Rubin, end of discussion!

Rubin's dogmatic management style placed the institution in a kind of internal self-contradiction. I myself took hours with a Swedish psychoanalyst between

1948 and 1950. I believe Rubin's fundamentalist attitude formed part of my wish to try it out. I was curious to learn what it was about Freudianism that could be so abhorrent. Yet, my psychoanalyst and I had difficulties finding common grounds. To him, all that mattered were childhood experiences from long ago. This was the kind of understanding in which he had specialized. To me my not-so-long-ago experiences from Porta somehow seemed more urgent – while at the same time they were difficult to put into words. We never really managed to make it work between us.

Instead I benefited from psychoanalysis in a theoretical way. During those years and ever since, it has served me as a framework for grasping the interconnectedness of what may appear disparate. When scientific literature was presented to us at the University, its subject matter had already been taken apart, split into tiny pieces. The University had 'come between' our understanding efforts and that which we were meant to understand. In the end, what was left was some kind of mental gymnastics. Whatever particular misgivings one may have about Freud – that he was overemphasizing certain points, etc. – still, he *was* seriously attempting to paint a full picture. What he talked about was *real people*.

You've talked about Outze as the ideal leader. Rubin is nowhere near your ideal. You do not seem prepared to give him any excuses. Looking back at our interview sessions as a whole, it seems that most leaders you encountered belonged to the Rubin category...? Or are we being biased?

... (thinking pause) ... In my opinion, Eric Trist, managing director of the Tavistock Institute of Human Relations, was also a good leader. Working for him gave me no problems.[15]

Further, I'm reminded of the year-long period when I worked for the National Council for the Unmarried Mother and her Child. During that year I experienced two leaders both of whom were gynaecologists. Comparing them, they stood in a sharp contrast to each other. One of them I saw as a brilliant leader. He made work flow smoothly in the institution. At staff meetings he was good at keeping focus on the primary task of the National Council, namely to help women. By his side he had the managing director of the institution – a lawyer who thought like lawyers and officials do. She represented the administrative viewpoint, reminding him, whenever needed, about the legal facts of the matter. He would thus be free to concentrate on the case from the woman's perspective. On that basis, he would guide staff discussions. Everyone felt listened to – which

---

15   We shall hear more about Eric Trist in Chapter 2.

doesn't, of course, imply that everybody would have an equal share in the final decision concerning a given petition. The central goal of the discussion seemed clear to everybody and was in practice honoured by everybody.

Comparatively speaking, the second leader I worked for actually had a higher professional reputation than the first, in the relevant circles. Still, in my opinion he hadn't much to offer, neither in his professional leadership capacity, nor his management capacity. He was far too eager to please the administrative management, meaning the lawyer, giving her far too much power. And he stuck to hierarchy. An argument would carry weight not only as a function of its content, but also based on the rank of the person who put it forward. The higher up in the hierarchy, the more you would be listened to.

I really did my best to let professional values guide me, also after the leadership change. 'What serves the woman best?' At times this would bring me into conflict with the new leader – e.g. if I told him his conclusions were completely off the mark since, in no way, they matched with my investigations. A general sense of mutual mistrust developed between us. After one year's employment it was time to renew the contract. I wanted to change from part-time to full-time employee. The workload was clearly there to justify such a change, but they were unwilling to upgrade the position. That made me resign. I had my permanent position – also part-time – at the Military Psychology Work Group. Shortly after my resignation they decided, after all, to upgrade the psychologist position. It wasn't upgrading as such that had bothered the new leader, but rather me as a person.

In an indirect manner, then, a conflict between you and your boss was responsible for your losing that job?

Yes – and this incident was a repetition of what had happened earlier on, when I changed from Hindholm Occupational High School to the Military Psychology Work Group.

I was pleased to get the job at Hindholm. It was my first 'real' psychologist job and I liked teaching. I was particularly happy because, here, I got a chance to *use* psychology in a *practical* context. Hindholm was an occupational high school, meaning that, ideally speaking, my classes should enable the girls to work with children in a professionally enlightened manner. All that suited me well. It was perfect. And yet, in the end it all went wrong. Slowly but surely not only I, but Berit as well, felt increasingly uncomfortable by staying and working at the school. It had something to do with the way they treated their students – the school's general perception of its task vis-a-vis its students.

The very idea lying behind such a high school, its primary task, is highly commendable. By staying at the school young people are meant to acquire a foundation that will help and guide them later on, not only in work, but also in life affairs. Their self-awareness will grow, and thus their awareness of their place in society and of the choices they have at their disposal. But then, what we saw happening time and again was that the institution and its principal acted in ways that ran strictly counter to the school's task. Young people need acceptance and emotional support from grown-ups. They need nursing as well as challenges from their surroundings. The relationship between teacher and student will never succeed unless nourished by some kind of love – but a love that doesn't make you blind or make you take over the student's will power. The student must be seen the way he or she actually is, and as fully capable of managing her own affairs. What we kept experiencing at Hindholm was the exact opposite – that the institution would behave towards its students as if they were irresponsible and *most probably* even naughty children.

A succession of events, big and small, gradually soured the relationship between the two of us and the school's principal and teachers. As an illustration, I remember one episode that began as a mere triviality but ended in a clash. During meals at the high school, a teacher would be sitting at the end of each table; the principal would head the main table. One day they observed that a girl – from Copenhagen of course! – put cheese *and* marmalade on her bread. She had broken the rules: this was definitely not allowed, and she was firmly requested to admit her guilt and promise never, never to do it again. This she refused. Things escalated, and her expulsion was considered as a possible solution. The teaching staff was sharply divided on the issue. I threw myself into the conflict speaking for the girl's right to stay on. Incidents like this made my relation to – most importantly – the principal increasingly tense. Neither did I particularly like the internal climate in the staff group: intrigue making, reciprocal outmanoeuvring ...

Looking back today, it is easy to see Hindholm as a replication of my University experiences – the main difference being that my position had changed from that of student to that of teacher. Of course it is possible to point out many aspects that made the two organizations differ. Still, as educational systems they were alike to the extent that much available energy was spent on things unrelated to the task with which society had entrusted them.

The Danish military: a training ground for the applied social psychologist to be

At first glance, Gunnar definitely did not strike one as being militaristic, neither in his way of being, nor his way of thinking. On this background it is interesting that, during our talks, the Military Psychology Work Group was very often referred to as the workplace which professionally speaking, apart from *Information*, he had held in the highest esteem. There were several reasons for this.

The place was filled with action. An inspiring place to be in.

During those years, the Military – as an institution – was undergoing radical changes and with many among the military staff you found a keen will to reform. A large group of young officers had experienced how the organization had compromised itself during the war: had gone morally bankrupt. Certain initiatives were taken in order to curb the 'old men's' influence or have them removed from posts insofar as they stood in the way of reforms. Furthermore, sizeable financial resources had been granted for the purpose of actually realizing the 'new' ideas in practice.[16]

This also explains why the Military Psychology Work Group was formed in 1952. We were four psychologists in the group when it started. All of us had graduated from the university, but only two of us were civilians. The two other members – who became the group's formal leaders from the very start – had, so to speak, been appointed by their superiors to study psychology as part of their military careers.

Definitely, during the early fifties the military was a very challenging, exciting and creative workplace. And the best part of it: *here it was absolutely impossible to keep theory and practice separate.* Job requisitions kept coming in. One day, we might be asked to go and investigate certain problems that kept cropping up in one of the battalions. To do that, we must first get hold of existing knowledge concerning group or team work. All sorts of things that had been written about groups suddenly became extremely relevant. During those years, the literature on small group research was skyrocketing. I still have my old copy of *Handbook of Social Psychology* – with all the underlinings I made back then.

---

16 In June 1997, Gunnar told one of us: "In many articles written about the Military by psychologists, the system is primarily described as reactionary. I do not agree. In my experience it is progressive". Cf. also Hjelholt, 1997.

But the job wasn't finished simply because we had succeeded in gaining some kind of *understanding* of what had happened – *why* some situation had reached a deadlock. We also had to find a solution to the problem. We had to develop the necessary tools, acquaint ourselves with the literature on methodologies that had been developed here and there and on that basis we had to design our own methods. That Work Group functioned like a small psychology course all by itself. It made sense, it was meaningful *because it was meant to be used*. Indeed, that was the only reason why it took place.

The Work Group also gave me my first serious opportunity to get acquainted with the consultant role. One well known risk inherent in that role is that you may be swallowed up by the system you're supposed to help – somehow forgetting that, in the first place, you were sent there to help *them* solve some of *their* problems. Once you've become swallowed up your value as a helper to the system has gone down the drain. Then you belong to the system. Concerning these issues, I did notice quite some differences between the civilian group members with no military rank and the two members having ranks – even though they were psychologists like we were. Those two carrying ranks were accustomed to *knowing their place in the hierarchy*, so to speak. You obey those above, you give orders to those below you. We civilians found it easier to participate on an equal footing in all kinds of situations – to take on the attitude of the observer, to ask silly questions. We were 'the outsiders', we kept a 'natural distance'. From a consultant point of view, it gave us certain benefits.

Likewise, if some situation had gone awry, it would often be easier for us civilians to see what was going on, and to hold on to our picture of what went wrong. For better or for worse, our two colleagues were old hands in the system. Work-wise, the system had socialized them – they had it under their skin, much more that we strangers. Looking at problems with innocent eyes, getting ideas about ways in which traditional problems might be solved by untraditional means, being truly curious – at times, this was not easy for them.

Falling out with management

Gunnar's employment with the Military Psychology Work Group helped him carve out for himself a niche that matched his professional development needs nicely. His respect for the military institution was also based on organizational appraisals of a more general nature – showing once more his persistent focus on task and task consciousness.

Just as we have not succeeded in abolishing crime, we've not managed to abolish war and violence. This given, we need systems that deal with these things – who see it as their job to handle these social problem. Many examples, contemporary as well as of the past, bear witness to the fact that the army may overstep its boundaries with regard to its proper function in society's division of labour. Military persons may elevate themselves into being the ones who set the political agenda, rather than submit to it. That, of course, won't work at all. However, as far as my concrete experience with the military institution goes, it showed good understanding of why it was there. No doubt, the extensive reform undertaking in which the Work Group was involved gave rise to lots of tension and conflicts, often harsh ones. Still, generally speaking, it remains my impression that conflicts and tension were dealt with in ways that paid respect to *the issue of relevance*: 'How do we find the best possible solution to the task with which we have been entrusted?'

In view of the above statement, it is telling that Gunnar's final exit from his military workplace was due to an incident where he felt himself forced to confront a colleague – at the same time his boss – who in practice betrayed the military ideals of moral integrity.

So, you had no ideological qualms about working for that system?

Well, no. I took care to follow my own, rather than the military dress code, striving, so to speak, not to appear as 'a military man'. We remained outsiders, civilians. It belongs to the story that my decision to leave was taken that one day when I heard myself clicking my heels entering a general's office: 'Hey, what's happening now? – Blimey, it seems the system's getting its hold on you. Must be about time to get out of here!'

Well, that was just one of my reasons for leaving. Another reason had to do with the kind of role I ended up playing in an episode which finally led to the sacking of one of my bosses – in fact, the very same man who, originally, had asked me to join the Military Psychology Work Group.

It all started when my other boss noticed some apparent irregularities concerning the accounts. We talked it over, internally in our unit to begin with. To the rest of us it quickly became pretty obvious that the boss who had appointed me was the responsible, or guilty one, if you like. Within our small group, however, he kept denying he had done anything wrong. He saw himself as being victimized. It may very well be that some kind of personal rivalry or competition motives played themselves out between the two bosses. Be that as it may, what finally happened was that the three of us, his Work Group colleagues, felt obliged to take the case higher up in the system. Formal investigations later on confirmed our original hunches that something irregular had been going on. As a result my boss had to resign.

Were you at any time in doubt as to whether you and the others did the right thing?

No. I saw it as a clear-cut case. Mainly it was about selling paper. A lot of paper was lying around in our system, due to all the tests we were administering. After shredding, it was sold back to the paper mills for recycling purposes. The selling price did not figure in the accounts, but the money had been paid, so where had it gone, and who had taken it? Well, my boss had!

I don't really think his motives were about personal enrichment. As a person, my boss liked to do things in style. I believe he has seen the embezzled money as a kind of personal expense account. Admittedly, the spending rules of the military system are rigid and very bureaucratic when it comes to entertainment expenses and "special measures". In situations where common interests were at stake, he might have found it useful to have 'a little something' to make things work smoother.

At a personal level, I did feel sorry for him. I was aware of a wide array of motives that cluttered up the case taken as a whole. But formal investigations did prove that the money had disappeared. He had dodged the general organizational control. You're not allowed to do that!

This incident turned out to become one important reason behind my final decision to leave the military. I didn't blame myself for what I had done – but others did! Many people around me held strong opinions, not only about the case as such, but definitely also about the part I had played in it.

The whole case became a bit of a shock for the entire military institution. Among other things, the formal investigations that followed resulted in a general tightening of procedures related to grants administration. A large number of consulting psychologists had their contracts abolished. Quite likely, professors and other psychologists lost a couple of million due to this. Definitely, my role in the case made me less than popular among some colleagues and co-psychologists – a fact which many among them made no attempt whatsoever to hide! According to them, I had been far too rigid and dogmatic in my way of handling the affair. I had failed to let *personal* considerations guide me. I had helped the system butcher a person who in many respects was greatly esteemed by me as a workmate and colleague. And yes, there's no way of denying that as an outcome of the whole thing many high-quality projects were either stopped or reduced – projects valuable not only to the military, but also to psychology broadly speaking. Grants were held back or were not renewed. Some people saw me as the person to be held responsible for these consequences. Many among them could only see it as a very bad idea, indeed, to push that case forward towards its bitter end.

These events made me feel more and more uncomfortable about staying on in the military. And then there was that experience of clicking my heels to the general!

Gunnar left the military, but with no great risk of becoming unemployed. University graduated psychologists were in great demand. Gunnar was no longer a novice. Besides having taught for a year at Hindholm Occupational High School and been part time caseworker at the National Council for the Unmarried Mother and her Child, his CV now told of a five year long job experience as a pioneer and professional trendsetter at one of the most highly esteemed workplaces for psychologists in Denmark.

The story comes to a temporary halt

Gunnar's next employment was as a staff member at the Danish Technological Institute. Earlier we described how the Institute management saw their newly employed psychologist as part of a long-term development plan aimed at including management consultancy in their business portfolio. This plan was not, however, immediately disclosed to Gunnar ...

So, what were you supposed to do at the Danish Technological Institute?

Well, at first I had some trouble figuring it out. When I was to receive my first monthly salary, I went out of my office to look up the people in the pay office. I asked them what my job was supposed to be. No one knew. Indeed, it seemed that no one had taken any notice of my presence. I then asked them about the size of my salary. I was told my salary equalled that of a primary school principal.

For many months to come, my situation felt strange. Up to the time of my employment I had been working a lot. Suddenly I had nothing to do. Sometimes I invited Berit and the kids to visit me at work. My office was an old classroom. They would use the blackboard for drawing and we would have lunch together. I tried to make the manager of the Institute tell me what he wanted me for. "Well, well, well … " – he kept saying. He would like to think about it. Somehow, we had to dig up something.

What finally became the result of the Institute manager's thinking was a trip to the United States and a post-graduate training course. However, this story will not be told right now, since it forms the starting point for Chapter 2.

Handling organizational value conflicts – as an insider or outsider

Taken together, the present and subsequent chapters cover the period in Gunnar's life which, in the introductory chapter, we described as his *professional apprentice years*. During this period he picked up a rich experiential load, creating for himself a space from which his later professional life could develop. His apprentice years ended in the United States. Here Gunnar met a professional environment with which he – almost unreservedly – could identify and from which he could learn. The ten year long period preceding this encounter – i.e. the period covered by the present chapter – had engaged him in learning experiences of a much more varied nature.

During one interview in Vust, we asked Gunnar to do a general appraisal of his organizational encounters during the years 1948-58 – with special emphasis on their more troublesome aspects.

> *Going over the material we are struck by the fact that conflicts between you and your social surroundings seemed to arise in almost any place you worked – Information being the only clear exception. The Technological Institute doesn't really count here – you barely arrived before you left for the United States. Do you recognize yourself in that description? Does it say something important about you?*

Sure enough, that's the way it was. And each time these conflicts, or, more importantly, their side effects, ended up forcing me to take my leave from the workplaces in question.

To tell you the truth, I've been doing quite a lot of thinking about this fact. Why is it so difficult for me to belong to an organization? Each time, I reach a point where I simply have to collect my things and walk away. It's a certain kind of impatience within me. I start noticing that other people fail to live up to the stated values or goals of the organization. Agreement no longer exists between what people say they do and what they actually do. I see it as failure to honour the task. That's what makes me put on my rigid self. I cannot accept it. As long as I'm still part of the organization, I cannot compromise.

This trait of mine has pushed me into a lot of difficulties – which doesn't imply, though, that I regret my ways, or feel I should have been more flexible. Important matters are at stake here, goddammit. Are humans meant to serve the systems, or are systems supposed to lend service to human beings? What counts most: the system's need to remain the kind of system it is, feeling comfortable in its own self-importance? – or rather, the needs of the people for whose sake the system originally came into being?

The interviews certainly do present you as person with a keen, critical eye for that particular developmental risk of organizations that make them end up regarding themselves *as their own purpose – in reality striving for nothing but their own survival?*

Precisely. And their own *unchanged* survival, at that. This kind of organizational self-sufficency or self-adulation is apt to catch my attention whenever I come across it. And I do seem to come across it constantly. The municipality is there for its own sake, not for the sake of its citizens. The hospital is there for the sake of the doctors, not the patients. During my time at the National Council for the Unmarried Mother and her Child I learned that this particular institution was there for the sake of the legal rulings, not for that of helping the mothers for whom it had been established in the first place. Well, and the university is there for the sake of science, not for the people who might benefit from science – surely, you two must know all about that!

When as a consultant I work in organizations where this tendency is strongly marked, I have a habit of thinking – and sometimes I say it aloud – that in this society of ours *organizational and institutional post-mortems are working at far too slow a pace.* Can't you see it? – death has already come about for these organizations, at least if you look at the original motives for bringing them into existence. What's missing is for somebody to actually have the courage to sign the death certificate. Certainly, you can't expect any such thing from the organizational members themselves.

We could easily dismantle the union-run unemployment insurance systems. They served a useful purpose when they were invented. In many respects today, they're just dead tissue on society's body. Yesterday's solutions for yesterday's problems. If they – and all other equally deserving systems – were dismantled, it would force us reflect on how best to handle all those problems within the organizations' task areas *that still remain unsolved.*

The public sector has a wealth of such examples. Consultants often meet them. But the client's true problem is seldom mentioned as part of the official requisition to the consultant. '*Please come and help us, we are no longer needed, our system has outlived its day*' – have you as consultants ever been asked to deal with this kind of problem? Still, very often these problems will form the essence of what the consultant actually addresses. No wonder! – it certainly serves people no good to stay inside such an empty organizational shell, having to spend a lot of energy to try and make sense out of something that has in fact outlived itself, become senseless. It can only contribute to their demoralization.

Under such circumstances, what usually happens to organizations is that they become rule governed rather than need and value governed. Contact and interaction between organization members and the outside world become increasingly predictable and ritualized. An increasing number of standard procedures, formal and informal ones, are invented so as to monitor the organization members' internal and external activities. Standard answers are worked out for all sorts of problem situations, actual as well as potential. Little by little, the inclination to pay heed to the exact content of questions asked by simple minds or ignoramuses disappears. I experienced this as a teacher at Hindholm in relation to its students. In some measure, I experienced it from the student position during my years of study. I definitely experienced it when my own children attended a well-renowned and allegedly progressive school where – *so they said* – 'the pupil' was in focus ... To me it rather seemed that focus was on whatever strange *fantasies* the teachers entertained about something called 'pupils' and 'children'. Nobody seemed to bother much about those small-size human beings who *actually* happened to live part of their lives at the school and of whom it was supposed to take care.

The kind of problems you now talk about obviously mean a lot to you. When talking about them in relation to systems that had yourself as member, you get very upset. Your voice tells that. Those same problems somehow seem easier for you to handle when you meet them as a consultant, i.e. a person moving back and forth across the system's boundary line. In that context you tell about them in a humorous vein – even though at times the humour turns grim. Still, it seems you're more forbearing in your professional role.

Definitely! As a professional you keep your distance. You don't share any responsibilities. You only spend a short time with the people you're dealing with. You see how they're stuck in their problems and you want to do your very best to help them out of those problems. That's the whole point of being together with them.

This kind of freedom – freedom to observe, freedom to act – I lose when I am part of the system myself, as was the case in the stories I told you about my workplaces. I couldn't help getting entangled in all sorts of conflicts, and it was stressful to me at a personal level. My family always knew when something was wrong. I could not let go of it. And at some point I had to resign. That was the only choice available.

I have met people who did not react like that. Who were not gripped or controlled by that kind of impatience. Who retained their capacity to think and act strategically within the organizational context, even when the organization was their own. They were not dominated by the kind of indignation and mental dissociation that makes you unable to see the possibilities of the situation. Instead, when they notice that actions are no longer in accord with stated values and the task at hand – and it happens all the time, you know – they feel inspired and start making plans for organizational changes that may set things right; so that, once more, the team will be able to attend to the task.

I can't do that. I doubt if I'll ever learn it. From my time at the Danish Technological Institute I remember talks I had with one of my bosses concerning the future of the Institute. We shared many ideas about problems that messed up the organizational process: its way of being out of tune with realities of the day – all that pointed backwards in the organization, empty rituals. I became kind of resigned by making all these analyses, whereas he saw the challenge. He was stimulated by our talks. I sensed in myself the urge to demolish the whole thing and start all over again.

I told you I've been thinking a lot about possible backgrounds for my being so rigid in these matters. Is it an indication of my wish to, quite simply, take over the organization? Is it a kind of megalomania that I don't want to admit? – given that I never announce my candidature for any kind of managerial role. Do I wish 'everyone else' to see things exactly the way I see them – based on the same values? Those who aren't prepared to do that – because they have different values – I just give up on, thus cutting off contact and precluding mutual influence?

Now you really get into the self-critical attitude. 'Gunnar is a bad person, he makes all kinds of mistakes' – at least when in the membership role. Could there be other explanations? We have often discussed how the concentration camp provided you with certain basic organizational experiences. Could there be a link from these experiences to your impatience and rigidity?

Well, there may be a link. It may be that a stay in a concentration camp makes you particularly scrupulous – and in a certain sense also narrow-minded – in matters relating to faithfulness towards your personal values. Much of what goes on in the camp is distinctly inhuman. Earlier I've talked to you about the issue of personal guilt, which invariably invades you as a camp inmate. Ugly things happen around you and you let them happen. Afterwards you ask yourself: 'Am I responsible? – I didn't interfere! – could I have prevented anything from happening?' In view of the *actual* circumstances, thoughts like these may not be very logical. Still, they pop up. In this way, the camp does make you focus attention on moral values and personal responsibility. Oh yes, you do become scrupulous – for the very simple reason that the camp system, in all its formalized aspects, is based, through and through, on a *lack* of responsibility.

Fine distinctions related to your action and choice become extremely important. As a camp inmate, you desperately need to know the boundary line of what the camp can make you do. Certain camp situations I still remember, due to specific things I *did not* do, even though I *might have* done them. It is important to remember such situations. *'No, this particular thing I will never do* – that would take me beyond my personal boundary line!' Situations like that help you find out who you are. Some of the people coming back from the camp were not, in this manner, able to point at their personal boundary line. Those committing suicide and the alcoholics will be found in that group. Well, alcoholism in itself is some kind of suicide.

The camp may very well have contributed to my rigidity: made it hard for me to accept when members of *my own* organization – my *own 'relatives'* so to speak – act irresponsibly. Because I know how important it is to hold on to the position where you can still face yourself and respect yourself – resisting at least *some* of the temptations that invite you to make compromises with what you believe and hope is *the meaning of it all.*

References

Barker, R.G. (1968). *Ecological Psychology*. Stanford (Calif.): Stanford University Press.

Borish, S.M. (1991). *The Land of the Living. The Danish Folk High Schools and Denmark's Non-violent Path to Modernization*. Grass Valley (Calif.): Blue Dolphin.

Dollard, J. (1949). *Caste and Class in a Southern Town* (2nd edn.). New York: Harper & Brothers.

Hjelholt, G. (1997). Forskeren og systemerne. In G. Graversen (ed.) *Et arbejdsliv. Festskrift tilegnet Professor dr.phil. Eggert Petersen fra hans venner og kolleger*. Århus: Psykologisk Institut.

Madsen, B. & Willert, S. (1996). *Survival in the Organization. Gunnar Hjelholt Looks Back at the Concentration Camp from an Organizational Perspective.* Aarhus: Aarhus University Press.

West, J. (1945). *Plainville.* New York: Columbia University Press.

2 THE BOUNDARY KEEPER

Gunnar Hjelholt on group dynamics and consultant roles

By Benedicte Madsen, Denmark

During 1958, Gunnar Hjelholt stayed for eight months in the USA where he was introduced to the Lewinian theories on group dynamics, in particular the laboratory method. Chapter 2 tells about this stay and the impact it had on his later professional life.

Gunnar remained professionally active until shortly before his death at the age of 82. Chapter 2 covers the period between 1958 and '70, the latter being the year when he turned 50 and – together with his wife, Berit, and their two sons – moved to a small farm house near Vust, a village situated in the north-western part of Denmark far away from the capital. This was also the house where, in a low-ceilinged room, Gunnar died around Christmas 2002.

The chapter opens with an account of Gunnar's stay as research fellow in the USA and we become acquainted with his critical views on the laboratory method in its various manifestations. Along the way we shall hear about Kurt Lewin's field theory and applied group dynamics. Furthermore, the chapter deals with Gunnar's understanding of groups and society; his own creation in laboratory design, the 'mini-society'; his consultant work in Denmark and abroad; and his participation in the foundation of EIT, an inter-European group dynamic organization. Finally, the chapter presents Gunnar's views on group structure including boundaries, as well as his personal preference for using the term 'boundary keeper' as a metaphor for the role of group trainer and process consultant. Over the years, Gunnar developed close professional ties with many internationally known representatives of the group dynamics movement. Among these, the chapter most importantly makes reference to relationships he formed with the following: Gordon and Ron Lippitt, Leeland Bradford, Murray Horwitz, Joseph Luft, Donald Nylen, Trygve Joenstad, Matthew Miles, Traugott Lindner and Eric Trist.

As was also the case in Chapter 1, Chapter 2 is largely based on interview data that I, together with Søren Willert, started collecting in 1992 as part of an ambitious biographical project, with Gunnar in the informant's role. Our aim was to use Gunnar's personal life story as a key to learning about the origins and historical development of applied social psychology in Denmark and elsewhere. Spaced over several years, we spent a dozen days in all interviewing Gunnar at his home in Vust. To this was added briefer visits, telephone calls and an extensive exchange of letters and documents back and forth. Each interview day resulted in a fairly long progress report from us. Sometimes we used a tape recorder, but most often we reconstructed the dialogue on the basis of detailed hand-written notes. For some of the interviews, though, we brought along a laptop computer and took down draft versions on the spot. Gunnar would read and make comments on our reports. From time to time he wrote short memos for the project. Until the publication of the present book, the material has only been made use of in two publications: an article on the mini-society (Madsen, Willert & Hjelholt, 1994) and a small book about Gunnar's stay in the concentration camp Porta Westphalica (Madsen & Willert, 1996).

Below, excerpts from the interview material are presented in a condensed and adapted form – either as indented paragraphs or quotes inserted in the main body of the text.

An invitation to the USA

Already during his student years Gunnar adopted a consistent social psychological outlook while at the same time he was constantly striving to relate theory and professional practice. This made him more strongly oriented towards the USA than towards the continental psychology even though the latter was considered a major inspirational source at his place of study, i.e. the Psychological Laboratory at the University of Copenhagen, cf. Chapter 1. In retrospect, Gunnar's stay in the USA can be seen as something that 'had to happen'.

In the Autumn of 1957, Gunnar had 18 months' employment at the Danish Technological Institute behind him. Professionally speaking, he was still on the lookout for a clear identity. He had tried out a number of workplaces – and left them again, often due to conflicts with his bosses. One evening he and Berit were invited to dinner by the director of the Institute. Another guest present was an American.

The American was Dr. Kight from the Fels Center for Group Dynamics at the University of Delaware in Newark. Fels was the name of the founder who had earned millions by producing soap and then invested his money in a university department. Before the dinner at Hotel Europa was over, Kight had asked me whether I would be interested in staying at Fels for a while.

My immediate reaction to his question was that I *would* like to go to the USA – most importantly because I felt professionally isolated at the Technological Institute. Yet, I was somehow reluctant to leave Berit and the children behind. My usually very intense working habits had made me accumulate a lot of guilt towards them – and Berit didn't have an easy life being an immigrant from Finland. But then, after having talked things over with Berit, I finally chose to accept the invitation. The Danish Technological Institute agreed to pay my salary for a period of eight months, the Denmark-America Foundation funded my travel expenses, and I was offered a position as research fellow at the Fels Center.

I left on January 2, 1958. They almost wouldn't let me into the USA. The passport officers stopped me in New York because my name had been entered on a list of criminals. I had to call Kight. They explained to him that they had this list from Germany and that it carried names of people who had been in prison or concentration camps. It seems that the Americans had not yet quite realized what the fighting had been all about.

It was only after my arrival in the USA that Kight told me the Technological Institute planned to make me head-of-department for a new management consultancy unit, to become established when I was back in Denmark. That had been their plan all along, but they'd never told me anything.

The staff at Fels included two full professors, three associate professors and three or four research assistants. The working style at the Centre was inspired by the Lewinian tradition for group dynamics – meaning that Gunnar was pushed into the practitioner's role right away. Anybody who has, at some point in time, been exposed to him as a teacher, trainer or consultant will know about his characteristic intervention style where practice precedes theory and the would-be learner must plunge into deep water irrespective of whether he feels sufficiently prepared or not. In 1958, Gunnar, himself, was a would-be learner – tasting the medicine he would later prescribe to others:

At the University of Copenhagen I hadn't learnt at lot. But the Americans set me to work at once. Shortly after my arrival I was invited to a meeting between the Centre and a client: Pennsylvania Bell ('Penn Bell' for short), a division of the American Telephone and Telegraph Company. A five-day course for foremen and others had to be arranged. 'Will you make a programme, the deadline is February 15?', Kight asked me and added that at any time I was welcome to discuss the programme with him.

During the next month I had a lot of reading to do about 'the small group'. At that time a good deal of research had been published along with textbooks by Homans, Hare, Borgatta & Bales, and others.[1] Back home I had already read some of the material, but here there were people around with whom I could discuss it! My personal engagement was really building up – I wanted to show them my potential. The first meeting had already gone some way to specify the task lying ahead of me. I was all set to present a splendid programme on flip-over sheets when we met again on February 15.

At the meeting I presented my plan, and the client was asked to evaluate whether or not it was acceptable. Questions were asked and discussed at great length. Then, at some point, Kight simply tore all my nice sheets off the wall: 'Now start from scratch once again, Gunnar'. The psychological effect of his gesture was tremendous: here, the customer's interests were all that counted. To me, however, his action came as a shock. It showed something about the difference between the USA and Europe. At home, if my socks got holes in them, I would darn them. Here, less-than-perfect socks were simply thrown away.

At Fels, lots of experimentation was done and much practical consultancy work. Industrial clients would present the problems they wanted us to solve. They also had adult education programmes. And I was free to involve myself in whatever I felt like. Seldom have I become engaged in so many stimulating activities during such a short period of time. There was no end to my 'discoveries' – whether

---

1 The Centre for Systems Development at the Department of Psychology in Aarhus was the home of Gunnar's library since his death. Here one could find the two books Gunnar mentioned: one of them being *Small groups. Studies in Social Interaction*, edited by Paul Hare, Edgar Borgatta and Robert Bales (1955), the other being *The Human Group* from 1951 by George Homans.

relating to method, or theory, or a particular social encounter, or discoveries about myself and my reactions in a strange environment.

One of the characteristics of Fels was the open atmosphere. Plus their capacity for discarding anything below the highest possible standard, and their certainty that even the worst imaginable scenario wouldn't kill you. Gradually, however, I also realized that the place had certain shortcomings. To name one, it seemed characteristic that authority problems were never discussed and yet such problems did exist. Further, in their eagerness to *make things work*, they did not always care too much about *why* they worked. When it comes to theorizing and reflection, Europeans are definitely more sophisticated.

Gunnar put together a new workshop programme. By mid-March, together with the training department manager at Penn Bell, he arranged a pilot course for 12 participants. One participant came from the head office. His job was to find out whether the course might be useful in other divisions of the telephone company. Gunnar's programme design became a prototype, not only in Penn Bell, but in all of the states operated by Bell Telephone.

The course focused on employee objectives at individual as well as group level, on the handling of complaints, on conflict resolution and on professional development among employees. Methods used were hands-on exercises, instructional cases and role-play. Continued feedback to participants was included in the design, partly through external observers' reports on group process, partly through small mirror groups[2] towards the end of each day where mutual feedback among participants was exchanged. For each participant, the course started with a self-evaluation on a number of dimensions – the procedure being repeated at end-of-course allowing everybody to find out whether any development seemed to have occurred. Not only did the course become a great success. It paid off in other respects as well: when the company learned that Gunnar did not receive a special salary for running their courses, they asked whether they might offer him something or other. It being a telephone company, Gunnar suggested they gave him a long-distance call to Denmark. This they did, and even added a flight ticket for Berit to visit him. She crossed the Atlantic to celebrate Gunnar's birthday on April 30.

During evenings and in parallel with his course-making, Gunnar took part in a practice-oriented group psychology training course arranged by his colleague

---

2   Cf. Chapter 10, a translation of a Hjelholt-article from 1960 on mirror groups. See also the section on The Small Group in the present chapter.

John Lanzetta. His next external assignment – a job for the petrochemical company Dupont – was handled in collaboration with Lanzetta. In Vust, some thirty years later, Gunnar recalls it through the following incident – unmistakably carrying his fingerprints:

> We were to advise them on how to staff their giant computer – it was larger than the one at the Pentagon. We suggested they hire advertising people rather than mathematicians for the job. We feared mathematicians might be too professionally narrow-minded – to an extent that would make them unable to fully grasp the range of possibilities actually lying buried in that computer.

Already when designing his very first course, Gunnar had emphasized the systematic use of feedback as a training method and had set much time apart for this process component. At this point he was as yet unaware of the important role feedback processes had played in the birth and further development, ever since 1946, of the laboratory training method. More will be said about that later. When Gunnar tells about his first steps as a group trainer, these design elements were simple, reflecting his wish to activate all participants and leave nobody's observations out.

But what happened to the research component during his stay? Formally speaking, Gunnar's status at Fels was that of a research fellow. When asked this question, Gunnar replied that, indeed, he had started a project on the feedback phenomenon, but had not found the time to complete it before returning to Denmark. In the end Kight had availed himself of parts of his literature research – "… and then made use of it as his own – as I believe is a normal thing to do in those circles", Gunnar, somewhat wryly, added.[3] But then, why bother, the important thing was to gather experience – get wiser. The eight months flew past.

Training in Bethel

In June 1958, Penn Bell offered Gunnar a grant allowing him to participate in a training laboratory in the idyllic town of Bethel in the North-East state of Maine. The town was – and still is – the site of the NTL organization: National Training Laboratories. Gunnar had made use of some of NTL-based material in the course he had arranged for Penn Bell, and he had participated in one of their training groups. One of the professors at Fels, Jack Gibb, did research on the laboratory method. Furthermore the director of NTL, Lee Bradford, was a

---

3 The Fels data are mentioned in Chapter 10 below.

board member at the Fels Center. Just like three other members of the board, Dorwin Cartwright, Stuart Cook and Morton Deutsch, he had collaborated closely with Kurt Lewin. "But all that didn't mean a lot to me back then", Gunnar recalls. "It was Bethel and NTL that gave me a kick".

How, then, was a standard training laboratory[4] organized in those days? Which aspects did Gunnar consider particularly important?

What I experienced in 1958 was the original Bethel laboratory; later some changes were made. 150-200 participants travelled from near and far to participate in a three-week programme consisting of three major elements: experiential groups; possibilities for planned action – practice training, that is; and lastly the acquisition of generalized understanding – theory development, that is.

The participants were grouped in small experiential groups, each having two trainers skilled in process awareness. This basic group was called a T-group – T for training. Members from different T-groups would be brought together forming exercise groups. Each exercise used was designed with a specific purpose in mind and the purpose would be derived from problems T-group members were likely to encounter while in process. Participants might have difficulties getting the talk flowing between them – then the staff would come up with listening exercises.

In Gunnar's remark on the tailor-made practical exercises, an indirect criticism can be heard of the 'mindless', mechanical way in which NTL exercises would, later, be used – also by professionals trained by himself.

Each day started with joint theoretical reflection. The rest of the morning was spent either in T-groups or exercise groups. Lectures were meant to help participants to review and make generalizations from their experiences and provide them with a framework for understanding what went on – preventing them, e.g., from believing that 'it's probably just *our* group that behaves in a very special manner.' And when I say 'lectures', I mean lectures – pure and simple; but often they had an extraordinary quality. Just imagine me sitting there in a lecture

---

4   People tend to use different terms and this may be confusing. The umbrella terms are 'the laboratory method' or 'training laboratory', but in the beginning it was named 'human relations laboratory'. Later, terms like 'the T-group method', 'sensitivity training' and 'group dynamic courses' were used. Over the years, numerous further developments and specializations were added.

hall, one person among 150, listening intently to a lecturer – and compare it to what my study years at the University of Copenhagen had given me.

The joint evening meeting might include films. One night they showed *Twelve Angry Men* and afterwards the film was analyzed. The film has one character among the twelve angry men, a watchmaker, who happens to be an immigrant. I wrongly made that person into the main character of the whole drama – thereby elevating my own situation and current problems into central issues, but with no backing from objective reality. In many ways, Bethel taught me to what an extent I, myself, am subject to the dynamics shaping interpersonal transactions.

A fourth design component was named 'special activities'. It could be meetings for participants from the same line of occupation; or other activities according to participants' choices. At the very beginning everybody was given a small notebook he or she had to 'talk to' for an hour every day. The first two weeks of the laboratory would concentrate on experiential, here-and-now learning. During the third week participants would work with the application aspect: how to make practical use of your experiences in time to come.

As it turned out, Bethel had more in store for Gunnar than simply participating in a three-week training laboratory. As a kind of bonus, he was offered to participate, free of charge, in a subsequent trainer development programme, authorizing him, from then on, to work as a staff member in training laboratories.

Primarily, we were trained by assuming the trainer role in T-groups made up of members from among the experienced NTL staff. Thus, for instance, Lee Bradford, NTL-director and hence chief responsible for all laboratories, would play the role of a quarrelsome, utterly nasty group member. During certain periods of time we would also, in pairs, act as observers in real-life T-groups being part of a concurrently running training laboratory. To end it all we were given the task of planning and implementing a town-hall meeting in a small village somewhere in the state of Maine.

So, you see – it was the same old story, once again repeated: if you want to learn something, first you must try it out in practice. Openness to experimentation was also demonstrated by our theory teachers. They were jointly working on a book on the laboratory method. We received pre-print copies of various chapters thereby helping them, through our feedback, to develop the book for final publication.[5] During those three weeks it was just hard work round the clock.

One teacher, remembered by Gunnar with special delight, was Gordon Lippitt, professor at Washington University. Gordon's position in the circle around Lewin had been more marginal than that of his brother, Ron Lippitt, who had been one of Lewin's closest collaborators since the 1930s.

> Later Gordon and I joined forces in a project requested by a small town. We were to set up a programme for a town meeting. When it came to theory, Gordon was no match for his brother Ron, but then he was a very practical man. He was a master of design ... [pause – and then with a crooked smile] – in that respect we are two look-alikes. I also happen to be a bit of a design master, myself.

Eventually – and in collaboration with Gunnar Hjelholt, among others – Gordon Lippitt founded the International Consultants Foundation (ICF). According to Gunnar, as a consultant he was much acclaimed internationally, and during the 1980s a membership of ICF was a 'must' if one wanted to consult for international organizations. However, when Gordon Lippitt died in the late 1980s, the ICF went downhill.

Complying with pre-existing rules or patterns was never one of Gunnar's strong points. Bethel he experienced as a place where nearly everything functioned according to his taste, meaning that he felt free to place himself right in the middle of things rather than – as was his wont – at, or beyond the boundary line. Yet, at this place, too, he made himself initiator of a small programme novelty, namely unofficial T-groups and training exercises for 'the wrong people'.

> Most participants brought their families with them to the summer stay in Bethel. One day the children asked me whether I would make a T-group for them – all the time they heard everybody talk about T-groups, and what was it all about? The reason they put their question to me may have been that, as a non-American or foreigner, I was seen as the easiest one to contact. I liked the idea, so I skipped some trainer programme classes and, together with one of my course mates, I made the world's first T-group for teenagers. Then the wife of my own trainer asked me to make role-plays for the spouses, something that turned into another parallel activity.

---

5   The book edited by Bradford, Gibb & Benne was published in 1964.

Did you ask for permission, so to speak?

No, I just did it. Incidentally, these activities gave me a particular status within the staff because I became acquainted with their families. In the end, it did give me privileged relations to some of the US pioneers within group and human relations training. I stayed in touch with many of them.

Having finished his own training, Gunnar for the first time experienced serving as a staff member at a training laboratory. His T-group co-trainer at this laboratory, Murray Horwitz, is one person he remembered with much veneration. As a Ph.D. student at Kurt Lewin's Centre for Group Dynamics, Horwitz had been a member of the research staff in the renowned event (soon to be heard more about) where the laboratory method was born. According to Gunnar, Horwitz was Lewin's favourite student. During the 1960s and '70s Horwitz paid visits to Gunnar in Denmark.

After his summer in Bethel, Gunnar returned to Fels and, by late October, continued to Denmark. Still, his American connection remained strong. In 1964, 1966, 1972 and 1987 he was a staff member at training laboratories in Bethel and elsewhere in the USA, on each occasion staffing two or three courses in a row, because (as he put it) 'they wanted value for money, now that they had to pay for the long journey'. In 1966, he was elected associate member of NTL and in 1969 full member, a status he retained until he resigned in 1992.

The Lewinian tradition

After the war, when Gunnar Hjelholt made his choice to become a psychologist, many of his personal characteristics found a potential joint outlet: his idealism, his wish to improve society and to help other people, his action orientation coupled with an untiring desire to understand the underlying dynamics. Yet, as was also shown in Chapter 1, his working years in Denmark leading up to the Fels adventure had not allowed him to find the right synthesis.

To get at the background for the inner turbulence initiated by his eight months stay in the USA, we shall now make a detour to the Lewinian tradition, paying special attention to certain themes and ways of understanding that were of vital, lasting concern to Gunnar: a tight link between theory and practice, action research, group processes, social involvement and democratic principles.

Kurt Lewin was born in Germany in 1890. For many years he was attached to the psychology department at Berlin University where he developed what was later named field theory.[6] In 1933, he left the country as a Jewish refugee and for the last 14 years of his life lived in the USA where he died in January 1947, 57 years old.

Lewin dedicated his life to the study of complex change processes, trying to understand any kind of movement or locomotion as a result of the dynamic interplay between a disparate set of forces. Other characteristics were his interdisciplinary orientation and his passion for relating theory and practice. The latter is reflected in his famous *bon mot*: "There is nothing so practical as a good theory".[7]

Lewin's key conception is *the psychological field*, also called *life space*. The field is defined as a multi-dimensional unity of the person and his psychological environment. This unity is comparable to an experiental or phenomenal field in which the physical and social environment and the person himself are mentally represented. The field is criss-crossed by multifarious motivational and cognitive structures including boundaries and barriers that define the 'spaces of free movement'. At the same time the unity is a tension field in which dynamic interactions between field forces result in mental as well as behavioural movements. The field constantly changes; however, it is also seeking temporary states of stability, by Lewin called quasistationary equilibria.

Together with his students in Berlin, Lewin carried out a series of experiments that soon became classic. Content themes were, among others, recall of unfinished tasks, the importance of substitution objects for the individual's goal-directed behaviour, psychological satiation in connection with monotonous repetition of a task, reactions of anger when the person's goals are blocked. Taken as a whole, this research programme may be described as a general psychological investigation of the dynamic role of tension building.

---

6   Having countless versions, the theory is presented in three publications by Lewin: *A Dynamic Theory of Personality. Selected Papers* (1935), *Principles of Topological Psychology* (1936) and *Field Theory in Social Science: Selected Theoretical Papers* (1951, posthumously edited by Dorwin Cartwright). Cf. Madsen, 2001, 2003.

7   According to Lewin's biographer, Alfred Marrow (1969: 171), the sentence appeared in an article that Lewin published in 1945 in the journal *Sociometry*. The purely biographical details in this section of Chapter 2 are based on Marrow's book *The Practical Theorist. The Life and Work of Kurt Lewin.*

But then, from the very moment he set foot on American soil, Lewin's research interests underwent a change, now becoming focused on groups and society. During a period of 25 years, his influence on experimental *social* psychology was remarkable, and he was intent on having psychology play a role in the development of society. He was passionately yearning for the world to become a better place to live in and wanted science to serve this purpose – while at the same time he envisioned scientists' efforts in grappling with practical problems as an important challenge and incentive to theory development. His work became a unique source of inspiration for American social psychology, not least indirectly in that his pupils and close collaborators became pioneers and trendsetters for decades to come.

Among American scholars of the 1930s there was widespread interest in interdisciplinary work. Human Relations faculties were established at the Ivy Liege universities and influential research groups were formed, being staffed by philosophers, psychologists, sociologists and social anthropologists. These trends reflected a growing social engagement and a felt need to make practical use of the Social Sciences and the Humanities. Gradually Americans – partly as an offshoot of the massive pre-war brain drain from Europe to the USA – became aware of the Fascist danger, resulting in strong democratic currents within the scientific community. These trends influenced the development of social psychology, and applied social psychology in particular.

Lewin's contribution to this development was considerable. Around 1935 he and Ronald Lippitt started a series of experiments based on club activities for young boys. This research examined how group atmosphere and tension building would depend on leadership style: *autocratic*, *democratic* and *laissez-faire* leadership (cf. Lewin, Lippitt & White 1939). Lewin's concept of democracy not only referred to political institutions and forms of government but first and foremost to a cultural pattern that, ideally, was to saturate all parts of society and the value systems of individual citizens.[8]

In addition to the above research programme, Lewin was initiator of another pair of famous experimental investigations, one focussing on the relation between frustration and regression, the other on the importance of group discussions in relation to change of food habits. The latter investigations came about as part of a war-dictated effort to economize on the use of scarce resources, and gave rise to important theoretical developments, most notably through

---

8   In the epilogue of the present book, Steen Visholm criticizes Lewin's understanding of democratic processes.

the coining of concepts such as *change agent, gatekeeper, resistance to change* and Lewin's famous change model *Unfreeze-Move-Refreeze*.

Clearest evidence of Lewin's preoccupation with the problems of society and their solution is found in the book *Resolving Social Conflicts*.[9] Also in this book the concept of *action research* was, for the first time, introduced to a larger public. Action research may be seen as an articulation of Lewin's wish to link science with practical problem solving. In its fully developed versions the action researcher will be involved in the planning and carrying out of the very same change processes as, at the same time, he studies as his 'object of research'. Action research implies a farewell to certain demands traditionally put on the researcher, namely those of distanced objectivity and non-committed neutrality. Instead, by actively involving himself in the role as change agent the researcher wilfully influences his research object. What is lost with regard to objectivity (traditionally speaking) is gained through the researcher getting access to interesting, true-to-life change processes – an access which is not easily achieved in any other way.[10]

Group dynamics, general and applied

According to Lewin, the group is the most important intermediary between individual and society. During his last years, he founded a new discipline – in fact a movement – which he called group dynamics. Lewin, himself, never came up with any strict definition or delimitation of the discipline, but my own definition goes like this: group dynamics is research on, interventions in, as well as the planning of interaction processes and change at group and organization levels, guided by the general assumption that such processes result from the interplay between complex forces.

In 1944, Lewin founded the *Research Centre for Group Dynamics*, the first of its kind. The Centre had four principal aims: to develop scientific methods for the study of changes in group life; to develop group dynamics conceptually and theoretically; to educate researchers; and to help furthering the training of practitioners (Marrow 1969). In the last year of his life Lewin wrote a theoretical manifesto: 'Frontiers in Group Dynamics', and had it published

---

9 *Resolving Social conflicts* (1948) is a collection of articles written by Lewin and posthumously edited by his widow. The concept of action research is introduced in Chapter 13.

10 A 'softer' action research version is that of practitioners and workshop participants helping each other to investigate their own activity. Gunnar's mini-societies exemplify such a version, cf. Chapters 6 and 13.

in the first issue of *Human Relations*,[11] a journal founded in 1946 through the joint efforts of Kurt Lewin and Eric Trist. Trist was one of the most prominent figures from the Tavistock Institute of Human Relations in London.

Reflecting his strong credo concerning the mutual interrelatedness and inspirational links between theory and practice, Lewin never distinguished between general and applied group dynamics. Soon, however, splitting tendencies showed up. On the one hand an academic tradition emerged, specializing in research on the general occurrence of group phenomena such as cooperation and conflict, processes of decision making and management, cohesion and diversion, stagnation and change (see Cartwright & Zander 1953). On the other hand, a number of professional, and thus intervention-oriented specialities, developed as instances of 'applied group dynamics'. Today, the concept has turned so vague that 'group dynamics' is no longer a valid label for any remotely cohesive discipline.

Incidentally, Gunnar Hjelholt and many others have talked about applied group dynamics as being almost identical to applied social psychology, while others (including the present author) view applied social psychology as a much broader field.

Nowadays, two distinct areas play a particularly dominant role within applied group dynamics. One is linked with consultants' efforts to bring about planned change and organizational development (OD). The laboratory method, described earlier, is the other. It belongs to the professional field of adult education, its name ('laboratory') emphasizing the strongly experimenting spirit pervading it. Within the Lewinian tradition, a training laboratory is a residential course that – by means of experiential learning – will ideally increase the participants' ability to cooperate as well as their understanding of group processes and democratic values.[12] This laboratory method is what initially sparked Gunnar's enthusiasm.

Originally, the laboratory method was seen as a method for democratization. Lewin saw society as badly in need of democratic reform, and (re)education was

---

11   The article referred to is printed as chapter IX in Lewin 1951. The journal *Human Relations* still exists.

12   Cf. *T-Group and Laboratory Methods: Innovation in Re-education,* edited by Bradford, Gibb & Benne, 1964. Lee Bradford and Kenneth Benne worked with Lewin during the last year of his life. This was also the year when the forerunner of the laboratory method first saw the light of day. Lewin himself talks about workshops as 'cultural islands' (1951:232).

his number one means towards that end. While autocracy is forced upon the individual from the outside, democracy has to be learned, he said. And when democratic values are weak – as World War II had shown them to be – some kind of popular re-education must be undertaken. According to Lewin, the most effective strategy to attain the desired goals would be to direct one's pedagogical efforts primarily at leaders, change agents and gatekeepers at all levels and in all sectors of society.

During the early years, research activities were included as an explicit part of training laboratories. Many PhD students, who later became 'names' within social and organizational psychology, wrote their theses on training laboratory data. Research was considered a means towards enhancing the quality of practice (in the training laboratory setting and elsewhere), just as the real-life world of practice (e.g. in the laboratory) enhanced the quality of research.

The seeds of the laboratory method were sown in 1946, shortly before Lewin died. The Research Centre for Group Dynamics had been given the assignment of managing a workshop on 'intergroup relations' for some fifty members of the Connecticut State Inter-Racial Commission.[13] Every night the staff would meet to compare observations, to evaluate and to make plans for the next day. One evening, a few participants lodging at the centre asked for permission to participate in such a meeting. Somewhat hesitant the staff invited them in – a move that should prove to have far-reaching consequences for the integration of joint reflection and feedback procedures in the design of future training laboratories. Many years later Marrow (1969: 212-213) quotes Ronald Lippitt, member of the original 1946-staff, for the following evaluation: "The evening session from then on became the significant learning experience of the day, with the focus on actual behavioural events and with active dialogue about differences of interpretations and observations of the events of those who had participated in them … In addition, the staff discovered that feedback had the effect of making participants more sensitive to their own conduct and brought criticism into the open in a healthy and constructive way".

A year later the first regular training laboratory was launched in Bethel, and in 1948 the 'Second Laboratory Session' followed. By then NTL had already been founded. Eventually, the method was spread to other institutional settings and other countries, but NTL still exists and Bethel is still the domicile of a number of annual NTL training laboratories.

---

13   Having slightly differing versions, the following "creation myth" is reproduced in various sources, see e.g. Bradford, Gibb & Benne, 1964:81ff and Marrow, 199:210ff.

The Laboratory Movement

In the book about his concentration camp experiences (Madsen & Willert 1996), a quote from an interview with Ken Benne was included at Gunnar's specific request.[14] The interview had been reprinted in the context of a memorial ceremony for Benne who died in 1992. Gunnar saw it as an 'unofficial' programme statement for the group dynamic movement: "What motivated us above all was the democratic idea and the necessity of preventing Nazism from ever occurring again." Here follows the Benne quote:

> After the war, we wanted to develop practical methods to preserve and enhance our democratic social values. Kurt Lewin, our spiritual leader, was fully dedicated to this. We believed that we, as behavioural scientists, could best contribute to this purpose by *applying* what we had learned in our research on leadership and small group dynamics to real-life community and organizational life. We believed that any kind of intentional change – not driven by raw power or economic and political coercion – involves *learning* on the part of everyone involved. Change is always occurring. We wanted to learn to use groups to support individual creativity, rather than to suppress or make everybody the same. We were quite convinced that if we created groups with the norm that *everybody values differences*, a group atmosphere would develop in which people would become more of the individuals that they potentially are, rather than just become copies of the same model. The original NTL was *not* focused on individual development; we were interested in *social change*. In the long run, you're not going to have stable, secure and healthy individuals unless you have a social environment which develops and supports the individual. Democratic values call for intervention at the *total social system* level.

'The *original* NTL' had concerned itself with society and world affairs, Benne said. But that value orientation did not stay unrivalled within the laboratory movement. During our conversations with Gunnar, he was preoccupied with the rift between an East Coast and a West Coast culture gradually developing in the USA. Connecticut, Delaware and Bethel are East Coast localities. Here active bonds continued to exist between the laboratory method and the scientific community. And the basic orientation stayed social psychological. When the method spread to the West Coast, it met the therapeutic community and humanistic psychology, this mixture resulting in an orientation towards individual personal growth.

---

14 Kenneth Benne (1908-1992) founded the NTL together with Lee Bradford and Ron Lippitt. He was one of the three editors of the major work on the laboratory method: Bradford, Gibb & Benne, 1964. He was interviewed in 1988 by Arthur Freedman.

Since its beginning, the laboratory method had been linked with active social commitment: community development, adult education, democratic cooperative methods etc. By contrast, in the Personal Growth movement the individual is the main focus. The distinction shows in the kind of interventions undertaken. The laboratory method focuses on the function and roles of the individual within the group. The other tradition used the group simply as a setting for individual therapy – often with a strong, and to my mind problematic, element of seduction, since participants in this type of group may well move further into self-revelation than they actually feel like doing. Today the Personal Growth tradition has become predominant as a consequence of the current individualistic trend.

The same developmental trends became apparent when Lee Bradford – as director of NTL – set out to combine the Bethel East Coast perspective with the West Coast perspective. The West Coast was not interested in the programme components dealing with theory and exercises; they just wanted the small group work. Bradford was intent on keeping the two worlds together, but also insisting on the original East Coast standpoint. In 1972 he recruited me for a large meeting in Carmel, California, where all the groups from the West Coast were assembled. Joe Luft and I were to be spokesmen for the East Coast values such as obligations vis-a-vis society – as opposed to self-realization, gestalt therapy etc. The conflict began in the early 60s and you might say that the West Coast perspective came out the winner – in Europe as well.[15]

Earlier we have referred to Lee Bradford as group trainer, director of NTL, chairman of the board of Fels and co-editor of the major work on the laboratory method (Bradford, Gibb & Benne et al. 1964). We found on Gunnar's bookshelves, after his death, an unpublished report by Bradford: *National Training Laboratories: its History 1947-1970* (1974) – and with a personal dedication: 'To Gunnar Hjelholt who did more than anyone else to use and spread NTL concepts in Denmark and in Europe – with great fondness, Leland P. Bradford'.

A couple of years before he died, Lee stayed with us for some days in Vust. He then looked back at his life. During the war he and his wife had volunteered to teach needy children and this was how he had made contact with Kurt Lewin. And then he ended up becoming an empire builder: the organizer, the admin-

---

15   In Denmark, T-groups have for a long time been known as 'sensi-groups'. In the popular parlance of today, a 'sensi-group' is understood as a place where personal intimacies are revealed and scrutinized by other group members and a 'sensi-trainer'.

istrator, the one who glued things together, manipulated, attracted the 'right' people, never gave up. A very interesting man!

One other person mentioned above is Joseph Luft. A book by Luft, *Group Processes. An Introduction to Group Dynamics* (3rd edition 1984) was also found in Gunnar's library, likewise with a dedication note to Gunnar. At one interview session in Vust, Gunnar told us: "Today I got a letter from Joseph Luft – the man, you know, after whom the Johari window, or half of it, is named.[16] From time to time I get letters from the people with whom I got acquainted in the USA. Strong, emotional and important contacts". In 2003, Joseph Luft sent us a mail regretting he was unable to attend the Gunnar Hjelholt memorial conference – after which he added: "Gunnar and I were friends and colleagues for many years, working together for NTL in Bethel, Maine. Also, I had the good fortune to visit him and his wife, back in the nineteen seventies, with my wife and two children. Gunnar was one of a kind, a pleasure to know and to work with. I will remember him in mind and spirit for ever".

We now move on to Gunnar's views on the laboratory method. For him, ideal working relationships were symmetrical relationships. That preference stayed with him, even when he found himself in asymmetrical role relations per se, like those between teacher and student, consultant and client, researcher and researched. Opting for symmetry implies a striving to have the interpersonal power aspect reduced, while at the same time acknowledging its de facto existence.

> The laboratory method was based on a 'transactional' learning theory. Teaching and training were understood in terms of the transactions involved, i.e. as dependent on *cooperation* – but a tricky kind of cooperation. Just as is the case for the trainee or participant, the teacher or trainer enters the situation armed with curiosity and a quest for learning, yet also anxious as to *what* he may learn, not least about himself and his own conduct. He should be open to feedback concerning his effect on the group – just as he hopes the other group members will be open to feedback. At any time he must be prepared to share his observations and knowledge with anybody else, participant or staff – as he must also respect and value the knowledge and contributions any participant has to offer.

---

16 'Johari window' is a much used matrix model consisting of two dimensions of awareness: (a) known to self vs. not known to self and (b) known to others vs. not known to others. It is called 'Johari' because Joe Luft's co-inventor was named Harry; see Luft, 1984.

The kind of relationship between trainer and participant is what matters the most: whether it is based on power differentials or on equality. All sorts of complications arise when two persons want to make use of each other, without, however, using – or possibly misusing – the power differential inherent in their relationship from the very start. As trainer, you may use your power, e.g., as an instrument helping you to keep a distance: you may want to stay neutral or to avoid burdening others with your own needs. Likewise, and for a variety of reasons, participants may well try to push you into the power position. All of this makes it imperative that the trainer-participant relationship be made an object of public investigation and be scrutinized so that the symmetrical relationship can be preserved.

My view of power is inspired by Max Pagès.[17] The relation between trainer and participant is characterized by inequality, and the inequality is due in part to the economic factor (the trainer is being paid), in part political (the trainer decides the programme and the organizational arrangement), in part ideological (the trainer's ideology and methods become the dominant group ideology). Furthermore, both parties depend on the institutions that support the training activities. Certain forms of intervention will preserve, or even augment the existing power imbalance – definitely this is what happens when interaction processes are dealt with in an individualistic manner.

In his professional role, Gunnar tended to be a man of action who tried to *do* something. According to himself he was apt to lose patience if he experienced participants talking themselves away from, rather than in the direction towards what was important. 'I may be too quick. At times, I'll inadvertently end up giving people the solution instead of helping them to reach the conclusion I have reached a long time ago'. At the same time – and this sort of self-criticism apart – he greatly valued reflection and always took care to have it included in his design work.

People may lose themselves in action – they just plainly enjoy getting things done and never bother to reflect. As for me, I do have that basic curiosity making me keen to know *what is there*, and *what has been*. This requires reflection.

From the very beginning, laboratory design roughly divided the available time in three equal parts, or thirds. During one third, participants would be experiencing human interaction in the raw. One third was set aside for

---

17   Later we will hear more about the relationship between Gunnar Hjelholt and Max Pagès, cf. also Chapter 9.

generating general, though experience-based understanding. During the last third, they were meant to reflect on how, in their home surroundings, they could make personal use of their new learning and knowledge. As I told you earlier, in Bethel we would hand out small notebooks to the participants, and they were supposed to 'talk to' these for an hour every day. After that would come plenary meetings where everybody would have a chance to generalize his or her learning.

Later adjustments removed all that. The tempo wasn't fast enough, not enough 'action'. Further, three-week courses are expensive. Shorter versions are a lot easier to sell. Firms and institutions sending, and paying for, their employees cannot – so they say – do without them for very long. Consequently, the third week was cut away. Nowadays they even try to finish it all in three days. In this way, reflection and generalization components disappeared – even though we had empirical data confirming the quality of three-week laboratories.

So there was a change of tempo and important issues were lost. They 'forgot' that boredom is full of tension. This is what matters: setting up conditions so that tension is preserved, to be made use of for reflection purposes. The only way to change a system is to make it experience things in a new way. Reflection, meaning a certain way of handling data, will bring about change. The power of reflection is linked to the fact that *one has to travel the road*.

Looking back at this part of professional history, the very concept of time has changed as well. We used to be more flexible, to give things the time they needed. Nowadays, to keep the spaces open while changes take place requires a lot of energy.

The shift in tempo happened parallel to a change towards utility-oriented success criteria for the training work and a downplay of the research part and the social commitment. Gunnar deeply regretted this development.

The small group

Having received his research training in a gestalt psychology environment, and thanks to his epoch-making Berlin experiments from the 1920s, Lewin had been much revered at the Copenhagen Psychological Laboratory – but only the 'early Lewin', not the social psychologist he had become after moving to the USA in 1933. Thus, during his student years, Gunnar Hjelholt had been introduced to field theory, but not to group dynamics.

Our child psychology classes were based on Carmichael.[18] That book, for the first time, acquainted me slightly with the writings of Kurt Lewin. Some other teacher did lectures on the psychology of the feeble-minded and made use of Lewin's graphical models – you know, the characteristic oval drawings of the psychological field with its field forces or vectors. They did appeal to me, those models. Their peculiar simplicity helped my comprehension along.

Generally speaking, at the University of Copenhagen they took no interest in stuff coming from the USA. As to newer research trends within social psychology, I hardly believe they had heard about them. One explanation might be that in the USA – a melting pot of immigrants and people from different nations who had left familiar surroundings in favour of new ones – a natural focus developed on how to live your life together with your own group and other groups. This made social psychology relevant. In Europe, focus was on the individual because our culture was more homogenous and we sensed less tension.

When Gunnar looked back upon his professionally formative years in the 1950s, it became clear that groups had interested him all along.

From my time at the Danish Technological Institute I remember the wonderful feeling when discovering that *it actually worked* – all those ideas coming from the group theories. It even worked better than in the research laboratory. To sense, deep in your heart, that some theory – which had looked reasonably sound on paper – actually holds true in the real world, goddamit! Most books I bought in the 1950s were written by Americans. Besides the more sociological issues, I was particularly stirred by psychoanalytical writings, e.g., on the way summer camps and other institutional settings could further observation and treatment work. In this literature, groups and their social psychological aspects became of central theoretical concern.

Looking at my ways of organizing group selection in the Military Psychology Work Group – or at my active concern for the fates of young people – or at my work with the enlisted privates as well as the sociometric measurements: all of this makes it evident that groups and group life had been one stable focus area of mine right from the beginning. Likewise, when employed at the National

18   Carmichael, L. (ed.) *Manual of Child Psychology*. New York: Wiley, 1946. The book's one chapter authored by Kurt Lewin ('Behavior and development as a function of the total situation', pp. 791-844) is extensively marked in the copy owned and read by young Gunnar Hjelholt. The chapter by Lewin is reprinted as chapter X in Lewin 1951. Incidentally, Lewin (1935) includes a paper on feeble-mindedness (Chapter XII).

Council for the Unmarried Mother and her Child, before making my report I used to do an interview with the couple, supplementing the habitual conversation with the woman alone. It was kind of unusual in those days.[19]

However, at the time I saw no links between my group related practice and Lewin. It wasn't until 1958, when in the USA I met some of his students and the training laboratories, that I fully realized his importance.

As described earlier, feedback processes are a key design feature of the laboratory method, and Gunnar had diligently taken care to integrate feedback procedures in his group work at Fels, e.g. in the form of so-called mirror groups or reflection groups. By the end of each day, course participants would meet with 2-3 others, giving each participant the chance to compare his own self-observations from diverse course settings with those of his co-participants. Mirror groups became a permanent feature within Gunnar's adult education programmes. Also, he experimented with the use of tape and video recordings:

> At some of the early laboratories and courses we tape-recorded the T-groups – or their course-equivalents: unstructured groups – and subsequently designed exercises where the participants would make joint analyses of what was on the tape. During evenings the tapes would be available so that participants were free to listen to themselves.

> On some occasion I had watched myself as the trainer on a video recording – seeing how there were wide discrepancies between my verbal expressions and my body language. Enlightening! That started my use of the video camera for certain training purposes. One of the most efficient ways I know of using video-recordings is to let participants take turns at operating the camera, afterwards having them discuss what they observed and focused upon in the situation, and what they did not want to see.

During his professional life, Gunnar spent a large amount of time as T-group trainer. We asked him what he saw as the most important background factors shaping the efficiency of this particular learning tool.

> Goal, leadership, norms …! When you remove these three elements from a group – which is exactly what happens in the beginning of a training laboratory – in-group fighting must necessarily start evolving around them. And then things start happening! What pleases me the most is getting the opportunity

---

19   These concerns are elaborated on in Chapter 1.

to follow the entire developmental cycle of a group, from the time it is born until it dies.

Preferably, as a group trainer, Gunnar would direct his interpretations and interventions at group level rather than at the level of the individual.

Often I say that I take no interest in the individual, but only pay attention to the system. If I possibly can, I will make interpretations at group level rather that at the individual level. Group interpretations are about participants' roles, their mutual relations and common goals. When making interpretations of unconscious processes at group level, my psychoanalytical background becomes particularly useful.

When working with a group, I first have to take care that it becomes established as a unity. You help a T-group become a real group by using the same words as those used by group members – then these words will become group property.

Through interpretations or suggestions, you may help a work team start looking at itself like a family. States of competition and fighting may then become transformed into a state of mutual consideration. In India I managed to do this in a newly formed Monitoring and Evaluation Group (MEG) of which I was the only foreign member.[20] One evening I asked them to find out about their mutual family roles. I chose the uncle role myself, and, mind you, I did this with a somewhat manipulative intent. I had looked into the matter beforehand and found out that, in India, if family members disagree, an uncle is consulted and the family must conform to his verdict. From then on, the group was called the MEG Family.

One important reason behind Gunnar's 'group level strategy' was his theoretical understanding of individuals as not being 'inside', but, rather, 'outside' the group.[21]

In systems thinking – especially within sociology – a distinction is made between psychological systems and social systems. Individual humans constitute part of the environment of the social systems! Being the complex psychological systems we are, we construct the social systems on which we are, then, dependent,

---

20 The large-scale Danida project in India took place between 1980 and 1985 and will not be mentioned further in the present chapter dealing primarily with the period until 1970. As early as 1974, Gunnar Hjelholt was a visiting professor in India for a couple of months. Cf. also Chapter 8.

21 Cf. the discussions in Chapter 16.

and which influence our way of viewing the world. But we also stand outside them – while, at the same time, of course, we are the ones who make them function by our role performance and by taking up positions within their hierarchies. Gradually, as the system complexity increases, our psychic system complexity increases, too – enabling us to sense our outside position more acutely. And the individual may start reflecting on the way he or she acts in social settings.

This way of thinking, including its distinction between psychic and social system, should influence your practice – e.g. by focusing your attention on group functions and patterns: on structure, roles and communication, rather than on individual persons and patterns.

The mini-societies showed this feature very clearly. We participated in them as role players belonging to social systems in interaction with other systems – while at the same time, as individuals, we constituted the environment of these systems, meaning that part of our own complexity would be made into objects for our reflection. I believe much of the participants' learning during these events can be explained in this way: not only were they observers of themselves while acting, but – since their whole being was not taken up by the action – they were also able, afterwards, to reflect on their actions.

Over the years Gunnar did a lot of reflection on the professional and ethical aspects of his role as group trainer.

One of my colleagues, Traugott Lindner, once made the observation that my T- groups would typically be the ones that arranged social events for the lab as a whole – such as inviting everybody to a party, or taking other, like initiatives. His observation troubled me a bit. It made me start reflecting on the influence coming from the trainer's personality and I tried to make up my mind concerning the positive versus negative effects of this influence – and whether such an impact is likely to stay with the participants even after you have left them. As an outcome of all this reflection work, I actually changed my trainer role into a more passive one – the result being that I, as a projection screen, became the target of all the attacks and aggressions. I believe Traugott had made his remarks during the mid-60s – after which I made my change-of-style. I started thinking that my most important task might be that of simply *being there* – i.e. being the boundary keeper.

Later, we shall see how the idea of boundary keeper was unfolded, analogies being also made with the role of process consultant. But for now we will return to the historical chronology.

Back in Denmark

After returning to the Danish Technological Institute, offices were set aside for Gunnar Hjelholt's new department. The directors looked forward to drawing on his experiences from the USA. On his part, Gunnar could hardly wait to try out his new skills. One of his first accomplishments was to translate the NTL material: "A very large part of the written lab-manuals circulating in Europe during the 1960s came from the NTL portfolio I brought with me from the 1958 laboratory." Soon, Gunnar made professional contact with study group leaders teaching labour union representatives in the organizational setting of the Danish Workers' Educational Association (WEA, in Danish: AOF).

> During winter season, 1958-59, and onward, we organized evening courses for study group leaders and adult educators in Copenhagen. We did two three hour long courses per week, including group exercises, role play, a bit of theory and a lot of enthusiasm. Our main objective was to communicate to them *the teacher's basic task*: activate the learners, get them to trust their own observations, their own experiences. In one word: Democracy! March 1962, the whole thing culminated in a mass meeting at Christiansborg.[22]

> During the years following, a large part of my work focused on teaching and democratization within the labour movement. T-groups, in my view, were clearly an opportunity not to be missed by the unions – an opportunity to create truly democratic organizations. Make Utopia come true. At courses for union representatives and other WEA-members, experiential teaching formats seemed the obvious choice. And they understood what I wanted to give them – or had to offer. Some few steps were taken in the direction of organizing autonomous groups.

Meanwhile – Gunnar told us – antagonism was slowly mounting at the Danish Technological Institute. Gunnar's department was moving fast, its many newly recruited employees viewed the Institute's internal policy matters differently from its old-timers. Proposals in favour of far-reaching changes – e.g., a suggestion that research activities be re-introduced at the Institute – were either shelved or turned down.

In April 1960 Gunnar chose to hand in his resignation. Then he spent a very long vacation period with his family – after which he registered his own consulting firm, "meaning that, from now on, I was a self-employed social

---

22 Christiansborg Castle in Copenhagen is the home of the Danish Parliament (Folketinget).

psychologist". Soon, other professionals became attached to the firm, the first being Hanne Sjelle Ernst, the next Gori Ehrenskjöld. As psychology students both of them had had their practicum at the Danish Technological Institute while Gunnar was still there. The staff expansion also became the occasion for giving the firm a name: *Applied Social Psychology – G. Hjelholt Associates.*

For Gunnar it proved not that easy to be the top-man in an enterprise: "Being a firm gradually made it more difficult for us to choose the position on the boundary line. We tried, but somehow the effect was rather the opposite." After ten years the associates split up. Gunnar became a freelancer, kept the firm's name and its international clients, established some sort of network organization and moved from Copenhagen to the farm cottage in Vust. In a folder written in English the new network organization presented itself as follows:[23]

> Applied Social Psychology undertakes projects for international, state, and local agencies, organizations and private enterprises, and applies the knowledge of social science to the human problems of to-day and tomorrow ... We are, perhaps, in our working methods a strange mixture between the consulting firm and the university. As social scientists we are basically not researchers but searchers ... The work is done in close collaboration with the client by our staff, psychologists and sociologists, employed fully or part, sometimes borrowed from other institutes ... Gunnar Hjelholt is president of the organization and a steering committee supervises the work. The steering committee consists of (Mrs) Hanne Sjelle Ernst, Gurth Higgin, Gunnar Hjelholt, Trygve Joenstad and Donald Nylen.

In 1971, this same organization sent out an invitation for a twelve-day international Organizational Laboratory in Denmark.[24] In the invitation they asked:

> Can organizations survive the 70s? Can the organization be saved, be made alive, meaningful, worth devoting a third of our lives to preparing for and living in?

---

23 We only have scant interview material covering this phase of Gunnar Hjelholt's life and career. For this reason we are not sure of the status of this 'network organization', nor of its duration. The source here is a folder from around 1970.

24 Besides Gunnar Hjelholt, the staff members of the mentioned laboratory were: Hanne Sjelle Ernst, Donald Nylen and Max Pagès.

Generally speaking, the cited formulations are typical of Gunnar's working ethos. He saw himself as a 'searcher', and, in this capacity, wanted to link academic theory and research with practice. He wanted to revitalize the institutions, an idea that, in condensed form, we also find represented in an excerpt from the introduction to the book *The institutions and the people*.[25]

> Society is a complex thing, and difficult to decipher. It has lots of systems that either grip us tightly, or do not let us in ... Our institutional systems – and, here, we are not only talking about the prisons – often build walls around themselves. The average citizen approaches the institutions in a state of awe, or even fear. Behind the gate or counter sits somebody representing power. By only looking at it through the eyes of their system, the institutional employees run the risk of creating imaginary pictures of the surrounding world.

Autonomous groups

Once again, we move backwards in time. In 1959, Gunnar had done some leadership training courses and laboratories for the Lauritzen Shipping Company. This became the beginning of a long-lasting involvement.[26]

> The Lauritzen contract gave me an opportunity to use the entire NTL repertory. I implemented management training in the form of eight-day laboratories. At every one of them, the participants represented a cross-section of the organizational structure. From 1959 until around 1963, these 'in-company laboratories' were run three times a year. That period was the shipping company's golden age.

> At some point while working for Lauritzen, Berit and I signed on as steward and stewardess on board the 'Frida Dan' in the Kiel Canal. The ship was bound for Italy to unload paper pulp and then for North Africa to load phosphate for Aalborg in northern Jutland. The idea was to give me some first-hand knowledge concerning life on board the ships.

> The leadership training included T-groups, exercises, role play and theory. During the last days of the course, the spouses would join in. Knud Lauritzen, the owner-manager, joined the course for one afternoon and evening so that

---

25 This is a translation of the Danish title of Hjelholt & Berg 1974. The translated quote is from page 9. Editor Berg is identical with Harald Berg, author of Chapter 7 in the following.

26 Cf. Chapter 12 in this book: Training for Reality.

questions could be asked. It was my job to make sure he did not evade the tough issues. Before the war, you know, managers just stated what needed doing, period! After the war, the notion arose that employees must be consulted and have a say – but the managers did not know how to go about it. Then this company brought in a psychologist. In the 60s these ideas proliferated enormously. Lauritzen, himself, thought it was great fun that his company had been a pioneer in this field.

My last job for Lauritzen was a piece of research leading up to a conference about drilling ships. The company entered that line of business in the beginning of the 1970s. During the late 1960s our contact had been somewhat sporadic – namely after the shipping company had joined the Danish Shipowners' Association and had their staff trained by the Association's training division. The rebel shipping company had become compliant.

My cooperation with Lauritzen was fruitful, and one of the things I did that really went well. Yet, I was not satisfied. Their financial situation improved and ships started functioning better due to our setting up autonomous work teams – but, then, in the end all these new activities became too much of a challenge for the shipping company, and we had to close down our activities!

Einar Thorsrud from Norway is often credited for being *the* European working with autonomous groups. During one interview, Gunnar brought in a correcting remark:

When it came to setting up autonomous groups, actually, I was the one who started it. Thorsrud only began a couple of years later. Like me, he worked with ships. He did not, however, dare to go all the way. At Lauritzen we didn't spend a lot of time on preparations. But since it was the crew that had made all decisions about the procedures, they were also the ones who could change and update them, as the need arose.

Gunnar's remark seems to hold an implicit critique as to the de facto-sustainability of Thorsrud's much acclaimed programmes.[27] He also told us that, as

---

27 Gunnar Hjelholt's library includes a small book by Einar Thorsrud & Fred Emery in cooperation with Eric Trist: *Industrielt demokrati – noen norske og utenlandske erfaringer* (1964). An English version was published in 1969: *Form and content in industrial democracy – Some experiences from Norway and other European countries.* Gunnar participated in a large memorial symposium after Thorsrud's death in which people from all over the world partook. "He *certainly* knew the right people", Gunnar exclaimed on one occasion.

a spin-off of his involvement in the Lauritzen Shipping Company, he subsequently became regarded as an expert on anything concerning the sea, tankers in particular. This reputation led to major assignments with, among others, the oil company Esso.

On the first floor in Vust, in Gunnar's study, we would always sit around a hexagonal table, or rather: one hexagon was made up of two half hexagons. The table had been designed by Gunnar specifically for Lauritzen's conference room. Such tables could be joined into all sizes and shapes depending on the occasion. The design expresses his omnipresent effort to create flowing and flexible structures that were conducive to task resolution without, however, pinning participants down to particular positions.[28]

Working in Europe

Gunnar Hjelholt had always been interested in other nations and cultures: "I am actually a stay-at-home person but I can see why open boundaries are a necessity". This attitude was strengthened during his stay in the concentration camp. Porta had held prisoners from 15-20 different nations. He was one among few in that camp who were able to 'build bridges'. His stay in the USA further broadened his international view.

> After my stay in the USA, my life almost entered a missionary phase. What I had learned must be made use of! And then I was seized by the great demand for change. Waves of democratization flooded Europe, Germany included. So much happened during the 1960s. Europe opened up, things must be built anew. I became part of this, and I influenced this European movement in various ways, not least through a large number of training laboratories. While Americans turned individualistic, we wanted laboratories to be reflections of society.

> Being one of the few who were actually trained in the group dynamic tradition – and being, on top of that, very action-oriented – I played an important role in the transfer of the NTL movement to Europe: getting it adjusted to European conditions, keeping the American dominance at bay.

> I guess it's natural to feel attracted to places where they appreciate you – and I did feel more appreciated out there, in the European setting, than here in

---

28 After his death, the mentioned hexagon was moved to 'Gunnar's library' at the Center for System Development at the Department of Psychology, University of Aarhus.

Denmark. I really know, deep down, that other nationalities are different from us, but at the same time like us. Other nationalities don't scare me. I suppose I am good at sensing where to tread carefully, so as not to offend other people, and good at making use of whatever I discover and understand concerning other people's qualities. Further, I'll tell them things about myself that will make them see me less as a stranger. Never have I felt myself shunned or rejected by foreign cultures. When in India, for instance, I always got on well with the Indians because I travelled the same class as they and never stayed at the posh hotels.

The list of activities, clients and geographical sites covered by Gunnar during the 1960s is truly overwhelming, quantitatively, in terms of the number of items, and qualitatively, in terms of diversity. Presenting the full catalogue would be pointless. He himself summed up his work during the said period by pointing out four major areas; below, summary presentations are given:

1. Attempting to influence adult education, not only in Denmark (cf. assignments for the labour movement referred to earlier), but also Germany – most notably through the ambitious Schliersee project that dealt with democratization of the educational sector.
2. Building organizations and organizational units based on the concept of autonomous work teams. His assignments for Lauritzen Shipping Company (cf.above) and the Hammerfest project (soon to be described) are major examples.
3. Introducing the laboratory method in Europe, including his own design, the mini-society.
4. Efforts at making EIT a viable organization.

The Schliersee project

In May 1963, a three-week laboratory and later follow-ups were held at Schliersee. The participants were 35 young teachers from the German region, Hessen, with all levels of the educational system being represented. The laboratory had been arranged as a joint venture between the *Institut für Sozialforschung* in Frankfurt, the Ministry of Cultural Affairs in Hessen and the Ford Foundation. The international staff included three NTL associates from the USA: Kenneth Benne, Donald Nylen and George Lehner. Europe was represented by Traugott Lindner, Tobias Brocher and Gunnar Hjelholt.[29] In the years following Schliersee – so Gunnar told us – many of its participants were to be recruited into leading positions. Another offshoot was the journal *Gruppendynamik: Forschung und Praxis*, appearing for the first time in 1966.

A few words about Don Nylen who was a member of the staff. Nylen was somewhat older than the others. American by birth but of Swedish descent, he held a doctoral degree from Vienna. He had been attached to the laboratory movement since 1949, and during the 1960s he served as professor in Organizational Behaviour in the USA.

> On several occasions Don Nylen and I visited psychology departments at universities and other institutions in order to raise money for the Schliersee group. I had met him in 1962 in Lausanne where the European Forum for Human Relations Training had been established as a forerunner of EIT. We shared a room and since then I have kept in touch with this old pioneer – a warm friendship.

The Hammerfest project

The Hammerfest project took place during the years 1966-68, it being a collaborational project between Gunnar and Trygve Joenstad from Norway. The project's client was an international company situated in a small fishing town in Northern Norway, north of the polar circle.[30] In addition the project included the trawler fleet and the entire community. While the project was running, Gunnar suffered from concentration camp after-effects and was periodically hospitalized. By reading his project description, we learned that

---

29 "Was für ein team", Inge Kähling recently exclaimed. She participated as a young teacher in the 1963 laboratory. Shortly after this she was appointed headmaster of a school and later became qualified as group trainer and EIT member. Our section on Schliersee, including the Kähling-quote, is in part based on an unsigned memo from 2002 that we found in Gunnar's study after his death. The memo is written on EIT note paper and refers to a visit to the said Inge Kähling. Incidentally, Gunnar did not mention the Ford Foundation, instead he referred to the fact that the American Jewish Committee put pressure on Volkswagen with regard to financial support. As for *Institut für Sozialforschung*, he mentioned the renowned trio Horchheimer-Adorno-Mitscherlich, of whom the latter, later, became an EIT member.
30 Cf. Chapter 15 below the title of which is North of the Polar Circle. The Hammerfest project is also referred to in Joenstad (1979), *Det sosiale samspillet: Trekk fra nyere europeisk gruppedynamikk.* [Social interaction: Trends in recent European Group Dynamics.] Oslo: Universitetsforlaget, pp. 112-131. At that time, Joenstad was director of Norigo, Institutt for Gruppeutvikling og Organisasjonspsykologi A/S. [Dept. of Group Development and Organizational Psychology Ltd.].

Gunnar's professional links with the project field had at times been indirect rather than direct: using a telephone from his hospital bed he had interviewed his colleague and participant observer Joenstad. It also appeared that his role as remote observer, rather than involved actor, had actually entailed certain benefits, making it easier for him to grasp underlying patterns in what went on. We asked Gunnar to elaborate on this idea.

> Yes, I definitely believe it gave me an advantage – because I was not that involved. But then, part of the difference between Trygve Joenstad and myself also stemmed from a contrast between my own habitual and critical focus on task-related capabilities of systems and Trygve's inclination to accept things the way they were. It has happened that I had to leave a project for the simple reason that I couldn't keep sufficient distance. A consultant's strength depends on his ability to ask the simple questions and to keep a distance – while still being engaged and possibly having personal preferences. Too much involvement may bring you so close that you will no longer be able to take the detached view that allows you to see things from another perspective. As consultants we must stay outside the system. I have always emphasized three things: you get in, you make them work, and then you leave again.[31] Over the years it has gradually become easier for me to follow these principles, without the members of the client system feeling betrayed.

Trygve Joenstad was a psychologist. For a period of time he had been head-of-department at the Danish Technological Institute in Denmark. While still colleagues, Trygve and Gunnar had promised each other that the one who died first was to be honoured by the other in the form of a funeral speech. "And then – you wouldn't believe it – but Trygve actually died before me", Gunnar told us, referring to his own failing health. The two of them had been excellent cooperational partners, a fact Gunnar ascribed to fundamental differences in their problem-solving style:

> As a consultant he had a quality I did not have myself: he was able to enter a system and be part of it, without being unpleasantly affected – as I typically would, by feeling 'swallowed up', etc. Things had to happen the way they happened, he said. That's why we worked so extremely well together in the Hammerfest project. I may even present you with a nice quotation from Joenstad: 'When an organization experiences disorder coming from its environment, it will contract and close the door to the outside world'. The important issue is whether such contraction will lead to organizational death, cf. the old entropy

---

31 Cf. Chapter 16 below.

principle, or, rather, to an inner tension that will again lead to expansion and new development.

The laboratory method and the mini-society design

A Danish training laboratory in 1962 – done together with Matthew Miles from the USA – turned out to become of crucial importance for Gunnar's later conception of the mini-society.

> In 1962, Miles and I arranged four weeks of training, targeting people from the adult education sector. Following this laboratory we wrote the article Extending the Conventional Training Laboratory.[32] We intended to develop *a European model*, meaning a model based on the participants' collaboration. By this design the small group was placed in an organizational framework. Subsequently the model became widely adopted by European laboratory designers.

> I had grown increasingly dissatisfied with the Bethel and NTL versions of the laboratory method. Certain things taking place in them were *not* subjected to the same kind of analysis as happened in the small T-group. Miles and I insisted that we must look at the entire organization. A group becomes what it is only in relation to the larger organization, or in relation to those who have defined it as a group. The organization itself must be critically scrutinized. In our article we discussed a possible transfer of power from the staff to the participants, and a change of perspective to that of society.

> *How did you get in touch with Miles?*

> I had met him at Fels, back in 1958 when he visited the centre. More than anybody else I met over there, he became a dear friend of mine. We developed close family ties as well, paying frequent visits to each other in the USA and in Denmark along with wives and children.

As a firm manager, Gunnar sent his first employees to the two-year Dutch training programme with Miles as the prominent staff member. Miles was among the founders of EIT, the European equivalent to NTL. He contributed to the classical textbook account of the laboratory method (Bradford et al. 1964). In 1959, he published a monograph on groups, and it appears that Gunnar was among the small group of people helping with comments when he prepared the first revised edition of the book. In 1964, Miles introduced

---

32   Hjelholt & Miles (1963), cf. Chapter 11.

the concept of temporary system and analysed the features of such a system by using the training laboratory as one example. In a preliminary form, this line of thought is also expressed in Hjelholt & Miles (1963). Under the subheading "The laboratory as a social system" they write: [33]

> We were much impressed by the possibilities inherent in examination of the lab itself as a system larger than a face-to-face group. Up to now, most lab staffs have preferred to ignore the fact that operation of the lab requires real people to function in a real organization, having real conflicts, satisfactions, emotions etc. in the process. Conflicts within lab staffs form part of trainer folklore, yet participants are carefully shielded from such phenomena as if they did not exist.

Turning now to the mini-society, invented by Gunnar a few years later, we find that the idea of laboratory-as-organization was further extended into that of the laboratory-as-society.

> All the early T-group evaluations confirmed that participants had indeed learned something, but the main effect seemed to be one of gaining increased *self*-knowledge. I pondered a lot on this, and finally arrived at the conclusion that in the group one learns about the individual, in the inter-group situations the group learns about itself, in organizations you learn about inter-group phenomena, and only when the organization is confronted with its external environment we may learn about organizations.

A mini-society may be defined as a social psychological laboratory, set up with the aim of investigating the relation between a large system and its groups. The underlying idea was to create a small-scale society that would mirror some of the structural features and procedural mechanisms of macro-society. Essentially, this was done by changing or adding the following structural features to the laboratory design as practised in Bethel: (a) a design with homogeneous groups of participants with similar real-life backgrounds; (b) a set of complementary groups, e.g. social workers *and* drug addicts, making up the total organization called 'mini-society' – rather than 'training laboratory'; (c) variable, participant-decided admission fees; (d) staff-arranged initial accommodation for participants, reflecting status or power diffentials; (e) a mandatory introductory plenary, not to be dissolved until a joint, unanimous plan for resource distribution has been agreed upon; (f) following that, staff no longer act as managers with formal power, but rather as researchers collecting data on the

---

33   The quote is slightly condensed compared to the original work which is reproduced as Chapter 11 in the present book.

proceedings and sharing their observations with the rest of the 'society'. More details on the design are available in Chapters 6 and 13 below.

I started thinking about it around 1967. 'We must integrate all aspects of society in a laboratory' – that's how I must have been thinking. Our firm, Hjelholt Associates, was based on the idea that money we earned, we also somehow had to spend. In 1967 we must have earned a lot of money – meaning that in 1968, when arranging the first mini-society, we had means at our disposal to cover possible losses. Thus, we could hire a place without knowing beforehand whether the participants' fees – which they themselves, as part of the design, were going to decide – could actually pay for the rent.

I mostly created the mini-societies for my own sake – to gain knowledge about systems and society. Fortunately, as it turned out, the participants learned something too. One thing that never stopped amazing me was the good effects it could bring to marginal groups. I'll be damned if we didn't manage to turn drug addicts – well, they started out partly detoxicated – into decent people. And, mind you, they stayed that way after returning home.

In a mini-society anything is visible or can be made visible. Who is paying for what? Who gets what? And with regard to status differences: either they are minimized or else made fully visible, e.g. as might be the case with participants' initial accommodation. Technically speaking, transference risk is low: the staff participates on equal terms with the other groups, presenting their images like everybody else.

I have enjoyed doing mini-societies a lot – and they allowed me to use almost all my talents. I experimented a lot with unconventional feedback formats and contents. I got a chance to work with a large number of groups in one organizational space – homogenous groups that is. This was done by abolishing the standard design principle of random recruitment to groups – a principle that, in fact, serves to minimize intergroup conflicts.

Yes, for me they became an occasion to *go all the way*. I tried to combine social psychology with sociology, guided by the assumption that insofar as we succeeded in having a true section of society represented in the laboratory, we would mirror society. You may say that I placed the traditional laboratory in a sociological perspective.

I trust that by using this method we got hold of the latent trends in society before they became manifest. I sensed it as a kind of prediction method – even though, admittedly, this idea was never put to a serious test. The mini-societies also demonstrated the ways in which individuals are affected by social-psychological and sociological conditions. Compared to the Personal Growth method, I much prefer working with structures and, in a certain sense, I do not give a hoot about the individuals. At least I do not try to change them. I like to work with reality as it *is*.

He also told us that in 1975 the sociologist Gurth Higgin from the Tavistock Institute wrote an article on his participation in a mini-society in 1970. The article was printed in the Tavistock Anthology with a postscript by Gunnar. The postscript concludes as follows:

> The minisociety plunges the participants, including the social scientists, into the psycho-dynamics of social systems, a field which – with dire consequences for society – has been avoided by most researchers. … The mini-society emerges as a useful arena for action research focused on the conflict between the desire for personal liberation and the need for social order (Higgin & Hjelholt, 1990:257).

Compared to the reprinted version, Gunnar told us, Higgins' original article text started in a rather more dramatic fashion – having this to say about the inventor of the mini-societies: "There was a man, a bit crazy, who got the idea to get society into a lab…" Somewhat mockingly, Gunnar added that "the article gave rise to heated discussions among social scientists, some utterly defaming mini-societies on the grounds that proper measurement methods had not been applied".

Gunnar counted the sociologist Higgin among his close friends. From the beginning of the 1970s the two of them had had a joint assignment for the Swedish glass factory Emmaboda.[34]

> Emmaboda ran labs for the staff. The training took place elsewhere, in Ireland for instance, in an attempt to change the management climate and create larger involvement. Many things followed in its wake. At one point, the owner of the

---

34   Apart from heading the laboratory training for management and staff at Emmaboda Glasverk, for a number of years Gunnar Hjelholt had many assignments in Sweden. Sven-Åke Lenning evaluated the Emmaboda project and its effect on the participants in a quantitative investigation with clear distinction between independent and dependent variables (Lennung 1974). In his dedication to Gunnar, Lennung wrote: "Ett varmt tack till en utomordentligt oberoende variabel" [Warm thanks to an extraordinarily independent variable].

glass factory financed a leave of absence for Gurth Higgin giving him time to write *Symptoms of tomorrow*.

The referred book (Higgin 1973) can be found in Gunnar's library and the dedication by the author goes like this: "For Gunnar, in lasting gratitude for all that you have caused to grow in me, and with a depth of love no other man can command".

European group dynamics

In France in 1965 the EIT organization – meant to be a European counterpart to NTL – was founded, and with Gunnar Hjelholt as its first secretary general. Preparing for this event, international meetings had taken place in Switzerland (1962), The Netherlands (1963) and France (1965). The organization defined itself as: 'EIT – The European Institute for Trans-National Studies in Group and Organizational Development – is engaged in gathering knowledge about the social problems of contemporary and emerging Europe – and applies this knowledge to organizations and institutions. Beside training activities also research and consultation projects are undertaken by EIT with this aim in mind'.[35]

Many heated discussions and conflicts between rivalling fractions complicated the founding and life of the organization. In Gunnar's words: "The very name of the organization indicates the tensions; we had to delimit our action field to international events or to cultural encounters so as not to offend national institutes". Another touchy subject related to criteria for membership recruitment. Was the organization going to have theoretical and educational leanings towards psychoanalysis or pedagogy? – psychiatry or psychology? – Europe or America? Authorization was yet another issue to consider. At times, the project almost capsized.

However, the need for mutual support in the difficult work – actually I was the only one formally trained according to NTL standards – was the strongest. Further, EIT reflected a wish to create something with its own characteristics that would not be dominated by NTL. Before starting, we had made an agree-

---

35   Excerpt from a 1968 folder that will receive comments further on. The folder shows that at that time great emphasis was attached to information gathering and research, no doubt under the influence of the secretary general: Gunnar Hjelholt, that is.
It is worth mentioning that the Hammerfest project took place within the EIT framework, meaning that the client company set up a business contract with EIT. EIT has survived until today.

ment with Bradford that NTL would not admit European members before EIT had been established.

As secretary general my main task was to keep things from falling apart, to work out compromise solutions, to take responsibility. I think I did rather well – by making sure that all the others did what they were supposed to do. So that things kept moving. This is my way of dealing with an organization or a responsibility area that is subject to conflict and where things are politicized. In EIT, some people really got into fights and feelings were hurt. I would see to it that we moved forward with sufficient speed, that actions were carried out according to plan and schedule.

I am – or was – candid, even fierce. I'll do whatever has to be done and say whatever has to be said. I dare do it. Not particularly diplomatic but it loosens things up. That is also why I was elected secretary general. There was a need for someone who could say no, who could raise the tough issues – but, actually, it didn't happen all that often.

In 1979, a one-year group dynamic training programme was started, having three parallel branches: one in Belgium (in English), one in Germany and Austria (in German) and finally a Scandinavian line. "There were eight modules, and in the beginning I was in charge of the first four, while Trygve Joenstad was in charge of the last four. This programme – with revisions – is still being run in Belgium with Leopold Vansina as the driving force".[36]

It seems that those were busy years?

Yes! We wrote a short report on our activities 'The first three years of EIT's life'. But it doesn't at all reflect our full range of Europe-based activities between 1961 and '68. I would rush from Tavistock in England to the Netherlands, from there to France and Germany. Attending meetings, doing training laboratories. I remember one time in Germany, I had caught a fever and yet I ran a T-group for German industry bosses: a giant flop, it became, with incredible amounts of collective repression as far as the Hitler era was concerned.

In the late 90s Gunnar sent us an EIT leaflet from 1968. The 1968 list of members included 35 EIT members from 10 European countries as well as 10 members from the USA. The following selection of names represent persons mentioned in the present chapter: Lee Bradford, Tobias Brocher, Gori Ehren-

---

36   See Lee Vansina's Chapter 3 below.

skjöld, Hanne Sjelle Ernst, Gurth Higgin, Gunnar Hjelholt, Trygve Joenstad, Traugott Lindner, Matthew Miles, A. Mitscherlich, Donald Nylen, Max Pagès, Einar Thorsrud, Eric Trist and Lee Vansina.

Every year EIT held an International Human Relations Laboratory. The first three took place in Austria (1966), Denmark (1967) and Italy (1968). The staff was recruited from the relatively narrow group of EIT members, and Gunnar joined the staff all three times. Participants would typically come from industry and enterprises, education and government. The EIT laboratories presented themselves as something unique by emphasizing two things: the intercultural dimension and the research affiliation. About the latter a folder states: "Research is done on the whole laboratory-group (micro-society) and the results are submitted for further processes within this group".

The folder also mentions research that had been done the previous year by Traugott Lindner and Trygve Joenstad: "A clear emphasis was laid on the organizational aspects of Human Relations Training. The staff used the total number of participants as an object for building a community, and its developmental processes was studied at the same time … The approach to consider a total lab population a suitable object for organizational investigation has proved useful. … It was possible to teach organizational dynamics by using action research methods focusing on the processes of an existing social reality". The fingerprints of the secretary general, Gunnar Hjelholt, are clear. When he mailed the copy to us, he added in telegraphic style: "Possibly useful as documentation material – concerning laboratory training, our attempts at integrating 'research' as part of the concept. Shows a training method we saw as distinctively European. Moreover, EIT model implies beginnings of mini-society".

Like it had happened in the USA, Gunnar's EIT activities resulted in a number of lasting professional and personal friendships: "Coming from the European continent were four young psychologists, more or less the same age. The four were Traugott Lindner from Austria, Leopold Vansina from Belgium, Max Pagès from France and myself. We were somehow meant to develop a European group psychology and organizational theory. That seemed to be what others wanted us to accomplish. It definitely was what we, ourselves, felt like doing".

Individual relationships within the quartet were described by Gunnar as follows: "I have worked and fought and achieved a great deal with Traugott and we had a warm relationship." Gunnar's relationship to Lee Vansina was extremely significant, but also full of contrasts – as is also evidenced by Vansina's contribution to the present book.[37] About Vansina Gunnar said: "Lee was very much the guardian of professional ethics and standards". And then there was Max Pagès:[38]

Professionally I didn't do so many things with Max, and yet I reckon that our relationship became the closest. He is my friend and source of inspiration. Somehow Max has an idea of what life should be like.

He raised so many important issues and his attitudes have been so uncompromising that I must make my own position very clear. Often, I had to let practical considerations guide me: 'Ideally speaking you are right, Max, but we have to make do with what we've got and get the best out of it'. Max dared to take action, sitting around and discussing wasn't enough. When the issue of criteria for EIT membership was first raised, the discussion was dominated by an anxiety theme: 'We must keep out the 'others', the 'unqualified'.' I remember Max suggesting that we simply leave the matter open, i.e. to let everybody decide for themselves whether *they* wanted to join *us*, whether *we* in *their* eyes seemed 'qualified company'. And he experimented with what he called 'flexible structures'. He was extremely good at spotting power relations. And he looked at organizations as defensive structures blocking growth, so better break them down. Max has always confronted me with serious questions that have brought me closer to various sorts of boundaries than I might otherwise have dared come.

Somewhere, he states that the whole world is a group and the rest are simply sub-groups. Perhaps this idea kindled my own interest in the *environment* of the group or the organization. When you work with only one part, you need always to bear in mind how this part is related to the other parts and how it influences and is influenced by the whole situation. You always have a choice as to where you posit the boundary line of the system you observe. In my way of thinking, the 'mission' became the all-important thing – the task, that is. The mission is what connects us to the world. I am almost morbidly preoccupied with the issue of task.

My concentration camp experiences helped me make sense of something Max used to say: 'My job as consultant is to destroy the organization – anything that has to do with defenses, restrictions and subordination'. To be able to

---

37 See Lee Vansina's Chapter 3 below.
38 See Max Pagès' Chapter 9 below.

destroy is important, a new organization will always emerge. Max was fabulous at destroying organizations, but perhaps he was not that good at building up. When it comes to that, I work differently. I see myself more as a realistic utopian. But I, too, do persist in asking the question whether the organization may turn itself into something different.

One of the European participants in the initial phase of EIT was Eric Trist (1909-1993) from the Tavistock Institute of Human Relations in England. When travelling around Europe, Gunnar was frequently in touch with this renowned co-founder of the socio-technical approach within organizational theory.

As you know there are three sides to Tavistock. One side is their research, the other is their training, and the third is their consultancy work, the aspect with which I was most closely involved. As regards the training, just like in Bethel it was based on Lewin's ideas. But Tavistock also has strong ties to psychoanalysis and Bion, and focuses on authority issues – on our relation to Daddy, that is.[39]

For me personally, Eric Trist is probably the one person who has opened most theoretical doors, helping me relate the psychological and the sociological levels. His way of engaging in the world, his belief that the social sciences had a significant role to play, his humbleness and emphasis on the importance of cooperating with 'the object' of research – people, that is. He strongly supported my own convictions that, as social scientists, we can learn much by cooperating with our clients, or whatever name we call them. Gains in knowledge come from shared investigations and shared involvement in task resolution. And then I learned from his way of applying the psychoanalytic frame of reference. For me, it became something natural to understand reality the way Eric did.

He had the gift of bringing out the best in a cooperational relationship – and for diligently quoting his collaborational partners in ways that opened up, thus

---

39 Between 1990 and 1997 a three-volume *Tavistock Anthology* was published. The anthology is edited by Trist & Murray and contains numerous contributions by researchers and practitioners. The Tavistock Institute was founded in 1946 as an independent research institution, inspired by Lewin among others. The first conference on group relations, arranged in 1957 by the Tavistock Institute of Human Relations, was led by Eric Trist. It was somehow imported from Bethel which means that it was very close to the Lewinian form. Pretty soon the English variety was influenced by psychoanalysis, in particular by the thinking of Melanie Klein and the group dynamics of Wilfred Bion (Bion, 1961).

bringing you to places you had not realized you were heading for. Trist, the system thinker, has planted seeds and thoughts everywhere. It was the whole world he was dealing with.

One thing I believe I have in common with Eric is a conviction that *we must carry on*: there are ways of solving our mess by somehow making systems cooperate. And also a conviction that, in a given problem setting, external and internal issues are always linked. For all these reasons I was so pleased with the title of the Tavistock publication from 1990: *The Social Engagement of Social Science*.

Great mutual respect seems to have characterized Eric and Gunnar's relationship. "I feel that Eric Trist was one of the few persons who really appreciated me", Gunnar told us on one occasion – later finding a book by Trist from his bookshelf and reading the dedication aloud: "To Gunnar, who pioneered so much of the way". He also spoke of Trist as one of the few whom he might have accepted as his leader. Answering our question, whether he could see himself as adapting to a subordinate staff position, his reply came short and concise: "I could work for Eric Trist!"[40]

Structures and boundaries

The mini-societies became for Gunnar Hjelholt an opportunity to refine his understanding of the consultant role vis-à-vis the client system, or the role of group trainer vis-à-vis the participants in a group dynamic course. To Gunnar, one of several meanings of the boundary concept relates to the question of *how far one may go* – as is implied in the following statement: "The boundary keeper can tell the others where the boundary is. He thereby helps them to move and explore within the boundary". Using Lewin's terminology, the boundary defines the 'space of free movement'.

During one interview, Gunnar described the boundary keeper as the person who may help large leaderless groups to stay truly democratic and not end up as pseudo-democratic playgrounds for strong individual members.

The wish for participatory democracy is a good thing. However, I also realize that mass meetings can be dangerous unless a boundary keeper is present to make sure that moral standards are not lowered. Democratic phraseology may

---

40 The quote appears in Chapter 1, as well. See also Bridger, H., Burgess, S., Emery, F., Hjelholt, G., Qvale, T. & Van Beinum, H. (1994), Eric Trist Remembered: The European Years. *Journal of Management Inquiry*, *3*, 10-22. Sage Publications.

be used to suppress and control people – and then the need arises for a boundary keeper to say: 'Hey, stop, listen: three persons of the entire crowd do all the talking'. Or for someone to structure the debate, for instance by allowing time for small group discussions. Or for a chairperson who may separate the case-related issues from the person-related ones. When I take, or am given the role of boundary keeper, or when I act as leader at a mass meeting or a conference, I feel that my actions are on behalf of everybody else. I perform a certain function ensuring that 'the others' may feel free to move around, sensing at the same time that it is reasonably safe to do so.

He brought up examples from training laboratories where this sense of safety had not been properly secured. In one case, by way of introduction, he had announced that even though he filled the position of being responsible for the programme, he would not abstain from experimenting a bit. On another occasion, the staff had chosen a somewhat comic way of presenting the programme, the result being that tensions, aggressions and erotic feelings were set free in an uncontrolled manner. Looking back on this example Gunnar remembered:

It turned into an extremely dramatic laboratory resulting in almost psychotic events and breakdowns within the staff. And at the same time a laboratory in which I experienced myself as being guided by purely unconscious forces, making extraordinary and inspired interventions and interpretations. For many participants, however, the insecurity grew too big. The introductory symbolic act had made it doubtful whether anything at all could be relied upon. In a laboratory there *has* to be a boundary – a visible boundary. Otherwise people will either run away from each other in some attempt to locate the missing boundary – or they'll cling together and not dare let go of each other for fear of bumping into the boundary and getting hurt.

You cannot live without structure, and a life without boundaries is no good. Going beyond boundaries is good. But to do that – and now I talk about laboratory training and consultancy work – someone must be placed at yet another boundary line *outside* the first and immediate boundary, so that participants may feel free, possibly even tempted to extend *their* present boundaries.

We asked Gunnar to compare his own professional trainer style with that of the classical Tavistock variety, belonging to the so-called group relations conferences.

I rebel a little against their training methods. There, the boundary keeper is actually turned into God. In the mini-societies the boundary keeper was a helper, someone marking the boundary, and at the same time assisting in dealing with whatever was felt as disturbing. Tavistock has made the fight with the boundary keeper the most essential part, they have almost turned him into a prison guard. They see everything as related to authority. I do not agree – yet being fully aware that authority issues may always crop up.

The Tavistock design not only functions due to its positive content, but very much due to what's missing. Certain things have been removed – and in a much more radical way than was the case in the original training laboratories. But then – in many ways this is the key to understating the efficiency of any training group: compared to what goes on in the 'normal' external world, you have removed The Task, in the conventional sense of that term. And you have removed the habitual working methods of everyday life. By removing these essentials, you make their necessity become acutely visible.

Gunnar told us that Gurth Higgin – who was attached to Tavistock – had at some point nicknamed him the Bell Ram. Metaphorically, this name shares associations with 'boundary keeper', but has other connotations as well. Originally Higgin came from New Zealand, a sheep-farming country, and it is worth remembering that Gunnar and his wife Berit, too, became sheep farmers after having moved to Vust in 1970.

The Bell Ram is the male sheep of the herd who is most sensitive to upcoming weather change – he senses them before they actually happen. So, by keeping an eye on him, the sheep may hope to escape bad weather conditions and take themselves to places where grazing can be done peacefully. For this reason, the Bell Ram must stand all by himself, on a hilltop, so as better to be able to concentrate on his function.

However, standing there on the hilltop, or the boundary, is a lonely position and it may be anxiety provoking. You can only stay in your position and manage your role if you recognize that there is some system in what seems to be chaos. You have to believe that even though things are complex, they are still coherent. Ideas like these made me interested in modern chaos theory and its conception of the self-organizing universe.[41] In chaos, certain circumstances keep recurring, but which ones it will be, you cannot predict. It may also help you in your role management if you can activate genuine curiosity as to what goes on around you.

As I see it, three concepts are intertwined: the purpose or the mission, the structure or the organization, and the fluctuation. The system is related to an outside world. In order to fulfil our task, we must have *something*, a structure, some moral values. For instance: 'God will punish us', or even simple habits to live by: 'We must always do the dishes'. We must have access to certain resources and capabilities useful for resolving the task at hand. We must know what has to be done, by whom and when. This is how I understand structure. If there is no such thing, we 'drift'; then nothing but fluctuations affect us.

For me, problems arise when I no longer see the connection between structure and task. In some cases people are prepared to do *anything* to maintain a certain structure. Contrariwise, they may believe that *simply* changing the structure will in itself get the task done. Often the structure, not the task is seen as the essence: our reason for being here. If task and structure cannot co-exist, task is what must be safeguarded even if it means that the structure has to be discarded – but I admit, in this I may be too extreme. Yet I know that some new structure will always appear.

Final remarks

World War II had brought the social engagement of the sciences and the necessity of democratization up for discussion. Research should no longer be neutral and distant, but contribute to the creation of a better world. And professional practice, such as adult education and consultancy work, must relate to society's needs. These currents were particularly strong in the USA, not least due to the big brain drain of intellectuals and left-wingers from Europe across the Atlantic. Among other things, Gunnar Hjelholt's life story is a story of how Europe re-imported the social engagement.

I just happened to be ever so lucky back then, in 1958. In group dynamics and laboratory training, I was one of the very first Europeans. What I did was wel-

---

41   After his death, Gunnar's archives revealed that he had long wished to write a monograph on these issues. One draft we found was entitled *System i kaos* [System in Chaos]. The paper presented as Chapter 16 seems to be a spin-off from this unfinished work.

comed with enthusiasm. All over Europe people like me were in great demand. The post-war period was indeed the golden age for social psychology. The war made it obligatory that the sciences including psychology be made useful in social contexts. That was a challenge. Yet, staying true to the scientific attitude helped ensure that we were not altogether carried away by our engagement.

Gunnar Hjelholt's encounter with the group dynamic tradition gave him a kind of answer to his old quest for a personal mission: showed where and how to channel his international sentiment and social engagement in ways that were also compatible with his researcher spirit. During his younger years, the quest had given rise to visions of becoming a journalist reporter, placed at the hotspots of the world or stirring up debates that would change society. "I wanted to become someone influential, but – mind you – by *doing* something", he once told us. A political career, however, was out of the question: party membership would have tied him down to a degree far beyond his level of tolerance. Likewise, he was afraid the action part in him would become too dominant, and thus unbalance reflection and the gaining of knowledge. Instead he became an action researcher, a group trainer and a consultant. A Bell Ram and Boundary Keeper.

References

Bradford, L.P. (1974). National Training Laboratories: Its History 1947-1970. Bethel, Maine (unpublished).

Bradford, L.P., Gibb, R.J. & Benne, K.D. (eds.) (1964). *T-Group and Laboratory Methods: Innovation in Re-education*. New York: Wiley.

Carmichael, L. (ed.) (1946). *Manual of Child Psychology*. New York: Wiley.

Cartwright, D. & Zander, A. (eds.) (1963). *Group Dynamics: Research and Theory*. New York: Harper & Row.

Emery, F.E. & Thorsrud, E., in cooperation with Eric Trist (1969). *Form and Content in Industrial Democracy – Some Experiences from Norway and other European Countries*. London: Tavistock.

Hare, P., Borgatta, E. & Bales, R.F. (1955). *Small Groups: Studies in Social Interaction*. New York: Alfred A. Knopf.

Higgin, G. (1973). *Symptoms of Tomorrow: Letters from a Sociologist on the Present State of Society*. London: Plume Press.

Higgin, G. & Hjelholt, G. (1990). Action research in minisocieties. In E. Trist & H. Murray (eds.), *The Social Engagement of Social Science: A Tavistock Anthology, vol.I.* London: Free Association Books, 246-258.

Hjelholt, G. & Miles, M. (1963). *Extending the Conventional Training Laboratory Design*. Mimeographed version. (Regarding publication, see Chapter 11 in the present book).

Hjelholt, G. & Berg, H. (eds.) (1974). *Institutionen og folket* [The Institution and the People]. Copenhagen: Fremads Fokusbøger.

Homans, G.C. (1951). *The Human Group*. London: Routledge & Kegan Paul.

Joenstad, T. (1979). *Det sosiale samspillet: Trekk fra nyere europeisk gruppedynamikk* [Social Interaction: Characteristics of Recent European Group Dynamics]. Oslo: Universitetsforlaget.

Lennung, S.Å. (1974). *Meta-learning, Laboratory Training, and Individually Different Changes. A Study on the Effects of Laboratory Training*. Lund: The Swedish Council for Personnel Administration.

Lewin, K. (1935). *A Dynamic Theory of Personality: Selected Papers*. New York: McGraw-Hill.

Lewin, K. (1936). *Principles of Topological Psychology*. New York: McGraw-Hill.

Lewin, K. (1947). Frontiers in group dynamics. *Human Relations*, vol.I, 2-38. (Reproduced as Chapter 9, pp. 188-237, in Lewin, 1951).

Lewin, K. (1948). *Resolving Social Conflicts: Selected Papers on Group Dynamics*. Posthumously edited by Gertrud Weiss Lewin. New York: Harper & Brothers.

Lewin, K. (1951). *Field Theory in Social Science: Selected Theoretical Papers*. Posthumously edited by Dorwin Cartwright. Chicago: The University of Chicago Press.

Lewin, K., Lippitt, R. & White, R. (1939). Patterns of aggressive behavior in experimentally created 'social climates'. *Journal of Social Psychology*, vol.10, 271-299.

Luft, J. (1984). *Group Processes. An Introduction to Group Dynamics. Third edn*. Palo Alto, Cal.: Mayfield.

Madsen, B. (2001). Organisation og værdier i voksenpædagogikken – med inspiration fra Kurt Lewin. [Organization and values of adult education – as inspired by Kurt Lewin]. *Nordisk Pedagogik, vol. 21*, 251-262.

Madsen, B. (2003). *Dialogisk genbrug af Lewin: Konsultativ praksis spejlet i Kurt Lewins teori og forskning* [Dialogic re-cycling of Lewin: Consultant practice mirrored in the theory and research of Kurt Lewin]. www.psy.au.dk/cfs.

Madsen, B. & Willert, S. (1996). *Survival in the Organization: Gunnar Hjelholt Looks Back at the Concentration Camp from an Organizational Perspective*. Aarhus: Aarhus University Press (Translation of a Danish version published in 1995 on the occasion of Hjelholt's 75th birthday).

Madsen, B., Willert, S. & Hjelholt, G. (1994). Mini-samfundet plus minus 25 år. [The 25th anniversary of the minisociety, looking back and ahead]. *Psykolog Nyt 3/94*, 90-92.

Marrow, A.J. (1969). *The Practical Theorist: The Life and Work of Kurt Lewin*. New York: Basic Books.

Miles, M.B. (1964). On temporary systems. In Miles, M.B. (ed.). *Innovation in Education*. New York: Teachers College Press, 437-490.

Miles, M.B. (1981, orig. 1959). *Learning to Work in Groups: A Practical Guide for Members & Trainers*. New York: Teachers College.

Thorsrud, E. & Emery, F. (1964). *Industrielt demokrati: Noen norske og utenlandske erfaringer*. [Industrial democracy: Some Norwegian and International experiences]. Oslo: Universitetsforlaget.

Trist, E. & Murray, H. (1990). Historical overview: The foundation and development of the Tavistock Institute. In E. Trist & H. Murray (eds.), *The Social Engagement of Social Science: A Tavistock Anthology, Vol. I*. London: Free Association Books, 1-34.

Trist, E. & Murray, H. (eds.). (1990/1993/1997). *The Social Engagement of Social Science: A Tavistock Anthology, Vol. I-III*. London: Free Association Books.

PART TWO

PEER CONTRIBUTIONS

Preamble for Chapter 3

In Chapter 3, Leopold Vansina tells about the honeymoon period of the European Institute for Trans-National Studies in Group and Organizational Development (EIT); Gunnar Hjelholt's mediation between East and West Coast conceptions of human relations and group training; his critical-constructive view on the Tavistock approach; and their joint perspective on the role of the unconscious in social psychology and group dynamics. Finally, Vansina acknowledges Gunnar's creativity as consultant and group trainer: "That capacity of yours to get quickly in touch with the emotional life of the larger group I have never seen displayed so well... You had a particular gift to grasp the dominant dynamics of the context and bring them alive in a working-conference through simple means".

Leopold Vansina (b.1932) has a Ph.D. in psychology (1964) from the University of Leuven and he received his psychoanalytic training in the Belgian Psychoanalytic Society (1961-1965). He is the founder and head of the Professional Development Institute, Ltd. (Pro-Dev.) in Belgium, an independent firm involved in action research, consulting and professional development. And he is Associate Professor Emeritus of the Belgian Catholic Universities of Leuven and Louvain-la-Neuve. In the late sixties and early seventies, he worked with Gunnar Hjelholt on different projects. Leopold Vansina has acquired a rich experience doing organizational consulting in national and international organizations in most parts of the world. His writings have been published in various journals and books, most recently in Armado, G. & Vansina, L. (eds.), *The Transactional Approach in Action,* London: Karnac, 2005.

Leopold or Lee, as Gunnar used to call him by his American nickname, was one of the founders of EIT in 1965. Together with Gunnar and other persons mentioned in the present book they designed a professional development programme for group trainers. In 1973, the programme was redesigned to include organization consultants as well as group trainers and was subsequently, until Lee's retirement as director in 1997, organized by the International Institute for Organizational and Social Development (I.O.D.), an independent international research and consulting firm. Since then the annual International Professional Development Programme has been organized by Pro-Dev. Ltd. (www. pro-dev.be). Gunnar Hjelholt was a staff member of this renewed programme until one year before his death.

3   GUNNAR REMEMBERED

As a rope dancer, a clown, a rebel and a critical thinker

By Leopold S. Vansina, Belgium

Hi Gunnar!

It is not easy to have a talk with you now that you have moved beyond the boundaries of time and space. Yet, I would like you to listen and – if it is not asking too much – correct what I am going to say about you. In fact, it may very well be more about how I remember you as a professional than about you. My memories about our first encounters and the work we did together may indeed have become somewhat blurred. The hopeful years of the sixties and early seventies have long since gone by and I have only my recollections from working together during the honeymoon period of EIT, and in IBM's Executive Development Centre at Blaricum, the Netherlands and in B.P., UK. After those early years, you and I went our own ways. You distanced yourself from EIT and invested your money and creativity in more interesting works like pioneering mini-societies. I had to find myself and build an identity for my own Institute. Going my own way was not always easy. You had an engaging quality from which I had to break loose. This became evident when I caught myself somewhat imitating your gestures or voice, or wondering how you would have reacted in a particular puzzling situation. That had to stop. I had to find out for myself and in my work what was valuable: move on, explore and develop some of the thoughts that you may have left with me or invoked in me.

So, you and I went our own ways for quite some time. Except for meetings in the International Consultants Foundation, we did not work together until we re-established contact in the nineties. These became most interesting times. Your interventions in our *International Professional Development Programme: Leading Meaningful Change*, your comments on my articles/papers, and our discussions at your home will stay with me. It was in the tranquillity of your farm that I discovered and found a valuable, friendly colleague in the critical explorations of commonly practiced professional interventions and current social issues.

Gunnar, it looked as if you too appreciated our critical exchanges and that you too had regrets that we had not picked up our friendly relations somewhat earlier in our lives.

When we first met in those institution-building meetings, you were a quite calm, inconspicuous human being amongst those heavyweights: social scientists from America, e.g. NTL's director Dr. Leland Bradford, Prof. George Lehner, Prof. Howard Perlmutter; from the Tavistock Institute for Human Relations, e.g. Dr. Eric Trist, Harold Bridger; from ARIP, e.g. Max Pagès, Guy Palmade, and others like Didier Anzieu, Dr. Jan de Cock van Leeuwen and Prof. Dr. Charles Mertens de Wilmars. Although there were also other social scientists present without powerful institutions behind them, you seemed to manage quite well within the existing and changing power relations. Gunnar, I remember you, Eric Trist, Howard Perlmutter and some others wanting to create an institution to move beyond group relations training into action research in organizations and into improving intercultural relations. I shared that view but a sizeable group in those early days held on to group dynamics and group relations. At other times, most of the Europeans – with the exception of the Dutch delegation – closed ranks around our concerns about the Americans taking over the social sciences in Europe. EIT should therefore become a European Institute in which Americans could apply for a special, but not full, membership. Then, other debates led to other coalitions between those amongst us trying to bring group dynamics under the control of trained psychoanalysts, even psychiatrists, versus those who wanted to keep the field open for different frames of reference. Finally, there was that omnipresent concern how to benefit from the established institutes while creating sufficient space for other small centres, even individuals to develop and enrich the practice of social scientists.[1]

Gunnar, you must have learned quite a lot from your earlier experiences in that concentration camp. You did not behave like a rebel, you did not take an up front position, but you kept on that tight rope of your principles. You even managed to mediate between and reconcile opposing parties, and.... to survive that process. Surviving, yes, but not without suffering.

Gunnar, are you still with me?

Your experiences in the concentration camp were never that far out of your mind, were they? It was not only that awful smell in the abbey of Royaumont that reminded you of the concentration camp and made you sick?

---

1   Chapter 2 tells more about NTL as well as EIT.

In any case, it was you: the calm social scientist from Denmark, who became elected as the first Secretary General of the European Institute for Trans-National Studies in Group and Organization Development, a mouthful abbreviated as EIT. So for six years, you struggled with the Finance Committee that didn't generate finances, with keeping the boundaries between what was an EIT project and what was a project for your own business. On top of all this, you had an eternal problem with all those double bookings in your diary and with some difficult EIT-members.

Gunnar, … no, no, I am not excluding myself.

Despite all these difficulties, you did nice work. The conferences that you organized, the Professional Development Programme that you helped us design and re-design, and the ground work that you did in Egypt – without real pay – upon which, at a later date, Harold Bridger and myself could build.

Your professional juggling with conflicts, potential and real, caught the eye of Lee Bradford, director of the NTL Institute of Applied Behavioural Science in Washington, D.C. You too had direct experiences with the problems in the staff of the then famous two weeks Basic Human Interaction Laboratory, Gould Academy, Bethel, Maine. On the one hand, we had the traditional group dynamics (T-Groups) and human relations conferences for managers with an emphasis on understanding and working with the here-and-now and learning about oneself, in groups carried by social scientists with a background in social and/or clinical psychology. On the other hand, we had staff members with a wide range of different backgrounds and a 'missionary zeal' for personal growth. Things got kind of wild at Bethel: instant openness (disclosures) at any time, easy-honesty ("I will level with you and tell you my feelings about you!" and then came, most of the time, the negative feelings), marathon T-groups as if all boundaries had to be broken to get to one's real deeper 'selves' and the introduction of all kinds of verbal and non-verbal exercises. The objectives of the programmes and the target groups changed. Staff meetings became argumentative and the first legal suits for damage claims landed on Lee Bradford's desk. In this mess, Gunnar, you accepted the assignment to mediate between the West Coast (Esalen, Synanon etc.) favouring personal growth, and the School of Chicago (a.o. Morton Lieberman, Irvin Yalom, Dorothy Stock) with like-minded members from the East Coast (a.o. Matt Miles, Chris Argyris, Warren Bennis) favouring more rigorous and conceptually grounded group work followed up by research. Your appointment was a considered, political choice: a European removed from the highly complex mixture of cultures, ideologies and power plays and someone that Lee Bradford could trust not to make compromises at any cost. Gunnar, I only know that you travelled from East to West with some stops in between; that you made and kept some friends from all those places, but you never told me much about the outcomes of your mediation efforts. I won't make guesses. We'll consider it confidential material![2]

Gunnar, did I hear you laugh?

Who knows? It could have gone much worse if you had not been around!

Do you remember Gunnar that Jaap Rabbie from Utrecht and myself invited you, Traugott Lindner from Vienna and Harold Bridger from the Tavistock Institute to help us with the regular two weeks module on group dynamics which was incorporated in the much longer executive programmes of IBM in Blaricum? Here, I got to know you as a clown. Don't get me wrong, I say this in recognition of an important quality of yours, and of its value to that serious group of IBM managers who were neither allowed to have a beard, a moustache nor to wear brightly coloured socks!

First, you asked the participants to come out of the formal lecture setting and sit in a wide circle. In the middle was Gunnar, relating directly to some individual participants, responding to their behavioural reactions (not just their comments), breaking the anonymity of the group, while getting in touch with the audience as a whole. I have never seen that capacity of yours to get quickly in touch with the emotional life of the larger group displayed so well. Sometimes it got you in trouble too. "Gunnar is like an elephant in a china shop!", people whispered in the corridors or the toilets. You knew that and I felt you kind of liked that role, the drama and the fact that people were moved and remembered your interventions.

Second, while we used to give talks in front of the 'class', trying hard to keep their attention, you, Gunnar, moved around in that space surrounded by participants, in the real sense of that word, engaging them in a process. You were there with every move of your body, every gesture. Your fist with the thumb and the little finger sticking out, balancing the ends as if you expressed your ambivalence, or the task of reconciling different wishes or conflicting demands, or hesitation, vacillation. You questioned the participants,

---

2   Gunnar Hjelholt touches upon these events in Chapter 2.

gently probing: "Can you tell us something more?" while your outspoken facial expressions more than revealed what was going on inside of you. That wide-open mouth of surprise, wondering. And those thoughtful, reflective pauses of yours: I can still see you in front of me, as if you are still with us. Your twisted mouth and grumble after a surprising comment, a captivating metaphor or analogy or a revealing intervention of yours, often followed by throwing your arms wildly around your head in a desperate attempt to protect it from anticipated violent reactions as if the clown was going to be bombarded by tomatoes, apples or flowers. You lived with our emotional lives and we were living with yours: the boundaries between the audience and you seemed to fade away.

Gunnar, you could be a real clown – or is 'jester' a more accurate word to depict you in the large group? You did not stage an experience for the audience, you tried to find out where they were, making it somewhat more easy for the participants to express their thoughts, images and emotions. Then, you went a little beyond their responses and behaviour, to touch upon a possible meaning of which they might not be fully aware, while mirroring the emotional correlatives of shock, surprise, discovery, sadness or even naughtiness that goes with understanding or recognizing oneself.

That emphasis on facilitating the expression of what went on within the group and its members led to a hot debate with those members of staff who held on to a traditional Tavistock approach. In their role conception the consultant had to stay away from social interactions or better 'socializing' with his/her group members. One always had to stay in role and focus on interpreting the unconscious dynamics of the group without touching upon the *individual* behaviour of its members. All individual behaviour in the group was considered to be an expression of the unconscious or conscious processes of the group. In that conception of the consultants' role, one was not allowed to express differentiation in one's perceptions of and relations to individual group members. To my delight that particular debate was resolved in our programme, but then it re-emerged for many years. Even today, we have consultants who stick to dogmatic interpretations – often based on questionable data –rather than to facilitate the sharing and comparing of experiences as well as the sharing and comparing with the members of the consultants' sense-making efforts and meaning attributions.

Gunnar, your creativity stimulated the expression, on relevant dimensions, of what participants and staff felt at a particular moment in a particular setting. I'll mention only a few examples to make you smile: group paintings, distributing paper cups to express the degree of trust in the other members, or to visualize the power structure within the groups, socio-metric choices at several intervals in the programme, or requesting each member to keep the empty beer bottle in front of him after 'enjoying' the free drinks (of course not in IBM) in order to explore the evolving amount of anxiety or discomfort in the group.

Gunnar, my memory is failing, now. Did you as a staff member join in with the beer-drinking participants?

Gunnar, come on, did you or didn't you?

Gunnar, you had a particular gift for grasping the dominant dynamics of the context and bringing them alive in a working-conference through simple means. You may recall how you pointed to the north and the south sides of the plenary room at Ferme Libert and invited the international group of consultants to take a seat according to the geographical location each one came from. Then, you asked participants to formulate what each small group had in common. That setting was sufficient to explore how these groups defined themselves in relation to the other small groups North and South in the room. Great learning! But not everyone has that particular gift to get a good enough understanding of the basic dynamics of the context back home and work with the subsequent interactions in the here-and-now.

Gunnar, your exercises are easier to copy than it is for us to work with the emerging dynamics in front of us!

Once you told me, Gunnar, that you were a rebel. Walking around during the German occupation with a hand grenade in your pocket got you in bad trouble. Eventually, you landed in a concentration camp. That is nothing to laugh about. Yet, it could have been much worse! Imagine what would have happened if G.W. Bush had been around. You would have been labelled a terrorist and sent to Guantanamo! There, you would even have been deprived of learning from your fellow detainees about various practices of organizing to survive. You would have been kept alone, isolated and always exposed to inquisitive eyes, desperately searching for internal strength to face the next ordeal of an interrogation!

Gunnar, is it me? Or do I hear you rumble: people, whoever they are should be treated with respect for their dignity as human beings!

I recognized that little rebel in you, a rebel, yes, but not one without a cause. As long as I can remember you took an interest in exposing and changing power structures, an interest that you shared with Max Pagès.[3] At first sight, it looked as if you could not stand being dominated. In a certain way it may have been right, but I think that, underneath, a more serious concern kept you vigilant. When I saw your anger about social injustice, I realized that the rebellion in you was an endless fight for justice and the right of every human being to be free. 'Responsibility in freedom' and 'Freedom in responsibility' were for you basic conditions for and of human development. You saw it as a necessary but delicate fabric on which organizations and societies could grow. I still remember that sparkle in your eyes when you told us about the drug addicts who stopped taking drugs, once they felt free in your mini-society, and your disappointment, bordering on outright anger, with the academics who occupied the space for a free ride.[4]

Gunnar, the concern for social justice and human dignity that inspired your work may be the most important piece of heritage that you left with us all. It won't be easy to live with it, but it is too valuable not to try.

When my wife and I started visiting you regularly at your farm in Vust, that concern of yours expressed itself in your anger with consultants, social scientists and politicians who manipulated people away from constructive conflicts into that poisonous mixture of obedience and apathy and away from facing the social issues in front of them. I later used several of the cases we discussed as examples in my writings or talks. One turned into an assignment of yours and is kept in a beautifully recorded videotape of the work that you carried out in a sort of protest against the human negligence of another group of consultants: *Midt i en forandringstid* or *Living through changing times*.[5]

The same concerns emerged in our afternoon discussions and explorations, which were often picked up at breakfast the next morning – after a night of reflection – before we pushed off for Sweden. Gunnar, do you recall our explorations of the destructive impact of politics within professional associations and even in professional institutes. How professional standards become eroded by that combination of the pursuit of material interests, the wish to grow in size and power, and the unwillingness to face conflict. You had a brilliant memory and a stockpile of documents from the early years of EIT to inves-

---

3   Max Pagès is the author of Chapter 9 below.
4   The mini-society is discussed in Chapters 2, 6 and 13.
5   See footnote no. 2 in Chapter 4.

tigate further and verify our understanding of the various factors that could explain the deterioration of its original mission. Verifying our understanding always demanded an extra effort to move from that pleasant feeling to have found a plausible explanation to the tiring, time-consuming consultation of data and documents. Yet, here our minds met as critical, scientific thinkers... 'scientific' may be too big a qualification, but 'critical' is correct.

Whenever I brought up my concerns about the professional development of future organization consultants – and we regularly discussed that issue – you had an attenuating impact on me with your reassurances about the little we can do and your trust in human development if only ...we could get the conditions good enough and if only ... the potentials are present.

Your attention to potentials and conditions for development reflected the importance you attached to understanding the wider context in which all of us live... Pardon Gunnar, I should say: live at least on this planet!

Can I continue?

Our discussions at your farm often started after a welcoming cup of coffee in one of those leather chairs – your dog lying at your feet – with an almost classic opening: "Gunnar, I have been thinking..." And you sat back waiting for what was going to come. You listened and then joined the critical explorations with interest and encouragement. Do you remember that sunny summer day, Gunnar, when after the classic opening, I came up with the provocative statement: "Gunnar, I think that people learn the wrong thing in the group relation conferences in the Tavistock tradition. They only seem to remember those sweeping dogmatic interpretations by the staff and not ways of exploring the possible meaning of behaviour in its context". You lit a cigarette and calmly waited for me to bring up some incidents. "At our last ISPSO symposium, after having listened to an incomprehensible paper full of Freudian jargon, my wife commented on this contribution in the subsequent, large plenary session. Her intervention was followed by, you know, that usual silence and then by a change of subject. On our way out, a member approached her and said (I assume as a compliment): '*You spoke for all of us!*' Marie-Jeanne, my wife responded with vehemence '*And why didn't you speak up?*' Statements like 'you spoke for all of us' are all around, and no one seems to realize that in this way one legitimises not speaking one's mind, thereby *undermining the social impact* of an individual's courageous statement. And so we started our critical analysis of group interventions by group consultants, the assumptions on which that delicate balance between – what is often called – 'development and teaching' are based, the important distinction between reality creating versus reality-testing interventions and how right R.D. Laing was when he wrote about the politics of interpretations. You shared your ideas from a psychotherapeutic perspective underlining the importance of insight and awareness of unconscious elements and processes. I talked from a consultant's perspective in which understanding is a basis for a conscious action choice as opposed to letting things ride, and the importance of strengthening the reality-testing capabilities for human development. We argued, we looked at shared incidences and experiences, and we explored alternative ways of balancing 'development and teaching' in order to make practice more valuable. How consultants can share their observations and hunches, make them available for reality testing to the other participants and engage them in coming up with their own sense-making, their own interpretations, while exploring the conditions that favour this kind of interactions. In so doing people gain access to the consultant's way of processing information as well as a feel for his/her sensitivities.

Gunnar, I believe you kind of enjoyed surprising people with some of your understandings. You kept them short and simple. I remember, you once said after the breakdown of the Soviet Union: "Lee, we may come to regret it. On whom is the world now going to put the blame for all its problems?" There are many versions around of that comment of yours. Some are more complicated with explicit reference to splitting and projecting the bad and good parts on to nation states. Some even include a prediction that Europe and the USA would move apart.[6] Well, the international developments became another issue of shared concern.

This discussion started again as usual. "Gunnar, I have been thinking…do we really need this kind of psychoanalytic interpretations to understand international developments or do they, rather, keep us from exploring and doing something about the changing realities in the world?" First, we scouted the noticeable changes in the power structure of the world brought about by the collapse of the Soviet Union. The USA no longer had a strong military opponent. The economy of the Soviet Union had become too weak to support its ideology in the rest of the world. Its relations with China were often strained. China itself was only starting its economic development and one could but catch a glimspe of its future power and strength. The USA no longer had to support Europe as a first battleground against the 'communists'. The American concern that 'those European socialists' might turn into real 'communists' – the distinction between socialism and communism was never very clear in their

---

6   The same type of remark on Gunnar Hjelholt's part is elaborated on in Chapter 8.

minds – had vanished. The USA had acquired a power position to impose its will, interests and ideology on the rest of the world. The unification process of Europe, however slowly it was developing, raised new concerns in the USA and new hopes for us Europeans. From a military and economic viewpoint we were becoming less dependent on our old ally. Thereby, it became easier for a lot of people to see how the USA was and had been exerting its power in other parts of the world: think about Cuba, Vietnam, Chile and Iraq. A large number of Europeans became critical and new alliances between and across nation states were in the making. Are we not confronted with redefinitions of *social identities* within a radically changed and changing power structure of this world?

Gunnar, I can't recall all the changes in the power structure that we explored together, but we came to a point where we both seemed to agree that, before settling for an explanation in terms of collective, unconscious processes, we always had to check the changing realities and social interactions. And then you lowered your voice for a penetrating question: "Lee, do you think we need the unconscious (the notion) to understand social and organizational behaviour? I think we do!" I could not answer that question immediately. After a pause, I think I said something like this: "Yes, we do! But, it is a much larger notion than the one Freud constructed, not just that garbage bag of repressed, infantile drives, but one that is constantly in development through social interactions. There are a few questions that we can't let slip out of our minds. Why do we focus so much, even too much, on defence mechanisms, labelling them without any genuine attempt to understand the reasons, reality based or not, for these unconscious processes to interfere with our interactions? Should we not pay more attention to the healthy, equally unconscious mental processes that allow us to be in touch with the realities around us, and the conditions that enable us to adapt to change and to develop? Important, too, is to sort out whether *interpretations of unconscious processes* in social interactions are deepening our understanding in terms of *appropriate action* or, rather, covering up our ignorance of complex social and organizational behaviour!"

These thoughts led us to the most important part of that afternoon. We delved into the relevance for the development of organization consultants. To what extent are sweeping psychoanalytical interpretations, or classic group relations, interventions that impede processes of inquiry by providing some gratification of understanding, albeit hindering other kinds of exploration of what kind of action could be taken to move systems in a more desirable direction? Exploring realities and interactions in their context generates ideas about what conditions may be modified. Managers, consultants, and social scientists not only need to understand, they need to become proficient in doing things, in creating conditions so that development and more appropriate behaviour can lead to more social justice and well-being for the persons concerned and society at large.

Was it in this context Gunnar that you dropped that notion of 'reality-acceptance'? That capacity to accept those realities that we can't change and the courage to change those that are changeable through our efforts. Gunnar, now that you are closer to the Lord, can you prod Him to grant us the wisdom to make that distinction in time!

Gunnar, are you getting tired? Or do you want a smoke?

"Not anymore, Lee... but, do you?"

Preamble for Chapter 4

In Chapter 4, Veronika Dalheimer describes how deeply she was influenced by the way Gunnar Hjelholt bridged the gap between systemic and psychoanalytic approaches. Incidentally, several of the chapters in the present book voice the same point. Material in the earlier Chapter 2 hints at the possibility that Gunnar's Lewinian schooling may have nourished his noticeable talents as a mediater between the two intellectual traditions. As an example of a psychoanalytically inspired method she recalls how Gunnar made members of EIT make drawings of their feelings and experiences after a visit to companies behind the former iron curtain, thereby illuminating how much one's perception is influenced by one's inner pictures. Whereas the psychoanalytic background is important as a means toward gaining an understanding of oneself in the professional role, Veronika – with reference to Gunnar Hjelholt – argues that it is inappropriate for consultants to offer direct psychoanalytical interpretations of their client systems, even when asked to do so.

Veronika Dalheimer (b. 1949) has a doctorate from the University of Vienna, Austria. She is psychoanalytically trained (1980) and she is a member of the Viennese Psychoanalytical Society. Being a consultant with her own network organization of colleagues (DalCo) she is a lecturer at the University of Klagenfurt as well, teaching courses in group dynamics as well as work and industrial psychology. In addition, she lectures on mediation at the Institut für Interdiziplinäre Forschung und Fortbildung (IFF) and on leadership programmes at Hernstein International Management Institute. A recent publication is Dalheimer, V.R., Krainz, E. & Oswald, M. (eds.), *Change Management auf Biegen und Brechen?* Wiesbaden: Gabler-Verlag, 1998. Her latest contribution is for Falk, G., Heintel, P. & Krainz, E. (eds.), *Handbuch Mediation und Konfliktmanagement,* Wiesbaden: Verlag für Sozialwissenschaft, 2005.

Veronika Dalheimer recently withdrew as Secretary General of EIT: The European Institute for Trans-National Studies in Group and Organizational Development. As we have learned in Chapters 2 and 3, Gunnar Hjelholt was co-founder and the first Secretary General of this organization. Veronika first met him during her training at EIT and ever since they kept in close contact. She was instrumental in securing the economic support from EIT when *Survival in the Organization: Gunnar Hjelholt looks Back at the Concentration Camp from and Organizational Perspective* (Madsen & Willert 1996) was to be translated from Danish.

www.dalco.at

4 SEEING WITH THE HEART

Gunnar Hjelholt's influence on consultants in Europe

By Veronika Dalheimer, Austria

In EIT – a European network of consultants[1] – Gunnar Hjelholt quite often reminded us of the need to perceive and to respect the boundaries between persons and nations *and* to build bridges simultaneously. Being a founding member of this association, he left to us the enthusiasm for a European network. Today we still sense his legacy, not as a nostalgic feeling, but as a heritage for which we feel actively responsible – or, as Goethe (1821) wrote: "Was Du ererbt von Deinen Vätern hast, erwirb es, um es zu besitzen" ("Of that which you inherited from your fathers you must make use, to make it truly your own"). This lesson may have become somewhat neglected over the years. In today's globalized world, tending to make geographical boundaries obsolete, while at the same time reinforcing mental frontier-lines everywhere, it becomes more and more important.

In my contribution, I will try to describe the influence Gunnar had on my colleagues, not only in Austria, but in EIT as a whole.

The essential

It was in Vienna in the early nineties. At the beginning of a workshop, Gunnar quoted the secret given as a present to *The Little Prince* (Saint-Exupéry, 1945): "It is only with the heart that one can see properly – what is essential is invisible to the eye". The first time I read that phrase at school (On ne voit bien qu'avec le cœur – l'essentiel est invisible pour les yeux), I was only 11 or 12 years old, still rather innocent, but curious to understand everything – and, above all, to understand my own inner world. Saint-Exupéry's sentence left me with some kind of itching tension that confused me at the time – and still does nowadays, sometimes, when I meet clients.

---

1   EIT is the European Institute for Trans-National Studies in Group and Organization Development, www.eitnetwork.net

I do not remember exactly what the said workshop was about, but I do remember a long discussion about boundaries. We tried to find out how much consultants should be emotionally involved in the client's system or world. Some of us (the proponents of systemic approaches) were talking about the necessity of differentiating ourselves and of maintaining an outside perspective. Others (the proponents of psychoanalysis) talked about abstinence, transference and counter transference. At a certain point Gunnar – till then more a listener to our Babylonean squabble than a teacher – said: "I don't know the meaning of all this for you, but I often find it difficult to decide which approach is the best one – aren't they quite often just two sides of the same coin?"

As it happened, Gunnar's question has had a serious impact on my further professional development. With the support of another teacher of mine – Fritz Simon from Heidelberg, Germany, a psychoanalyst in former days and now a consultant – I began to appreciate the tension of ambiguity and to cultivate it rather than always search for a final solution.

Emotions

In my practice as a psychoanalyst, as well as in my capacity as a consultant in organizations, I have learned to *use* my own emotional reactions towards social systems – be it individuals, groups or organizations – as an instrument for gaining a clearer understanding of what is going on. Awareness of emotions also helps me build up my professional commitment. The more I allow myself to have all kinds of emotional reactions – friendly or not so friendly ones, and sometimes a mixture of both – the more I feel responsible for the people I work with.

Similarly, *not* reacting emotionally has become, for me, a sign that I am *not* in touch with my client. But emotional reactions demand to be handled. Once they emerge, boundaries become important and have to be actively maintained. Starting from there, we slowly – step by step – establish those ties which make the professional work rewarding.

Gunnar taught us the importance of exchanges between partners in a network, reminding us, in implicit and explicit ways that a network is not a sales department or a company, but consists of colleagues I can trust.

Some of my Austrian network partners are educated as psychoanalysts, some of them have undergone psychoanalysis, and some of them are simply making use of their natural talent to explore and to reflect. The work we do together aims at making us aware of why, when confronted with a client system, we sometimes feel so proud, sometimes so happy or angry, and sometimes so shocked. Subsequently, we make these feelings available for professional purposes. I am convinced there is no other way to get in touch with and to see 'the essential'.

During the last years I often had the opportunity to discuss all this with Gunnar: within EIT, when the book *Survival in the Organization* was translated (Madsen & Willert 1996), and when I saw the video *Living through changing times* (*Midt i en forandringstid*).[2]

I was reassured by Gunnar's style of intervention. Often without a lot of words, he built bridges between the emotional flow of his clients and his own experience. In this way he established ties.

One famous example of Gunnar's silent influence on consultants in Europe was a workshop in Portugal in the eighties. I was not there myself, but I have heard about it so many times. An association of Portuguese farmers had to make a decision on how to schedule the use of their jointly owned agricultural machinery. The consultants were Maria Heineke and Martin Siegler from Frankfurt, Flavio Neves from Brasil, and Gunnar (whose Portuguese was rather rudimentary) acting as their supervisor.

When, in a plenary session, Maria had to comment on the contributions of some small groups, it proved painfully difficult for her to complete her sentences, Portuguese not being her mother tongue. The audience was highly attentive (because nobody wanted to be misinterpreted) but, as it turned out, also very helpful. Approximately 40 farmers kept throwing the possibly missing words at her like flowers – it must have been lovely. After having engaged concentratedly in this activity for one hour or so, they had reached a common understanding on how to schedule the use of their machines.

Gunnar had hardly understood a word of what was going on. Nevertheless, he made a comment on this wonderful cooperation – something like "It obviously helps to invite a German woman". Sometimes the essential can be sensed as being there, even though it is not heard or understood in its meaning aspect. My German colleagues told me later that this was one of their most important

---

2   Video *Living Through Changing Times* (Danish with English sub-titles): www. arbejdsmiljobutikken.dk (Danish Kr. 425/Euro 57).

training experiences. German discipline, orderliness, eloquence and precision are desirable virtues, but sometimes dispensable!

The inner and the outer reality

In 1990 Gunnar showed us in an EIT forum how much our perception of 'the reality' is influenced by our inner pictures. In the year following the fall of the Berlin Wall and the Iron Curtain we met in Hernstein (Austria) and took day trips to companies in Bratislava and Sopron. Instead of just talking about our experiences we painted the feelings we had experienced.

Of course, Gunnar did not intend this to be a therapeutic intervention, e.g. as a framework for making us work through our emotional confusion. My guess is that he simply wanted us to identify in ourselves the tendency to project our inner world onto those outer reality circumstances we do not really understand.

My colleagues and I have included this idea in our own work with organizations as well as in our supervision with trainees wanting to become consultants. In organizations we use intervention strategies where the diverse perceptions, anxieties and hopes of participants are explicated and allowed to make an impact. By working this way, we avoid the tiredness coming from having to invent new designs all the time as a means towards the disclosure of organizational realities. Instead, the stage is handed over to the members of the organization themselves. They indicate not only the spectrum of values and attitudes by which they are guided. In presenting their ideas and themselves, they also demonstrate a richness of expressive and stylistic variety, as soon as they have left their regular jargon behind.

We keep insisting that the speed of communication be slowed down and that time-outs are taken at regular intervals – as also promoted by Peter Heintel in his books (e.g., Heintel, 1998) and in an association called 'Verein zur Verzögerung der Zeit' (Association for Slowing Down Time). We create in organizations the appropriate space and structures where experiences and emerging emotions can be expressed – among the participants and between them and us.

I have always considered emotions the motor of communication rather than just their frame. In this I am at variance with Luc Ciompi (1997) and Rosmarie Welter-Enderlin (1998), although we owe them much for their efforts at reviving an interest in the emotional life of organizations after long years of a purely systemic approach. Further, I find it extremely inspiring when the fantasies of and projections onto leaders can be explored, as has also been described by Kets de Vries (1998).

In some cases, such fantasies and projections can even be spoken out loud and made the object of discussions in the organization – all the time remembering, of course, that such discussions must be planned and executed in a 'respectful way' (see Sennet, 2002), i.e. with a maximum of discretion.

As we have learned from Gunnar, it is inappropriate for consultants (even when they are asked to do it) to give psychoanalytical interpretations. For me, on the one hand, my psychoanalytic background plays an important role as a means towards gaining an understanding of my own – conscious and unconscious – reactions. As an organizational consultant, on the other hand, I find it impossible to establish a relation that is strong enough to carry interpretations of the client system's unconscious.

Still, relationships of a wide variety are formed between consultants and their clients and very often these relations reveal what is going on in the organization.

I remember a client who called me because of the high attrition rate in the company. Quite soon, the contact with this client made me feel utterly exhausted, too. As something remarkable I noticed that I felt consistently guilty, even when I left at the agreed time. Something very important always came up just as I was about to leave. Once, when I felt just as drained of energy as the people who were actually employed by the company, I suddenly realized that I was on my way to becoming the over-protective mother of a large company – and a company, at that, dealing with baby equipment like dummies, feeding bottles and the like!

When working with younger colleagues in a supervisory setting (which is part of their education as consultants in OeGGO[3]), we make an effort to gain a deeper understanding of their (or our) emotional reactions. They appreciate being allowed into a space where they can freely explore their inner world, under no constraint from the various theoretical approaches to organizations. They develop a respectful curiosity concerning their own and others' emotional

---

3   OeGGO is the Austrian Society for Group Dynamics and Organizational Consulting (Oesterreichische Gesellschaft für Gruppendynamik und Organisationsberatung), www.oeggo.at

life. This I see as a good starting-point for a professional life that can, hopefully, lend support to the renaissance of emotions in organizations.

Communication across boundaries

I write the above with a great amount of optimism. I know.

In one of the banks for whom I am a consultant, a typical statement from its former general manager – and a statement which is still part of the culture – goes like this: "Für Befindlichkeiten ist hier kein Platz"! The statement is not easy to translate. "We are not interested in how people feel" would meet the contents, but the shortness and the strictness of the German sentence also conveys associations to phrases like "No pets allowed!" or "No Parking!"

Just before a seminar last year with the said bank, we were informed that they planned to dismiss some hundred people. At the outset, seminar participants were unbelievably reserved. When I shared my feelings with them, saying that I was not sure my contributions would be of any use to them, they breathed a sigh of relief: "Now you have understood. That's how we feel all the time!" And they started to explore their feelings of insecurity, their anxiety and their hopes.

Well, I have told stories about how I continue to sow the seeds called self-observation, reflection and awareness of emotions and of boundaries wherever I can – sometimes with 'Gunnar's sound', a near-inaudible "chchch" as an accompaniment in my mind's ear ....

As long as we continue to communicate across the mental boundaries and frontier lines, for which we ourselves are responsible, I retain the hope that we will somehow come closer to 'the essential'.

References

Ciompi, L. (1997). *Die emotionale Grundlage des Denkens.* Göttingen: Vandenhoeck & Ruprecht.

Goethe, J.W. von (1821). *Faust, Part One* (Translated by David Luke, Oxford World's Classics 1987, page 24).

Heintel, P. (1998). *Innehalten. Gegen die Beschleunigung – für eine andere Zeitkultur.* Stuttgart: Herder.

Madsen, B. & Willert, S. (1996). *Survival in the Organization.* Aarhus: Aarhus University Press.

Saint-Exupéry, A. de (1945). *Le petit Prince.* Paris: Gallimard.

Sennet, R. (2002). *Respekt im Zeitalter der Ungleichheit.* [Original title: Respect in World of Unequality] Berlin: Berlin-Verlag.

Vries, M.F.R.K. de (1998). *Führer, Narren und Hochstapler. Essays über die Psychologie der Führung.* Stuttgart: Verlag Internationale Psychoanalyse.

Welter-Enderlin, R. & Hildenbrand, B. (1998). *Gefühle und Systeme – Die emotionale Rahmung beraterischer und therapeutischer Prozesse.* Heidelberg: Carl-Auer-Verlag.

Preamble for Chapter 5

In the following chapter, Jørgen Steen Christensen takes his point of departure in the 1995 publication by Gunnar Hjelholt that is translated in Chapter 16 below. He further reflects on a case of professional intervention with Hjelholt in the role as a process designer, thus illustrating aspects of Hjelholt's working style. What is exemplified is the process of moving, first from complexity to simplification and then back again to complexity, with new insights gained through the process. At a general, descriptive level, Christensen uses Lewin's three-fased change model (unfreeze-move-refreeze) to acquire insight in the consultant's role as change agent.

Gunnar Hjelholt shared the conviction that social systems are characterized in depth by their primary task. The primary task is what gives the system its legitimacy and meaning and sets it apart from other social systems. He was convinced that loss of meaning, or prolonged exposure to social structures experienced as meaningless, may cause burn-out, stress and all the pathologies that follow from these states. Conversely, the sense of coherence and meaning is of vital importance. This was apparent already in Part One of the present book.

As Jørgen Steen Christensen observes, Hjelholt in the consultant role constantly looked for meaning, and he constantly created meaning. Perhaps the overall intervention design is the consultant's most important tool. In this domain more than in any other, he saw Hjelholt's creativity unfold. The case is an example of a brilliant design. It illustrates how Gunnar was able to establish shared meaning and a joint mental movement.

Jørgen Steen Christensen (b. 1943) has a degree in psychology from the University of Copenhagen, 1973. Since 1994, he has been a partner and active consultant in Proces ApS, a small consulting firm. For a decade, he was a board member of IFSI, International Forum for Social Innovation, located in France. He has been on the staff of the international professional development programme at Pro-Dev in Belgium, cf. the preamble for Chapter 3. Through the years, he has written and edited a number of reports, articles, chapters and books, most of them on environmental therapy and all in Danish. We would like, though, to mention his chapter on organization and consultation in a Danish anthology from 1995, edited by Per Krogager. Gunnar, too, contributed to this book, cf. Chapter 16. In 2004, Jørgen was awarded the Gunnar Hjelholt Prize. We, the editors, know that Gunnar considered Jørgen one of his true successors.

www.proces-aps.dk

5 COMPLEXITY, DYNAMICS AND THE SENSE OF MEANING

By Jørgen Steen Christensen, Denmark

In his article 'Too Strange' (Hjelholt 1995)[1] Gunnar Hjelholt raised the question, "Can we simplify our understanding of a complex and dynamic reality, and still avoid making it simplistic?" – a question that holds you captive and keeps popping up once it is put, and a question to which no clear-cut answer can be found. The question carries a dilemma with no solution. Yet continually, both in our daily lives and, not least, in our work as process and organizational consultants, we are forced to make decisions that somehow neutralize the dilemma. The answer to the question is neither 'yes' nor 'no' – nor, indeed, 'yes' and 'no' combined.

To simplify and to oversimplify

You may linger a bit with the two expressions. In Danish you can say 'at forenkle' which means to make something simple, less complex or complicated. And you can say 'at forsimple' having the sense of oversimplifying or making a simplism. When oversimplifying a problem, you reduce it to a false and thus misleading simplicity by ignoring truly complicating factors. In Gunnar's article he is playing games with the two Danish expressions 'at forenkle' and 'at forsimple'. This he can do because, meaning-wise, they are so close to each other.

In my own text below, the term 'to oversimplify' (at forsimple) denotes an operation whereby your understanding of something is not only made simple, but also bad or blurred – at the risk of becoming oversimplified, simplistic. Contrariwise, 'making something simple' (at forenkle) means making it *both* simple *and* clear. As it appears, the distinction has a definite normative intent.

---

1   A translation is brought in Chapter 16 below.

Complexity

The world surrounding us is characterized by complexity. Simplifying it means altering it. Often, when we try to simplify with the intent, e.g., of separating certain parts of the system from other parts, a paradox appears: complexity is in fact increased. New sub-systems appear. The image of 'The Chinese Box' captures this eventuality.

Still, as individuals, as members of social systems and as consultants we cannot evade the necessity of somehow reducing the complexity surrounding us – thereby choosing a focus. It is a skill you have to master in order to survive. Thus, complexity reduction is a central function in social systems. In order for us to navigate, we must reduce the total number of possible outcome events in the world we live in (Kneer & Nassehi 2003).

The term 'complex' is employed in many contexts. In daily life it is often used as a synonym for a state of confusion. Once a state of confusion prevails, it may move or be moved either in the direction of more clarity or, indeed, lesser clarity.

Within organizations it is a common notion that we must make the unclear clear in order for work processes to become more manageable. Often management theories take this quite reasonable starting point. They make their point by suggesting that attention should only be focused on certain segments of the organization – not on others. The important question is which segments are included and which ones are excluded by any given theory. If focus is only on the organization's mechanical and structural aspects, thus leaving organizational dynamics out, the result tends to be an oversimplification of the social systems' complexity (Krogager 1998). When this happens, simplifying equals oversimplifying. Complexity aspects, vital for understanding what goes on, are ignored or denied.

The term 'complex' is rooted in system-theoretical thinking. With some variations as to its precise signification, the term is used, e.g., in open systems theory, theories about social systems or about non-linear, complex adaptive systems, including conceptions drawing inspiration from chaos theory. Common to all such theories is an underlying premise stating that the full complexity of a system cannot be grasped in any one act of observation – carrying the further implication that as observers of social systems we can describe no more than some fraction of that which, in principle, is observable.

Applied Social Psychology, with its roots going back to Kurt Lewin's theories and experiments, is based on system-theoretical thinking. General systems theory is a theoretical framework lying behind what is named 'strategies for planned change' in organizations. This intervention strategy is understood as consisting of the following three interrelated phase events:

- A more or less defined input, reflecting a change agent's action strategy
- A process of input transformation, this process being a reflection of the organization's task, its way-of-functioning, its dynamics
- An output matching to a bigger or lesser degree the original intention and justifying the input-as-action

It is a common feature of theories lying behind applied social psychology that interpersonal, intragroup, and intergroup processes are seen as complex phenomena. Another feature of consultancy work inspired by these theories is that any state of complexity should be understood as a joint product of cognitively and emotionally justified action strategies.

Social systems are characterized in depth by their primary task. The primary task is what gives the system its legitimacy and sets it apart from other social systems. This makes it a valid attention focus for the consultant in search of an observational or descriptive focus: a simplification that does not entail over-simplification.

Once the consultant has chosen to define and understand the task *given to him* as a reflection of the more or less outspoken primary task of the organization, he or she then moves on to set up a plan for the subsequent intervention. Even though the chosen focus implies simplification, the consultant may still harbour the intention of 'stirring up' the client system – set it out of balance by confronting it with aspects of its own inner complexity. In this way possibilities are created for new avenues of development and for transformation of energy and organizational roles. Such an intervention strategy demands that the consultant provides an overall design – a framework for interventions – capable of containing the 'stir up' and the complexity aroused. Likewise, at various points along the intervention's duration time, the consultant must offer the client system a new or revised focus of understanding, thereby making the process comprehensible.

When Gunnar, in the above-mentioned article, talks about complexity, I imagine that he – as the discerning, well-read person he was – was basing his text on an extensive knowledge of system theoretical thinking. I further imagine that his own personal version of such theories lay behind the article's reflections on relationships between the social system and the individual.

Boundaries and unconscious dynamics

Social systems are dynamic systems, they hold energies such as those resulting from forces that either facilitate or go against the system executing its primary task – forces which in the long run will determine whether the system can stay alive or not. The dynamic aspect is seen and felt particularly when the social system is off balance – is moving or being moved.

Taking into account that 'forces' may refer not only to conscious and visible forces supplemented by hidden, albeit recognized, forces, but even to unconscious forces having their own inherent irrationality and logic, Gunnar's question – whether organizational dynamics can be simplified without becoming over-simplified – has to be answered with a 'No'. But at the same time we are bound to live and do our work in this field of tension and instability and carve out our identity across variations in time and space. As Gunnar was apt to say, we must draw some demarcation lines that exclude certain things and include others. We create structures hoping thereby to be able to monitor and control the system dynamics. In our daily life we often draw these lines without further reflection. The consultant may draw them consciously hoping thereby to simplify the dynamic complexity and open it up for reflection.

The consultant will – in the described sense – be 'drawing lines' and establishing boundaries when he designs an organizational intervention process. Parts of the dynamics of the client system are included and others are excluded. The system's resistance becomes visible to the extent that the consultant succeeds in including aspects of organizational dynamics which system members are unwilling to recognize and against which the system as a whole has established defence mechanisms and defensive organizational routines.

In this context, too, the problems surrounding 'Gunnar's question' give rise to certain professional dilemmas. As organization consultants, we have to be focused in our interventions – something that necessitates boundary lines and simplification – while at the same time aiming to stay in contact with the diversity and the unknown parts of the organizational life. If Gunnar were to comment on these issues, he might have said that what is hidden or perhaps unconscious to the social system and its members contains its peculiar magic and is as such an important part of its dynamics. The unconscious resists any kind of institutionalization. The unconscious cannot be fenced in, forced to move in certain directions, constrained, controlled, or predicted. It does not honour hierarchies, rules, procedures, or uniforms. It has what it takes to become the *enfant terrible* of the organization. Further than that, it does not respect corporeal boundaries. It seems to have elements belonging to other bodies' undertakings – even if they also belong to one's own body; at an unconscious level, the subject may thus ascribe to other bodies what belongs to the subject itself. The unconscious makes itself felt in both inner and outer spaces – and keeps popping up in places where you are not looking for it.

Through his verbal and often nonverbal interventions, Gunnar was able to establish a focus, a joint mental movement whereby perceived complexity was changed (either to a higher or a lower level) and underlying system dynamics were revealed. In the course of a meeting, for example, he might at a certain point get up from his chair, walk around a bit in the room, then stand still at a certain place not incidentally chosen… Having in this manner made himself the attentional and energetic focus of all participants, he would start using his peculiar mimetic, storyteller way of expressing himself to convey to everybody what he saw and felt. Often such monologues would lead up to what would be called a 'punch-line' in the world of theatre. This done, he returned to his chair, sat down in silence waiting for reactions. Gunnar had an extremely varied intervention repertoire. In a split-second he could transform himself into the uncompromising, external evaluative yardstick of the group or organization with which he was dealing.

To look and to ask for meaning

Gunnar once said that loss of meaning or prolonged exposure to social structures that are experienced as meaningless is what causes burn-out, stress and all the various pathologies – of mind and body – that follow from these states. Conversely, one may conclude that the individual's sense of coherence (Antonovsky, 2000) is the precondition for health. *Coherence* is experienced in the organization or the group when members *comprehend* what is going on and when their close environment is sensed as *manageable* – both phenomena are connected to the experience of *meaning*.

Gunnar looked for meaning; he asked for meaning. This he did in one-to-one dialogues, and he did it when working with bigger or smaller groups and organizations. He invented organizational events and learning designs that created possibilities to look for meaning, or at least to locate it, if so wished by the system. They were frameworks potentially making it easier for participants and staff to *comprehend* what was going on. Paradoxically, through his interventions he at the same time opened up for such complexity and dynamics as would pose challenges to the system's own self-image and self-understanding. This intervention aspect of his somehow resembles what Kurt Lewin called 'unfreezing', the first of three phases in a change process: a 'thawing out' of generally accepted attitudes, views, explanations, etc., that might prevent the system from reaching its own stated change or learning objectives.[2]

Developing a design that creates structures for containing the participants' emotions, hostility, resistance and possibly even their open attacks on the design and the role of the consultant is the main professional keystones in this phase of consultation work.

The second phase, not necessarily clearly delimited from the first, Kurt Lewin named 'move' or 'change'. It is concerned with issues related to the term *manageable*. 'Learning by doing', risk taking, having an experimental attitude, trial and error... – all these are central working modes in this phase.

It is well known that skills and experiences stemming from laboratory training such as T-groups, Learning Communities or Group Relations Conferences can be difficult to implement at home in one's own organization. As Gunnar Hjelholt expresses it in Chapter 2 and in the paper which is reproduced in Chapter 16, group training is satisfactory work, but its results at an organizational level are poor. This kind of training is more beneficial at the personal level and in family connections. The bigger social systems remain by and large unchanged. For these reasons, we must continually search for ways in which these weighty methods can actually be applied to 'the living organization' – at times in their original form, but more often built into tailor-made designs.

Gunnar was known and acknowledged for his wealth of ideas and his creativity in this phase of consultancy work. These talents, he would use in large-scale experimental designs such as his mini-societies,[3] in educational contexts such as post-graduate training of psychologists (e.g. "Today you will go out in the street, in offices etc. and ask people you meet there how psychologists can be best used"), or when he worked directly with employees in institutions and companies (an example will be given below). In all such contexts, he would make use of action research methodology in such ways as to make system and organizational processes manageable.

---

2 Kurt Lewin's theory is examined at greater length in Chapter 2.
3 Cf. Chapters 2, 6 and 13.

Finding one's life *meaningful* – in the areas of work and human relations at work – should not be understood as a value that can be gained once and for all and then stay with you forever. Rather, it must be regarded as an ongoing process, a continued looking and asking for meaning. The energy, the curiosity, and also the courage to look for the meaning inherent in one's membership of – and various specialized roles within – groups and organizations do not come by themselves, they must be nurtured and encouraged. This last design phase – 'refreezing' in Kurt Lewin's terminology – involves analysis and 'digestion' of new learning as well as its actual implementation in group and organizational life: implementation of new structures, new individual role enactments and new individual skills. On this issue, Gunnar wrote in the said article: 'I suppose that function and meaning are some of the consultant's most essential questions. In actual life, a number of actions will not be oriented towards the function that the system is claimed to have. Frequently it seems as if the people living in the system have forgotten or ignored the very function of the system'.

The troublesome difficulties here mentioned by Gunnar – related to staying in contact with the system's meaning or function – are probably what, generally speaking, make us more interested in methods and tools, in structures and procedures, than in finding ways to make concrete use of these components.

Focusing on the primary task

Given that the consultant must find ways of handling both the complexity and the dynamics belonging to the client system and to the contact zone between consultant and client system, he is obliged, through his actions, to weave together into one unified whole (1) the primary task of the social system (insofar as it can at all be revealed); (2) the task given to the consultant, and finally (3) the way he organizes and monitors the learning process.

The task given to the consultant is a vital source from which to obtain guidelines for the optimal structure and timing of the consultant's contribution – and here I include both its spoken and unspoken aspects, its obvious and its hidden aspects, those of its aspects that are directly communicated and those which are unconsciously transmitted. Implementation of the consultant's task in itself demands organization. Organizing his or her intervention, the overall organizational design, is the consultant's tool to bring about the wanted dynamics and to make the client system work with the task. As is well known, the consultant's creativity is crucial for this to happen.

In this domain more than in any other, I have seen Gunnar's creativity unfold.

It was often said about Gunnar that he was a master-craftsman in creating deeply meaningful designs, i.e. designs that gave participants unexpected insights and learning. Speaking generally, I can endorse this. In the present context, I would like to add that Gunnar's creativity as a designer seemed to stem from his intuitive understanding of the task.

Exemplifying Gunnar's creativity

The following case-illustration shows aspects of Gunnar Hjelholt's working style. For me, what is exemplified is the process of moving, first from complexity to simplification and then back to complexity, with new insights gained through the process.

It was my last experience of working together with Gunnar. An agreement was made with two mutually independent social institutions. They had recently decided to join forces in a two year long development project focusing on staff members' professional competences and practical skills in relevant method domains. Both institutions worked with the same client group, they had the same primary task involving a focus on institution-based treatment and environmental therapy. I was the manager of the development project and as such responsible for its overall design.

Halfway through the project, competition and rivalry – which for a long time had been mounting between the two institutions – reached their peak. Intergroup dynamics and tensions became a significant barrier preventing the two institutions from learning anything from each other even though mutual learning had been the central purpose behind the project being started in the first place. At this point, and in my capacity as project manager, I had asked Gunnar to be responsible for a two-day workshop. The general thematic issue of the workshop and the task to be accomplished were stated already in my written requisition to Gunnar.

The thematic issue was articulated by the phrase "If only we were free to decide, then …..", and the task was based on a double task model (Bridger 1990) allowing the two institutions to reflect on psychological and physical work conditions at their respective home bases while at the same time studying here-and-now patterns of interaction and collaboration in and between the two institutions as these processes were aroused and developed by the workshop.

Through the workshop setting to enable the staff groups of the two institutions – jointly and separately – to focus on organizational processes here-and-now and establish links between their workshop experiences and the work done in their home institutions. Main investigational target will be the institutional dynamics arising and developing between two systems: staff and client system – and their impact on the output resulting from the work.

Based on Gunnar's overall understanding of the project, its primary task and available data concerning the project as framework for learning, he had the task of designing and organizing the course of the two workshop days. In his introduction Gunnar reformulated the complex wording of thematic issue and workshop task into the following:

...look at the institution as a living society in time and space with a special focus on meaning and communication.

Starting the workshop, Gunnar first told a bit about himself, then disclosed a fantasy about himself in the shepherd's role,[4] and finally distributed a series of postcards among the participants; in groups of 3-4, they were asked to share their impression of what they saw. It was pictures showing the well-known architect, Hundertwasser's, architecture in Vienna – buildings having many forms and colours. The participants were mystified – "What was the meaning of this?" Gunnar collected details from the small group talks and spoke a little about how "buildings should be made for people – not vice versa".

Gunnar had constructed a workshop-design called *The two architect companies – an inter-group event* which he then carried out.

The formal construction of the design

Two architect companies were to be established. The two real-world institutional leaders should, each of them, function as leader of one of the prospective architect offices. The two leaders then chose 3-4 employees from their own institutional staff who were to take on the roles as architects within the office managed by their own institutional leader. Each office had a work territory at their disposal.

The remaining members of the two staff groups should 'play themselves', i.e. be staff members at the two institutions, A and B, which made up the devel-

---

4   Cf. Gunnar Hjelholt's reflections in Chapter 2 on his role as a bell ram.

opment project. Like the architect companies, each institution was furnished with a territory of their own. They were then asked to imagine themselves in a situation where, due to unforeseen circumstances, they had to leave their present institutional site – buildings and surrounding area – for good. A new institutional site must be found and constructed. Each site should be designed in accordance with its institution's primary professional task.

The two architect companies should *not* have 'their own' institution, but rather 'the other' as their client, meaning that architect office A worked for institution B and architect office B worked for institution A. Graphically it could look like this:

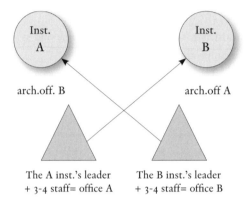

As part of his introduction to the event, Gunnar emphasized that, in each case, the primary task and function of the institution in question should be made clear as a prerequisite for the architectural design and be made recognizable in the layout and drawings for the new institutions.

The two architect offices were provided with lots of paper, crayons, scissors, glue sticks etc. The final result in the form of drawings and descriptions of the new institutional sites should be displayed the following day, i.e. the second day of the workshop. The (imagined) framework for the two displays was an exhibition, said to take place at the National School of Architecture and covering the theme: *Institutional design year 2000 – institutions as living societies in time and space*. Both architect companies were to display their designs, complete with drawings, measurements in square meters, etc., and both institutions would comment on the results.

Strategies and outcome

In both sub-cases of the workshop, cooperational relations between architect company and institutional client collapsed during the event.

One architect company had assumed an explicit policy of being supportive, understanding and client-oriented. "Tell us what you want, and we'll do our best to find a solution!" Its client institution perceived their primary professional task in dynamic and complex terms, a perception they vigorously tried to communicate to 'the architects' really wanting them to understand and reflect on it. The architects, however, more or less gave up understanding what was at stake for the institution. Instead, they withdrew to their office where they started to make drawings in line with what they thought were the institution's guiding ideas and philosophy – still keeping intact their picture of themselves as being supportive, helpful, etc., in relation to their client. The institution, on the other hand, was left more or less to itself with nothing to do, while 'its' architect company was overloaded with work.

The other architect company looked upon itself as change agents. Through active consultation it wanted to assist 'its' client institution in determining its professional task, all the while stressing the complexity and dynamic qualities of such an endeavour. As a necessary prerequisite to their putting a single line on paper, they wanted the staff members of the institution to develop and to agree upon a specific verbal statement of the primary professional task of the institution. This stance caused trouble for the staff members who – in the absence of their leader in his role as professional authority – tended to disagree amongst themselves concerning the exact nature of the institution's primary task. These events made them feel extremely uncomfortable and they turned to the architect company for help. As things turned out, they did not find the company's way of working helpful, so they sent the architects away and carried on discussions between themselves, and the architects were left to themselves with nothing to do for a long period of time.

These events notwithstanding, both architect offices felt obliged to present a product – in the form of an institutional building-with-surroundings – at 'the exhibition'. In view of the interaction that had occurred within each of the workshop's cooperation units, none of the client institutions showed any appreciation for the final product and they were not prepared to move into the new buildings. Rather than seeing the product exhibited as a reflection of what the two institutional groups had tried to communicate, they both experienced it as expressing the architect company's own ideas.

Reflections

The workshop design might at the outset look like a superficial role play or management game, but it ended up very close to reality. It became apparent that the architect companies' way of contacting their client institutions resembled the way the two "original" institutions contacted their own clients back home. Both architect offices tended to let their own understanding of the client institutions' primary task and their ensuing vision of how the new building therefore ought to look, guide them in a manner that barred them from true dialogue with the client.

Through the workshop, the dynamics that had so far built up between the two institutions in the course of the development project was made visible. It became possible for all participants to reflect on the two systems' interrelation and dynamics as well as on the group-projections each one harboured towards the other, and on their respective contributions towards facilitating and/or preventing the formation of a mutual learning platform.

Subsequently, it was possible for both institutions to reflect on the dynamics going on between staff and client system in their home settings. Differences and similarities between institutional habits of dealing with their primary task and handling the boundary between staff and client system became a focus of attention. Rather than making projections, each of them was able to use 'the other' in his own right as an external evaluative yardstick within the setting of a learning environment characterized by curiosity and the absence of organizational defences.

As simple as that – in spite of complexity and complicated dynamics.

References

Antonovsky, A. (2000). *Helbredets mysterium*. København: Hans Reitzel.

Bridger, H. (1990). Courses and Working Conferences as Transitional Learning Institutions. In Trist E. & Murray, H. (eds.), *The Social Engagement of Social Science*, Vol. 1. London: Free Association Books, 221-245.

Hjelholt, G. (1995). For-underligt – kan det komplekse og dynamiske gøres enkelt, uden det forsimples. In Krogager, P. (ed.), *Ubevidste processer i organisation og ledelse*. København: Dansk Industri, 88-99.

Kneer, G. & Nassehi, A. (2003). *Niklas Luhmann – introduktion til teorier om sociale systemer*. København: Hans Reitzel.

Krogager, P. (1998). *Konsulentarbejdet i komplekse omstillingsprocesser*. Aarhus: Systime/ Dansk Teknologisk Institut.

In Chapter 6, Ian Lauritzen tells us how, during the 1960s, the mini-society was developed by Gunnar Hjelholt as an extension of the Lewinian laboratory approach. See Chapter 2 and Gunnar's own articles in Chapters 11 and 13. Incidentally, this special design is spelled differently by Hjelholt himself; Ian Lauritzen has requested that 'Minisociety' is used in his contribution, rather than the spelling mode chosen by the editors, i.e. 'mini-society'.

In a mini-society, every participant has to earn for himself his position in the 'society' and everyone will be challenged to contribute in new ways. The design enables participants to learn about positions, roles and inter-group processes in the ordinary society, in an ideal learning environment. As was the case in the original NTL laboratories, the mini-society involves research or, to be more specific: action research methods with the aim of addressing complex processes going on in this societal micro-cosmos.

According to Ian Lauritzen, about 20 mini-societies have been conducted in Sweden, Denmark and elsewhere. Apparently, most of them took place during the 1960s. It is not quite clear whether any related activity has been going on in recent times, but Lauritzen suggests that the method be utilized in the future: "Globalization and internationalization will ask for new pedagogical models and training methods. Future minisocieties will take advantage of modern communication like internet and interactive multimedia".

Ian Laurizen (b. 1943) has a Swedish degree in psychology (fil.kand). He knew Gunnar since 1968, and they cooperated in the planning and conducting of four mini-societies in Sweden, Austria and England. From the time they met, Hjelholt and his family played an important role in Lauritzen's professional and private life. He started his own consulting firm in 1971, very much inspired by Hjelholt. As social psychologists, the staff of this firm focused on management and change using action learning, system analysis and laboratory approaches in order to involve people in sharing, learning and planning for their future. Nowadays Ian Lauritzen is well established as a senior advisor on complicated industrial and governmental changes as well as on community-based psycho-social services in humanitarian aid.

www.lauritzen.se

6 MINISOCIETY

Towards a Psychology of Society

By Ian Lauritzen, Sweden

This chapter aims at giving a short introduction to the Minisociety – its background, objectives and characteristics. I hope to encourage the professional social psychologist to use the model as a contribution towards the Psychology of Society.

Background

Minisociety was developed by Gunnar Hjelholt in the early 1960s as a laboratory approach using active research methods to address complex processes in the society. Experiences from the International Laboratories at NTL Bethel USA, working together with Erik Trist and Gurth Higgins on 'working groups' at Tavistock and Don Nylen's work on intercultural dilemmas in Africa gave Gunnar Hjelholt and his colleagues clear insights into the design of action learning workshops using intergroup dynamics.

As recently well documented in the book *Survival in the Organization* by Madsen & Willert,[1] already when deported to Porta by the Nazis Gunnar managed to keep his mind clear and to analyse the destructive but highly efficient Nazi Camp in terms of processes within a closed social system.

When you want to learn about leadership you need to see the individual as part of a whole organization. If you want to learn about groups you need to understand its interaction with other groups. To learn about processes you need to widen your perspective and include the environment.

Minisociety is based upon the assumption that people who find themselves within a well-defined and shared environment will bring with them values and attitudes from their traditional roles and positions. The design enables participants to study and learn from the behaviour of themselves and that of

---

1   References to this book are given in former chapters.

others, as individuals and groups. The intergroup dynamics give the partici-pants experiences valid outside the Minisociety as well.

Minisocieties of very different sizes have been established with 30 to 280 participants depending on the objectives. About 20 Minisocieties have been supervised and recorded by Gunnar Hjelholt in USA, Austria, England and in Scandinavia.

Being one of the pioneers within group dynamics, management training and action learning, Gunnar experimented a great deal with different techniques of learning about leadership, teamwork, organizational development and human relations. Not only was he interested in his own individual understanding and testing of theories within the science of social psychology. His main concern was how to create conditions for shared analyses and learning in an adequate and simple way. He was an applied social psychologist. He understood the strength of open shared experience. Lectures and training programmes in social psychol-ogy delivered to homogeneous groups will never provide as deep an understand-ing as that which one can obtain from active learning in intergroup relations and in confrontations when solving problems in real life situations.

In applied social psychology, practice comes before theory. The main contribu-tion from theory originates from understanding personally experienced events. Theories will only be fully grasped when they relate to your own world. The closer in time and space theories are to your own activities, the more they can help you make sense out of your own behaviour and guiding values and grasp even complex relations. Theories offer a language and, in addition, often a chance to compare one's own experiences with that of others.

In the Minisociety participants will learn from their own activities. In shared feedback sessions and discussions they try to draw conclusions valid also in the outside world.

Goals and principles

The characteristics of the Minisociety may be summarized in four fundamental principles that everyone involved will have to agree upon.

1. *Resources*. The Minisociety will have a defined amount of resources and occupy a defined space. All decisions regarding the handling of joint resources have to be made according to procedures agreed upon by the society itself.

2. *Time*. The Minisociety will start and end at a given day and hour.
3. *Moves*. At the outset, everyone is placed in a household/group by the planning committee. From a certain point in time participants are free to move from one household to another or to establish new households. All changes in households need to be reported and recorded.
4. *Research*. All participants must accept the focus upon action learning and the use of observations, feedback and open discussions as tools to reach a shared understanding about what is happening in the Minisociety. All agree to do their best.

The Minisociety is focused upon learning about society as a system, 'society' being defined as a structure of interdependent groups and sub-groups. It is not an arena for therapy or interpretations at an individual psychological level.

The laboratory approach of the Minisociety offers great opportunities to study complex processes from everyday society, such as intergroup reactions, power distribution, cultural and ethical dilemmas. Every Minisociety has specific goals. Participants are recruited according to that objective. The initial household consists of people sharing the same specific background, attitude, standard, occupation or other relevant sub-group characteristics. The forming of households helps strengthening and clarifying characteristics that would otherwise risk being less obvious or even hidden in the ongoing life of the Minisociety. Each household is requested to name itself.

- Minisocieties studying the question of rich and poor will establish households of different wealth.
- The question of age is more easily understood when a group of elderly people has the opportunity to meet a group of youngsters.
- The roles and conditions within social welfare can be elaborated when households of professional social workers and politicians can be confronted with groups of alcoholics, drug abusers, criminals or other socially exposed groups.

As an example, the Minisociety approach has been used to help a number of institutions for alcoholics by applying a multidiscipline approach that combines medicine, social training, group therapy, individual coaching and the sharing of all practical tasks in the institution such as cooking, gardening and cleaning. All obligations and tasks were seen as parts of a working whole in which the contribution of every individual was needed. The process of building trust and developing behaviour patterns of value to the society were set in focus.

The Minisociety technique has also been used to enable whole villages to study and redefine attitudes, working options and how to cope with the fact of having to live in a village totally dependent upon a single industry.

One village was inhabited by fishermen, workers at the fishery plant, their families and local village services such as stores, welfare workers and priests. Everyone was, directly or indirectly, totally dependent upon one single company. The whole village was represented in the Minisociety by groups of fishermen, administrators, top-management, merchants, workers at the plant, local politicians, families etc. The same approach was used by a local glassware industry, being the dominant working place in the village. Here, the company development programme involved representatives from the whole village.

Experience tells us that the duration can vary depending on goals and purposes, but the minimum seems to be four days. After 14 days, participants tend to become overwhelmed by the sheer amount of information they take in and are preoccupied with practical timeplanning tasks. Shorter Minisocieties have a tendency to operate more like an ordinary group dynamic laboratory or workshop. Participants need a few days to settle down and formulate their personal agendas and evaluate possible new options; preferences and expectations from ordinary life need to be changed according to the new situation. The difficulties of being a Minisociety gradually increase, enabling the participants to gain a deeper understanding and to transfer their insights to new tasks and responsibility areas.

Observation and feedback

The most important method of research within an action learning programme is observation and feedback. Everyone is encouraged to be active in observing and sharing all possible data helpful in order to understand processes and basic findings of importance for the Minisociety in fulfilling its goals and objectives. Action research means studying an ongoing process of which you yourself are a part.

In the Minisociety different techniques have been used in addition to traditional discussion and sharing amongst participants: techniques such as video recording by handycams, production of newsletters, interviewing, systematic observations and oral reports of individual findings.

Most methods have proved to be too slow, however. The delay between observation and feedback is consistently too long. The Minisociety is so busy and time runs so quickly that most information is out of date when fed back to the society. Data might be entertaining and interesting, like stories or tales from the past, but rarely of any use or influential in the present situation.

The only methods of presenting data that really have an impact upon the process are simple recordings of observations presented as statistics, graphs, drawings or maps. Updated information on economy, current households, migration, where and how people live, problems needed to be solved and immediate news always meet an attentive audience. Sharing of more personal perspectives and impressions like short stories, letters and anecdotes are welcomed, too.

To help generate a shared awareness of the importance of feeding back information about actions, reactions, plans and results, needs and efforts, trust and relations, open meetings called feedback sessions are arranged. Participants are frequently reporting that, comparatively speaking, during the Minisociety they have been much more aware of what was going on and they have been talking much more about processes and interference than ever before.

The planning committee

The Minisociety is organized by a planning committee that has to decide upon the framework of the program. Decisions on goals, staff, participants, time, costs and location – all kinds of administrative matters before and after the actual Minisociety – are to be handled by the committee.

From experience we have learnt the importance of a well-organized planning committee. The administration of a Minisociety is a difficult task especially when the Minisociety is not adapted to a given situation or a specific institution, organization or village.

Goals and objectives must be understood and found attractive by the potential participants and they must be formulated in terms of processes rather than expected outcome. Minisociety must be understood as an action learning project. It is arranged for participants venturing to learn about themselves, groups and processes. Except for the four rules mentioned above, the planning committee is not advocating any regulations other than existing national laws.

All decisions during the event have to be taken by the Minisociety itself. Communication between the Minisociety and the 'outside world' is to be handled by the society. In the course of the Minisociety the planning committee has no role to play. Its members can undertake new roles within the Minisociety or not participate at all.

One group/household in the Minisociety is appointed by the planning committee to work with the process, recordings, analyses and feedback. This household can add new members, but the original members are requested not to move. To this group, members from the planning committee are recruited, too.

As a team, the planning committee needs at least three talents:
• Sound knowledge in social psychology
• Sound experience in working with whole systems
• Sufficient administrative talents and backup

Location and costs

When the Minisociety does not have a specific territory, the planning committee has to find an appropriate location related to the goals and objectives of that particular Minisociety. It might be a holiday resort out season, a training camp, a boarding school, an empty village or a mix of B&Bs, hotels and shelters in the middle of London. There must be a place inside or outside where everybody can meet and plan together.

It is helpful when the different households/groups can be accommodated according to their starting positions in terms of background and status. Highest standard to the rich and lowest to the poor – as the Bible advocates. If possible, closely related groups such as social workers and their clients should be placed as far away from each other as possible. The size of a household might be used as a tool to reinforce starting positions. Soldiers sleep in a group together, officers in more luxurious and neat cabinets, fishermen together in boats, and CEOs in hotels. Variations in living conditions help the households to form their initial identities and present themselves to the rest of the Minisociety.

Dependence on the outside world should be minimized during the Minisociety.

All costs of the Minisociety have to be covered either by the participants themselves or by sponsors. Only payments collected in advance can be used. No credit or reserves are available. Late payments are returned to sender. The participants are not allowed to spend any additional money, either cash or credit.

After external costs for location, services and other economical relations with the outside world have been dealt with, the rest of the money is put in a bag, The Budget, and presented to the Minisociety at the first possible meeting. All participants must be fully informed about all available and prepaid resources and thereafter they may use The Budget, and The Budget only, to pay for all additional costs generated by the society.

As soon as the Minisociety has decided on how to distribute and use the money, The Budget is handed over to a "cashier" appointed by the Minisociety. Until the Minisociety has made a decision about money-spending, a person from the planning committee keeps the money and distributes a daily sum based upon the simple principle of 'total amount of money divided by amount of days and individuals', regardless of age or position.

Interdependency and balance in roles

According to a system perspective the concepts of interdependency and balance are vital. Studies show how identity formation depends on relations of interdependency. Power distribution is another example. Being powerful means that somebody else has got less power. The same applies to some of the roles we play in society. They are complementary. Rich-poor. Boss-subordinate. Social worker-client. Old–young. Man–woman. Employed–unemployed. Christian–Hindu. German–Swede. Black–white. Hetero-gay, and so on. In the Minisociety participants often experience how the strengthening of one group seems to weaken its counterpart.

- A group of young drug addicts, 'The Outsiders', had not taken part in any meeting in the Minisociety. After four days they invited all other households to a party. Almost everyone attended. Weak coffee, a simple biscuit, a troubadour and most of all just being together, sharing their friendliness made all households love The Outsiders. – Next day the social workers, i.e. the complementary group, opened a public bar, spending a capital reserve not known to anyone and breaking one of the four fundamental rules of the Minisociety.

- In London a household of seven top managers and company owners calling themselves 'The Seven-Ups' took almost all energy out of the open meetings by arguing why they needed a larger amount from The Budget. So far the Minisociety had not reached any agreement on how to distribute the money. All of it remained in The Budget. A suggestion was made to give The Seven-Ups a substantial amount, far beyond what could be recognized as a fair part. After a long silence the suggestion was approved and The Seven Ups disappeared in triumph. When they, after two days, appeared at the plenary discussion one of The Seven Ups had hardly opened his mouth before the statement: "You have nothing more to say – you already got your money!" was uttered in a low but clear voice. – For the rest of the Minisociety, The Seven Ups were silenced.

- A group of middle-aged fathers had a hard time coping with the fact of equal distribution of money, that is, same amount to each individual regardless of need, age or sex. They claimed the right to receive the special services and attendance they were used to. This, however, was totally ignored by their wives. – They had to find new roles proving their value instead of leaning on their old authority platform based on being the traditional breadwinners.

- The children between 10 and 14 opened a school for the younger children. – A group of parents made it impossible for the young teachers to continue by frequently interrupting and criticizing the teaching methodology and attempting to take over the teaching.

- A household of elderly enjoyed talking about old times and named themselves Good Old Days. After a couple of days they were getting quite annoyed with What's Up, a group of young boys and girls, because of their late night loud singing and dancing and their 'self-sufficiency'. One of the oldest broke the ice. Dressed in a 'young' way he thought would match, he walked over to What's Up. First they ignored him but after a while one girl asked him why he was dressed the way he was. She was told that his main interest was to get in contact with the young group and, he added, he was envious of their joy and friendship. After a while she explained to him that she liked him much better when he was himself, not pretending to be someone else. Following this episode Good Old Days and What's Up were hanging out together. The last week of the Minisociety the two groups merged and just called themselves Life.

Activation of forgotten skills

The need for practice is widely known from Education and Psychology. Not only to develop new skills but also to preserve familiar skills and learning. The brain seems to have difficulties accessing areas of knowledge that have not been activated for a long period of time. Knowledge once needed and welcomed by others as a contribution may disappear. An earlier requested talent will diminish when not asked for. Motivation and self-esteem go with it. Even very special talents and skills will be forgotten step by step when not practised and appraised. The Minisociety exposes the need for forgotten skills. When traditional services and roles are discarded the participants must find their own ways of solving emerging tasks and dilemmas in the society.

In Minisocieties most participants will have to cope with a much lower budget than what they are used to. They will have to live under conditions and standards they might not ever have experienced. Shopping, cooking, cleaning and other everyday matters have to be solved. Taking care of children and other traditional family matters appear in Minisocieties to be a concern involving others in the household than the parents.

The Minisociety has to set up rules and procedures on how to make its own decisions. Participation and responsibilities in planning, monitoring and evaluating how the Minisociety develops have to be clarified. The progress of the Minisociety will challenge everybody to contribute in new ways. Minisociety means hard work for all. Creativity and all kinds of skills are asked for. What can be eaten directly from Mother Earth? Which leaves, flowers, roots can be added to your salad? What sort of fish can be caught? How to fish and how to cook? In the Minisociety we will find participants having to prove their worth and talents in situations and roles new to themselves:

- John who recognized himself as an outsider after years of drinking proved himself to be an excellent grandfather loved by the children.

- Axel and Sven called themselves Old Lonesome Fishermen, referring to their favourite hobby. In the Minisociety they were highly valued because they could offer their catch to people instead of giving it to cats.

- Sonja was a depressed single mother, but proved herself to be an excellent writer. Her everyday letter, 'from a mother's perspective', nailed at the bus-stop and commenting on how the Minisociety developed, was read by everyone and had a strong impact on people's understanding and decisions.

Furthermore, some households must face the difficulties of not being able to rely upon their traditional status and authority. All positions will have to be earned within the Minisociety. Losers in the ordinary society can prove their value and show quite new attitudes and talents. The Minisociety will often substantiate the wisdom of how success creates success, trust is met with trust and acceptance opens new doors.

How to give people new choices is a key issue in all societies.

Perspectives for the future

Minisociety is in line with the logical thinking of a devoted applied social psychologist facing the need to understand a complex system even at the scale of macro-society.

All educational designs using a laboratory approach will have to clarify the structure and boundaries within which to work. Most failures in learning relate to an environment unable to provide the needed experience. Intergroup dynamics add new dimensions to the comprehension of whole systems. It makes it possible to understand society as a complex system. Separation and even segregation in roles and sub-groups are brought in focus in the experimental training within a specially arranged setting.

The Minisociety is a welcomed opportunity to learn about roles and processes in society, and it is of potential use for development and knowledge, important in ordinary life as well. Participants seem to remember and recall experiences from the Minisociety for the rest of their lives. They have memories giving hope, pleasure and energy to cope with smaller or bigger problems of relevance to their personal and professional lives.

Based upon experiences in minisocieties, companies and institutions have made major changes in their ways of organizing and solving their tasks. The experiences have inspired professional social psychologists when designing and conducting training programmes for international organizations such as NATO, the European Union, ILO and UNICEF on issues such as intercultural dilemmas, problem solving, decision making and conflict handling in an international context.

Globalization and internationalization will ask for new pedagogical models and training methods. Future minisocieties will take advantage of modern communication like the internet and interactive multimedia.

Training methods for strategy planning and society-building programmes using simulation and computerized data processing, such as management games, inter-business competition and the PC game Sim City, raise a demand for additional action learning relating to intergroup relations and society. Minisociety offers the requested format.

The main disadvantage of the Minisociety, however, is the needed planning and administration. The Minisociety renders hardly any monetary profit. It has to be planned and fulfilled in the light of devotion to applied social psychology and, in this regard, only highly dedicated professionals like Gunnar Hjelholt will be capable of managing to arrange a Minisociety.

Still it remains an exceptionally efficient and challenging design that generates learning about the dynamics of society, and probably one of the most inspiring formats for applied social psychologists wishing to develop the discipline Gunnar Hjelholt called the 'psychology of society'.

As Harald Berg spells out in Chapter 7, hidden forces, suppressed feelings and unconscious or subconscious levels persist in all social systems. They are revealed in the myths and stories, rituals and standardized behaviours. The social psychologist can, as Gunnar Hjelholt did, observe these patterns, interpret them, unveil them, make them less influential, help change them and assist groups and organizations in learning from them. According to Berg – and according to Hjelholt – knowledge and understanding of psychoanalytic theory as well as systems theory, in the broad sense of these conceptions, are necessary assets for the practitioner of social psychology.

Harald Berg reveals that Gunnar Hjelholt, in the last years of his life, was working on a book in which systems theory and social psychology were to be combined into a Psychology of Society, although "he did not win this game of wrestling. The book was planned but not written".

Regarding Berg's references to Kurt Lewin, NTL, EIT and Eric Trist, see also Chapter 2.

Harald Berg (b. 1937) has a master degree in psychology from University of Stockholm, 1966, and before that a master in language and archaeological studies. Apart from a long career as a consultant, he has held a teaching and research position in the field of Organizational Development at Stockholm School of Economics 1966-69. Through the years he has written a number of reports. Between 1970 and 1986 he ran numerous courses and training laboratories together with Hjelholt. In 1974, they co-edited a book in Danish on the relation between the institutions and the people, cf. Chapter 2. For many years, the two of them were close friends and discussion partners.

www.consider.se

7 GUNNAR HJELHOLT

Researcher and practitioner of applied social psychology

By Harald Berg, Sweden

Gunnar Hjelholt learned from Kurt Lewin, the psychologist, the innovative creator and integrator of coherent theories of personality psychology and social psychology, at the same time a great practitioner, the front figure of group dynamics and a great action reseacher. Lewin integrated the thinking of e.g. Freud, Köhler and Wertheimer, he used the concepts of systems theory, he built a creative and dynamic environment wherever he worked and he inspired a whole new generation of researchers and practitioners of what was to be called social psychology. Gunnar belonged to the young generation inspired by Lewin and he was among the first psychologists who brought these dynamic fields of research and practise in social psychology back to Europe. (Remember that Lewin was a European, fostered in the European intellectual tradition, and that he brought it with him to the USA where he met a climate which gave this tradition new wings).

Gunnar was, of course, at NTL in Bethel (another Lewin-inspired environment) where he worked with and learned from Ronald Lippitt, Kenneth Benne and Lee Bradford, just to mention a few of the pioneers in group dynamics and laboratory training.

Back in Europe, Gunnar cooperated with Tavistock people, both with those who developed socio-technical analysis, such as Eric Trist, and psychoanalysts, such as Ron Markillie. He was obviously influenced by Bion and Melanie Klein. He admired Max Pagès.[1] He did laboratory training with Harold Bridger, Tryggve Johnstad, Ken Bamforth, Leopold Vansina[2] and many others. In the Lewinian spirit he performed action research and development in the socio-technical environment at Lauritzen Shipping and in the Norwegian Trawler fleet.

---

1   See Chapter 9.
2   See Chapter 3.

This list of names shows the wide scope of ideas, influences and, indeed, research and development in the world of social psychology that flourished in the post-war years, all inspired by Lewin.

The involved and concerned outsider

Gunnar was a front figure in the European network of social psychologists. He was one of the founders of EIT, European Institure for Trans-National Studies in Group and Organizational Development.

With all his knowledge, all his experience and all the integrated influences from different schools, he was indeed a university himself. But he chose to be a researcher and practitioner outside the academic world. Or, rather, he chose a position where he looked into the academic world from the outside, rather than looking at the other world from an academic perspective. I talked with him about this towards the end of his life. Sometimes he regretted having taken this outsider position vis-à-vis the academic environment, sometimes he would say that university life would have bored him to death. Basically – to make a somewhat drastic simile – I believe that Jesus Christ would have preferred to stay outside the church. He too might have been bored. (All other comparisons excluded).

Instead Gunnar created his own arenas for transferring his knowledge and for discussing and developing ideas. He selected his disciples from young people he met in connection with his work, young people who joined EIT and people who actively sought him. He brought some of them into his assignments and he served as a mentor for them. He did not, though, take any action or responsibility to bring them together in a network and he would never dream of having them as a congregation.

The position of the involved and concerned outsider was one of his favourite ones. As a prisoner in the concentration camp, he had managed to survive by observation and reflection. He went his own way, independently. And so he did, all his life. A strong, involved, and concerned outsider.

This position also serves as a model for his professional role as a social psychologist. Today it is important and necessary to stress this role model. It gave Gunnar the freedom and the authority to choose his own perspective and to speak out about his observations and conclusions and contribute to his clients with an original and creative mind.

As a practitioner of social psychology, Gunnar served as a role model for his apprentices – 'the involved, concerned and reflecting outsider'.

The researcher, the trainer, the consultant, the personality

Gunnar was a researcher by personality and profession, even though he never took a doctoral degree. His method was observation and reflection. Most of his reflections were communicated as interventions and his interventions were part of the research process, hence he would be a researcher in the tradition of action research.

Unconscious structures and processes within groups, organizations and societies were essential and natural to him. Therefore, his weapons and tools were often metaphors and symbols, maps and drawings, dreams, songs and quotations. The primary object of his constantly ongoing research was the nature and features of social systems. The subject matters of his research were above all issues of power, fear and conflict. Gunnar was almost obsessed with the distribution and execution of power in all social systems. He had strong feelings about power, e.g. striving for power, fighting for power, defending and keeping power. He considered organization and bureaucracy as tools for distribution and execution of power. In his world power was always strongly related to fear.

His research methods were provocatively simple.

He was an impatient man who hated to be bored. If a group or a meeting bored him he would sometimes leave the room, but please, never mistake this for impulsivity, this kind of intervention was always calculated. He was by no means a cool and objective observer. Even when he showed a relaxed surface he could burn inside. He used everything he had, including his bushy eyebrows and the special sound of his voice that came from his lung problems. He frequently used his own dreams in his interventions and he would never hesitate to show his feelings, angry or satisfied. He could be quite scary – even for his young staff colleagues. All this often behind a good-natured face.

Gunnar Hjelholt has become well known as a man who walked the boundaries. These walks were in themselves adventures, since Gunnar was a true explorer and there is always a certain risk in exploring boundaries. He took many risks because he was a brave man who had the courage to challenge established theory and practise and established institutions. He was greatly rewarded in terms of respect, adoration, friendship and good words. He even made some good enemies and I think he would consider that as a reward, too.

He was not so well rewarded with official recognition and his work did not make him a rich man.

It takes some courage for a social psychologist to apply his knowledge. He or she is dealing with some dangerous stuff when working for organizations and for society.

Applied Social Psychology, for what? – for whom? In a plea for more and better use of it, Gunnar called both his art and his consultancy firm Applied Social Psychology. Why 'applied'?

1. Basically because our world desperately needs the knowledge and the art of the practising social psychologist in order to help individuals, groups, organizations and even society itself to understand and deal with all matters of social interaction.
    • We need to learn about ourselves and about the world that surrounds us
    • We need to know why people behave and act the way they do
    • We need to get things done in cooperation with others
    • We need to learn how to organize common efforts
    • We need to be able to deal with conflicts in non-destructive ways

2. Thus, the practising social psychologist helps his/her clients to understand and deal with
    • Basic raison d' être, values, norms and goals
    • Structure and processes for effectiveness
    • Management and leadership
    • Inter-group and intra-group dynamics, conflict, cooperation, culture and working climate
    • Learning and development
    • Identification of new knowledge, new possibilities, new situations and new needs
    • Adjustment or resistance to these phenomena
    • Ability to transform and change

Who wants to pay for the work of social psychologists, practising applied social psychology? Certainly Gunnar as a consultant often had to work very hard to find clients or customers who would help him earn his daily bread, especially as he chose not to seek any kind of position within the academic world which could have given him some economic security. The challenges for organizations today are as tough as ever. Applied social psychology and its practitioners have much to offer when it comes to making groups and organizations meaningful and successful and to help them create environments where people can enjoy work and life together. But there must be a body of interested and active social psychologists to do the job and thus demonstrate what applied social psychology can accomplish. And these people must be competent. They must build their competence on a broad and deep theoretical knowledge – just like Gunnar Hjelholt did. He had the advantage of personally knowing and meeting the forerunners. Together they combined studies and theory building with action research and consulting. That is how they learned, drinking directly from the deepest wells of knowledge. Using, reading, trying, testing ideas, speculating, teaching, writing, consulting, developing.

Today the hegemony of organization science and practise seems to belong to scientists whose knowledge and values are connected with logistics, management systems, controlling and control systems, i.e. ruling and running organizations by absolute power and bureaucratic control, disguised as self control and a climate for individual self-fulfilment.

Let's not complain or regret that. They have their values and they have developed their knowledge. But let us conclude: applied social psychology is needed today as much as ever. It cannot be replaced by anything like 'management science' and computerized management systems, business systems or standardized solutions to organizational problems. On the contrary, applied social psychology might provide necessary analyses, information, learning, experiences, knowledge and solutions to many of today's burning issues for individuals, groups, organizations and society. What can be more important than understanding ourselves and other people?

What can be said about the scope and knowledge needed by practitioners of applied social psychology?

Psychoanalysis

The unconscious or subconscious level of life in an organization can be explored. Hidden motives and forces can be revealed by the help of social psychologists. Groups, organizations and even society have an inner logic which often seems to be contrary to the outer logic. It is built up by forces and fields of tension within the organization. These forces and fields originate and develop from experiences like:

- Historic experiences. Events and episodes which have become symbolic and memories that one returns to, consciously or unconsciously
- Influences from strong personalities who have left or indeed still leave their marks or signs
- Old and new conflicts, fights for power and territories, old or fresh failures or wrongs or injustices
- Painful experiences of change, exclusion, fear and anxiety due to turbulence within the organization
- Traditional lack of confidence between different functions or levels within the organization
- Norms or conceptions, built up in one specific situation, which have been encapsulated and survive without ever being questioned or doubted

This kind of inner logic will create a specific pattern of psychological conditions and restrictions within the organization.

The past events and the suppressed feelings are represented in today's patterns. Unconscious or subconscious patterns are revealed in the myths and stories that are told within the organization. Often certain themes seem to be repeated in the thoughts and in the behaviour of the members. Certain conflicts seem to be very deeply rooted and to dominate or at least influence values, thoughts and behaviour. Certain values, officially abandoned a long time ago are still reflected in the culture of the group or organization. Or certain rituals and standardized behaviours may put the social psychologist on the track. Just like the psychoanalyst has methods of helping the individual patient make contact with hidden and suppressed levels of his mind, the social psychologist may use methods for the same purpose in a group or an organization. T-groups and organization laboratories are examples of such methods. Bion described an example of the unconscious or subconscious patterns in a group when he created his theory of 'basic assumptions', unconscious assumptions which may exist side by side with the regular work of the group and deeply influence the behaviour of the group members.

These conditions or gestalts form the field of operation for applied social psychology. The social psychologist can observe them, interpret them, unveil them and help change them or make them less influential. And he or she can help groups and organizations learn about them. Gunnar and his colleagues and followers did all that.

Of course then, knowledge and use of psychoanalytic theory in a broad sense is one necessary asset for the practitioner of social psychology.

Systems theory

Knowledge and understanding of systems theory is another necessary asset for the practitioner of social psychology.

Gunnar understood groups and organizations and even society as systems. Ludwig von Bertalanffy, the prominent figure of systems theory, says something like this: "general system laws appear to exist which apply to any system of a particular type, irrespective of the special properties of the systems and the elements involved. Compared to the analytical procedure of classical science with resolution into component elements and one-way or linear causality as a basic category, the investigation of organized wholes requires new categories of interaction, transaction, organization, teleology….".

This perspective seems absolutely necessary as a basis for thinking and research on human systems at all levels, from the individual to the whole society. Every practitioner of social psychology must know and understand systems theory. That is what Gunnar meant. In the discussion about an open or closed system he would be one of those who argued that, no matter what, social systems seem to have a strong need to close themselves. Boundaries and restrictions are inevitable. He meant that life itself is a constant struggle to cope with the boundaries of the system. In fact this struggle means hard work and this is the essence of life in every system. We could sometimes hear him talk about the organization as a prison. He did not have any bad feelings about this. He seemed triggered by his attempts to work and walk on boundaries.

Lewin's approach

Social psychology, psychoanalytic thinking and systems theory are fields that contain knowledge and ideas necessary for the practitioner of social psychology. To be frank and put it simply: Kurt Lewin almost has it all. He included most of this basic knowledge in his research, in his theories and in his teaching. His field theory serves even today as the most fruitful theoretical basis for social psychologists. His approach to research, mainly action research, is the best model and tool for the social psychologist's approach to understanding his client's situation and needs, as well as his ability to help the client system to improve/recover/develop.

Hopefully, students of social psychology today can be closely acquainted with Kurt Lewin's work and theories. And hopefully they will find wise teachers, mentors and brave researchers like Gunnar Hjelholt. Among practitioners of applied social psychology there should be no more room for amateur psychologists and people who compensate their shallow and narrow knowledge by being enthusiastic. There are too many of them already.

Psychology of Society, a further development of applied social psychology

In his last years Gunnar Hjelholt was wrestling with a concept that he called Psychology of Society. It would be – I think – a book where systems theory and applied social psychology constituted a basis which could contribute to exploring and understanding structures and processes in the system we call society. Gunnar would share his experiences from his consultancy practise, above all his work with mini-societies.[3] In his mind this was something that needed to be done. He saw it almost as his duty. He did not win this game of wrestling, however. The book was planned but not written.

The connecting line is clear between his scientific instincts, his values, his basic knowledge and ideas as a psychologist and his deep involvement in matters of society. This book still needs to be written. By whom?

Thanks to Gunnar and his contemporary friends and colleagues we know today that understanding social psychology in terms of social systems is a very important key to understanding organizations and their features, drives, forces and in the end the value of their performance. When we look at an organization through the perspective of systems theory we will find and identify basic conditions for its birth, its meaning and purpose, its growth, its structure and processes, its economy, its transformations, its relation to other systems and eventually its death. When we look at it through the perspective of social psychology we will find and hopefully identify some basic conditions and driving forces for its performance, its strength and weaknesses, its ability to fulfil its aim and its goals and its ability to change successfully. Gunnar and his colleagues practised a successful and unique combination of knowledge and ideas from systems theory and social psychology.

We know also that an organization needs a mirror to reflect all this. The nature of a mirror is that of reflecting. Thus the mirror must be external. If we could place a mirror inside our body to reflect the functioning of the liver it would tell us something about the functioning of the liver, but not about the system of which the liver is a part. In an organization all members are involved in important psychological processes connected with basic feelings, such as the joy of work, ambi-

---

3   See Chapters 2, 6 and 13.

tions and hope, power and dependence, anger and fear, conflict and other complex patterns of relations. The members themselves would be very biased mirrors and they would probably not be able to reflect on a system's level.

The mirror could be the practitioner of applied social psychology. And this magic mirror is an active mirror.

- It can move and it can shift focus
- It is a wise mirror, it has deep and broad knowledge and experiences
- It can reflect its own inside too
- It can think and analyse
- It can store pictures
- It can compare images – like the stepmother of Snow White
- It can be angry, it can laugh, it can cry

Be careful when you look into that mirror. It does not work like the mirror of Narcissus. Organizations: try that mirror! Students of social psychology: you can be that mirror!

As we have learnt in previous chapters, Gunnar Hjelholt had a notable capability to combine systems theory with the psychoanalytic approach, including a notion of the unconscious. In Chapter 8, the boundary between Eastern and Western Europe is one of Gouranga Chattopadhyay's illustrations of unconscious transactions between large systems. His second example relates to the Indian caste system. By means of specially designed group relations conferences (GRC) Chattopadhyay has worked with leaders from the untouchable community in India. GRC is a method inspired by the Lewinian laboratory method as well as the Tavistock tradition. The aims of the GRCs were to unveil and reflect on processes in the community such as denials, introjections and projections. These leaders eventually understood that they had unconsciously introduced organizational processes into their community which had lead to mismanagement of much needed human resources.

Please note that Chapter 8 contains political observations from the world scene as it appeared around 2003-2004 when the manuscript was prepared and submitted.

Gouranga Chattopadhyay (b.1931) from Calcutta (Kolkota) in India has a D.Phil.Sc. Degree from Calcutta University and has completed personal psychoanalysis in 1983. Being Professor Emeritus at the Academy of Human Ressources Development in Ahmedabad, he is in charge of Chattopadhyay Associates, Organizational Consultants and Personal Counsellors. He has held faculty and honorary positions in a number of countries and he has been a frequent guest at workshops and conferences all over the world.

Gouranga Chattopadhyay has published a great many articles and books on management theory and practice, in addition to poems and translations. One of his latest books is *Managing Organisational Process: The Individual, the Enterprise, the Nation & Beyond,* Kolkata: Eureka Publishers, 1999. See also his work from 1986: *When the Twain Meet: Western Theory & Indian Insights in Exploring Indian Organisations,* Allahabad: Wheeler & Co. An earlier version of the present Chapter 8 has been published in a British journal: Unconscious transactions across boundaries, *Organizational and Social Dynamics, vol. 4* (1), 2004, 133-150.

Twice Chattopadhyay had the opportunity to work with Gunnar Hjelholt in India. The first occasion was when an Indian Institute of Management, in the late 1960s, invited Hjelholt to work in Calcutta and Jaipur with groups of business executives. The second occasion was in the 1970s when on Hjelholt's recommendation one of the senior managers of the Danida project in India invited Chattopadhyay to work as a consultant along with Gunnar. Gouranga and his wife later spent a few days with Gunnar and Berit in their home in Vust.

8 UNCONSCIOUS TRANSACTIONS ACROSS BOUNDARIES

Two examples

By Gouranga P. Chattopadhyay, India

During various e-mail exchanges leading up to the conference: *Homage to Gunnar Hjelholt: Working on Boundaries*, its chief organizer Benedicte Madsen mentioned four interpretations of the theme *Working on Boundaries*. These were (a) the consultant or trainer placing himself on the boundary of the system while working with it; (b) the consultant guarding the boundary between a client system and its environment (Gunnar's favourite definition of a consultant was: a boundary keeper); (c) the consultant helping the system come to terms with its own boundaries; and (d) the consultant (or the scholar) reflecting and writing on boundary phenomena.[1]

The material for this paper comes from two sources. Its first part is actually based on a statement Gunnar Hjelholt made in a letter to me. That part accords with Madsen's fourth interpretation of working on boundaries, i.e. reflecting and writing on boundary phenomena. Gunnar Hjelholt was the one who started the reflection process by making a prediction about certain phenomena. I take over from there, furnishing data that may be used to assess the validity of his prediction.

The second part of the paper touches on all four interpretations. As one of the Joint Directors of a Group Relations Conference, I had to place myself at the system boundary of the Conference while working with it. Secondly, in our combined roles as Collective Management and consultants to certain conference events, my colleagues and I had to act as boundary managers – keepers or guardians of the conference boundary. Thirdly, when looking at the conference from the point of view of its membership subsystem, our consultative assistance offered to this subsystem was very much aimed at helping it come to terms with its own boundary. The fourth interpretation is evidenced by the fact that this paper has been written!

---

1   These and other interpretations appear in the prologue in the present book.

With these introductory remarks I shall take up my first example of working on boundaries.

EXAMPLE 1: UNCONSCIOUS PROCESSES UNDERLYING
POLITICAL RELATIONSHIPS ACROSS THE IRON CURTAIN

On July 24th, 2002 the veteran Indian journalist K.P. Nayar wrote an article in *The Telegraph*, one of India's national dailies, with a rather startling title: *It's worth thinking about whether the US is a communist country, but a successful one*. What he establishes in the article is that the United States of America today shows many of the features for which the erstwhile Soviet Union was known.

One part of Nayar's article concerns the individual level. If a Soviet citizen publicly raised his voice against what the government would like its citizens to believe, that citizen was hounded. Today in the US precisely the same phenomenon is at work as evidenced, e.g., by the way the tennis star "Navratilova is being pilloried from coast to coast in America for having spoken out her views on the values of American society (...) So far Navratilova has stood her ground, but safety for her has come only from numbers. By suggesting that she is being attacked because she is openly lesbian, the tennis star has sought the protection and the lobbying power of lesbians and gays, who are powerful forces in US". During a CNN interview, the channel's star anchor of the time, Connie Chung, told Navratilova to either love US or leave it, as though love for one's country may not include standing up against decadent values, even if they are espoused by the government.

Another illustration is based on a Nayar-quotation dealing with different matters. "*The Economist*, the standard bearer for everything that Western free-market democracies stand for", had in an editorial, early 2002, viewed the US business leaders' being knocked off their pedestals as a process that, today, is faster than Communist heroes being dragged down after the fall of the Berlin Wall. Nayar goes so far as to draw a parallel between the toppling of many Lenin statues in the erstwhile Soviet Union or Eastern Europe and the way "men of iron-clad reputation such as Jack Welch of GE have been discredited". Nayar continues to dwell on the parallel and comes up with the fact that the current evidence concerning corporate dishonesty in USA closely parallels events in the erstwhile German Democratic Republic while the Wall still existed.

In those days, on the basis of their records, the powers ruling East Germany had boasted that GDR globally ranked twelfth as an industrial power. After the unification of East and West Germany, the *Treuhand* agency was set up to privatize the former East German State enterprises. Their findings were that "Everything had been inflated. The books of state enterprises were cooked up, their inventories were maintained by sleight of hand, productivity had been exaggerated and many of the firms in GDR only deserved to be closed down. A close parallel to the above is the recent spate of bankruptcies of industrial giants in USA and the massive frauds perpetrated by falsifying records".

On the basis of such evidence as has been given above, and much more, a European diplomat posted in the US, but with long experience from earlier postings in Moscow, had said to Nayar that, "America reminded him every single day of the former Soviet Union. America is a communist country, but a successful one (. . .) The only difference with the Soviet Union and its east European satellites is that unlike in those societies, propaganda is very effective here. The people lap up all the propaganda in the US; in Russia they used to quietly put up with it and look for the truth elsewhere".

While thinking about my association with Gunnar Hjelholt, I first recalled, and then made a connection between these apparently tenuous parallels between the former USSR and the present-day USA drawn by Nayar and a statement made by Gunnar Hjelholt in a letter to me shortly after the Berlin Wall was dismantled. He wrote, "I am concerned about our own institutions and 'democracy'. With the Wall we could export our dark sides. Now that escape has been taken from us".

What Gunnar Hjelholt was drawing our attention to was that the Berlin Wall had all those years come to stand as a metaphor for the Iron Curtain. Its being dismantled signified the psychological collapse of the Iron Curtain. In his letter to me Gunnar had further written "So long as the Iron Curtain existed, the West unconsciously kept exporting the evils in their midst to those countries on the other side of the Iron Curtain. Now that the curtain has been dismantled, those projections will begin to come home to roost. I wonder how prepared we are to deal with those projections!"

This brief statement actually draws our attention to several unconscious processes around boundaries. While all boundaries need to be permeable in order that the system within the boundary survives through appropriate transactions with its environment outside the boundary, the USSR had tried to ensure that the boundary around the Communist Block of countries in Europe had an almost non-permeable quality. And while unconscious transactions, which broke no man-made or perceived boundaries, went on across the so-called Iron

Curtain due to lack of appropriate socio-economic transactions, the system within the Iron Curtain eventually collapsed. Among the unconscious transactions that took place, one major process was the so-called Free World of the West using the Communist Block as a projection screen for evils within it, which it was unwilling to acknowledge and explore.

After the collapse of the almost non-permeable boundary of the so-called Iron Curtain and the dismantling of its visible representative, the Berlin Wall, there were no longer two systems: the apparently free (democratic) and the apparently totalitarian system. Projections boomeranged back into the societies from which they had sprung. As a result, the media-hyped differences between the two also vanished making it easier to see that, perhaps, what Nayar and his diplomat friend had said was in a sense true.

Evidence of Gunnar Hjelholt's prediction seems to be more than fulfilled by America's so-called anti-terrorist war in Afghanistan. If the primary task of waging war in Afghanistan was to kill all Al Quaeda terrorists, it is clear from the result that the US has failed. It carried out carpet bombing of Afghanistan thereby killing and maiming thousands of peaceful Afghan citizens along with a handful of terrorists. Since many terrorists fled across the border to Pakistan, logically USA should have followed up its operation by sending its army there to wipe out all those terrorists who had slipped in to Pakistan. However, this never happened, and one wonders whether the covert purpose of American 'intervention' in Afghanistan was to ensure its presence in a country that has as its neighbours some of the world's most oil-rich nations.

The US war in Afghanistan has been followed by the Anglo-American war against Iraq. It was rather obvious to many people that the probability of Iraq being able to withstand the attack was near zero. First, Iraq was roundly punished in the Gulf War, with a tally of 35,000 civilian casualties alone. Then, 12 years ago, sanctions were imposed which broke its economic backbone and created near famine. One horrifying piece of evidence is a 700% increase in the child death rate per 1000 births between 1989 and 1999 combined with an estimated death toll due to sanctions of 1.5 million Iraqis, of whom 750,000 were children. Further, in 1998 the UN weapons inspectors claimed that they had already dismantled 90% of Iraq's post-1991 capacity to develop weapons of mass destruction.

On this background, USA must have been absolutely certain about the outcome of attacking a weakened Iraq. Consequently – as we learned from the media – no sooner had it started the war than it also started organizing the rebuilding of a war tattered Iraq along with imposing on it a new administrative infrastructure. Examination of that infrastructure reveals that, in effect, Iraq has been converted into a colony of the USA with the lion's share of the UN funds for rebuilding of Iraq allocated to powerful US business houses.

The same method was followed by the ex-USSR when promoting its agenda of 'liberating', one after another, the Eastern European countries like Poland, Czechoslovakia, Yugoslavia, Hungary, Romania etc. In effect, the operation converted these countries into colonies, even though, in polite political terms, they were described as satellites of the USSR. In the Middle East today, Syria already believes that it is going to be USA's next target after Iraq. Iran is busy trying to prove that it has no nuclear armament programme up it sleeve so as to avoid possible and probable US invasion.

It is also well known how the ex-USSR used to terrorize the population within the boundaries of the Iron Curtain by 'liquidating' any serious attempt to question the dictates of the powers that be.

Once more, it seems that the USA, for many decades, has been following the same policy, albeit in a somewhat different form. But this fact has been glossed over since the 'Democratic West' and its allies have held on to the belief that the policy of shutting people up or questioning them only existed within the countries bounded by the metaphorical Iron Curtain. Thus the supposed purging of communists in the USA in the 1950s led by Senator McCarthy, mass killings in Vietnam and Korea in the name of US intervention to stop the spread of communism, the death of an unknown number of Afghan civilians through carpet bombing, and the killing of many Iraqi civilians in the recent war almost escaped negative publicity, not to speak of open criticism in the 'Democratic West'. However, with the last vestiges of the metaphor called the Iron Curtain vanishing, namely through the dismantling of its visible representative, the Berlin Wall, the rifts in the so-called Democratic West are showing with countries like France and Germany openly condemning US action in Iraq. Such condemnation also highlights the fact that acts of terrorizing and purging dissidents for the sake of monopolizing economic resources, which was earlier thought of as the actions of the 'evil communists', are also taking place in the 'Democratic West'.

As I understand it, it was boundary-related phenomena like the ones described above that Gunnar Hjelholt in his wisdom was warning us to look out for. He was worried that the Western Democracies might not be properly prepared to deal with such phenomena. His worry seems to be quite justified.

I have given the above example to highlight how Gunnar Hjelholt could combine systems theory and the psychoanalytic approach as his means for formulating hypotheses about the unconscious interrelationship between two such very large systems as were created when the world became divided between the so-called democratic half and the so-called communist half. Now, years later, evidence in support of his hypothesis is surfacing.

EXAMPLE 2: UNCONSCIOUS PROCESSES ACROSS
BOUNDARIES IN A GROUP RELATIONS CONFERENCE

I will now switch to another side of Gunnar Hjelholt's personality which immediately drew me towards him as a human being, namely his compassion – that rarest of human qualities. It is well known to many how this quality led him to help groups that were poor in terms of access to resources.

Below, I will describe my work – accomplished with some of my Indian colleagues, and, indeed, still continuing – involving the so-called untouchable community of the Indian sub-continent. This community is economically at the bottom of the heap. Like many liberal and thinking Indians, all through my adult life and in my own small way I have fought against the caste system as an institution. Recently I was offered an opportunity to utilize my professional skills in the service of this lowest sub-system in the Indian caste structure.

We began our work with the untouchable community of South India by using the socio-analytic approach (Bain, 1998) in dealing with some of the major issues that emerged during a Group Relations Conference (GRC) held in Hyderabad, India, in February 2003. The GRC was jointly sponsored by *Learning Network*, a Bangalore based consulting and training organization, and *Dappu*, the umbrella organization of a large number of NGOs fighting for the provision of human rights to the so-called untouchable castes (the *Dalits*). Some of these NGOs have as many as 7,000 – 9,000 members.[2]

The Group Relations Conference design

A few words about GRCs are in order. GRCs (also known as Working Conferences) are temporary educational institutions for learning from the 'here and

---

2   Currently, Learning Network's director is actively supporting follow-up workshops.
    Dappu is the name of a drum with a leather surface used by some of the so-called
    untouchable castes. It has now become a metaphor for their struggle to achieve
    human existence.

now' experience. By 'here and now' one means working with experiences that are readily available to all the participants, both members and staff, within the conference. A GRC provides opportunities for its participants to explore their experiences – conscious as well as unconscious – in different events of the conference as it takes place.[3]

'Experience' in this context includes individual articulations of environmental impacts as well as participants' ways of dealing with the feelings and emotions associated with these. In the conference context, such issues are attended to in ways that are generally not possible in the hurly-burly of day-to-day life where one is constantly on the move from one role to another – from one location to the next. In the GRCs one gets the space to reflect on one's experience, including both outward behaviour and inner experience: thoughts and feelings. One conceptualizes and internalizes insights that appear useful for leading one's life. In other words, one accepts one's learning from experience on the basis of one's personal authority. In acknowledging one's new insights, one also has the opportunity to deal with problems encountered when using one's personal authority. Obviously, GRCs have neither a set of curricula nor any formal lectures or evaluation of performance. The participating members accept or reject learnings and insights based on their personal authority. In their role as a collective management, the staff provides and manages the boundaries of task, time and territory. In their consultant role during various events, they offer working hypotheses and other interventions on the basis of their 'here and now' experience, taking their authority from the task.

> The methodology (of the GRC) places experiential learning at the centre, without any fanfare of pampering the learning process; it instead gives complete authority to all – staff and members – in their roles – around the primary task(s). Stripped of pretences, the conscious and unconscious dynamics of individual and group behaviour surface as people engage in the tasks. This is a challenge as there is no garb of intellectualism or pretentious emotions. It is often frightening, as the group is confronted with its own shadows and what lurks from within the depths of the individual and collective unconscious. Experiential learning is thus far more powerful than what can be gathered in research papers and academic statistics. (I say this without negating the relevance of research in analysing socio-political phenomena). GRCs through the firm adherence to roles, tasks

---

3   Editorial comment: GRC as described by Gouranga Chattopadhyay is identical to the Tavistock conference that is briefly discussed in Chapters 2 and 3.

and their related boundaries create such a space that individuals in groups are confronted with their conscious and unconscious in a powerful way.[4]

GRCs create situations where it is possible for the trained and experienced consultants to offer hypotheses to the participants about unconscious assumptions possibly lying behind many of their intellectual and emotional positions, as these are reflected in the 'here and now' behaviours of the groups as they occur. Participants are encouraged to work with the hypotheses offered, not only by exploring the 'here and now' data available to all, but also their inner feelings and emotions, these being data of a different kind.

One common example of unconscious assumptions with a potential for getting a behavioural impact relates to the picture of authority that the average individual carries in his or her mind, partly at a conscious, largely at an unconscious level. These pictures are almost invariably projected onto whoever is or are perceived as authority figure(s) in any given situation – whether or not those people actually carry *the kind of authority* that they, according to the pictures, are assumed to carry. In GRCs such assumptions about authority are inevitably projected onto staff members, both in their role as collective management and, individually, in their role as consultants who – by offering hypotheses based on 'here and now' evidence – try to assist participants in understanding the nature of their projective identification and its impact.

In order for participants to actually work with hypotheses and other interventions offered by the staff, thereby learning worthwhile facts about their own behaviour and related societal phenomena, they must be able to deal with their inner resistance to confront various 'unpalatable' or 'indigestible' truths that may emerge in the events of the GRC. This ability is related to one's capacity to risk becoming exposed within oneself to one's untrue assumptions which in many situations lie behind one's hitherto unrecognized destructive behaviour – behaviour destructive to self or others or institutions to which one belongs, or all of these simultaneously. Consequently the process does become painful to those who muster the courage to learn worthwhile insights and realities.

The Dalits and their position in Indian society

Today there are about 160 million Dalits in India. Roughly 80% of these live in villages. A community numbering 160 million people is by normal stan-

---

4   This is a quote from a note prepared by one of the staff at the GRC, Rina Tagore, for her former colleagues in the Swiss Agency for Development and Cooperation (SDC) where she worked prior to her departure for New Zealand.

dards large. Still, in India, with its current population of 1 billion, Dalits form a minority community.

The word *dalit* has several meanings. These are, according to the standard Bengali–English dictionary (Dasgupta, 1989), "trampled underfoot, trodden, chastised, coerced, quelled". The same meanings can be found in most other Indian languages, including Sanskrit. In terms of the experience of the people belonging to these castes,[5] and also in the perception of a minority of liberal and *thinking* Indians – whichever caste or religion or socio-political group they may belong to – the socio-psychological conditions of these castes reflect most, or all, the meanings noted in the dictionary.

The great leader Dr B.R. Ambedkar (who was requested by Pundit Jawaharlal Nehru to make a draft for the Indian Constitution and whose draft version the Indian Parliament by and large adopted) coined the word *Dalit*. Ambedkar, himself, belonged to the so-called untouchable community by virtue of his birth in the *Mahar* caste, famous for its military prowess (though unrecognized as such in history books, presumably because of its low position in the Hindu caste hierarchy). He coined the term after rejecting the term introduced by Mahatma Gandhi. Gandhi had used the term *Harijan*, meaning the 'People of God'. Elevating the so-called untouchables intellectually by associating them with the term 'God' perhaps hid their problems from the general public more than it helped them. So Ambedkar chose a term which, rather, aimed at confronting all other communities of India with a very unpalatable Indian reality. He thereby lent a political voice to the issue of caste discrimination.

> Dalits are at the lowest rung in the caste hierarchy based on the twin concepts of purity and pollution. This societal position also limits them in terms of choice of occupations and puts them outside the *varna* system.[6] They have been oppressed throughout the recorded history of India, relegated to toiling and engaging in 'polluting' occupations like agricultural labour, disposing (of) dead bodies, working with leather, cleaning toilets and sewage etc. Many Indians continue to believe that others would be polluted by their touch, or even by their shadow. To avoid such 'pollution' Dalits were segregated and denied access to many community facilities like schools, temples, wells, water tanks, etc. To this day

---

5   Non-Indian readers who find it difficult to visualize the Dalits' experience of themselves in the Indian milieu may find some similarities in the life experience of Afro-Americans (also known as Black Americans), as described in books such as *The Ways of White Folks* (1933) and *Ask Your Mama* (1961) by Langston Hughes.
6   In traditional Hindu society, the four main caste groupings are called Varnas.

thousands of villages have a separate area for Dalit houses (including houses built for them by the government), separate wells for Dalits, class rooms where Dalit children sit separately, tea shops with separate cups and glasses for Dalits. Such discrimination occurs despite laws against those practices.[7]

One of India's tragedies is the acceptance of the hierarchy of groups based on the principle of birth-determined purity and pollution. This highly ascriptive system has existed for several millennia and is indeed very hard to make a dent on. In fact, many people belonging even to the so-called untouchable or other so-called impure castes of various degrees believe in this hierarchy. They do so not only because this social structure has been strongly associated with religious beliefs. For many millennia, the caste system has been based on a process in which every caste, from the topmost layer of the Brahmin *varna* and downward, has *projected the unexplored emotionally felt badness and even evil within their community onto the lower order castes.* In this way, the caste system, like the Berlin Wall, provides intercaste boundaries that are rather impermeable. Because most upper castes wield more socio-political and economic power, these projections more often than not end up as a process of projective identification. Obviously, under various kinds of economic and psychological pressures the lower order castes have introjected the projections. This process has led to a blinding logic with deep-seated anxieties based on unexplored feelings, such as guilt for example, that have been driven into the unconscious.

Many years ago in an article, I recorded my frustration arising from an experience where, in vain, I tried to persuade a family belonging to a caste that was rather low in the local caste hierarchy (the *Bagdi* caste of West Bengal) to offer me a cooked meal that included boiled rice. They considered it a sinful act *on their part* because eating a meal consisting of boiled rice cooked in their home would 'pollute' me! It was enough for the family that I have a Brahminical surname. Neither the fact that, according to Manu's laws, I am not a Brahmin but an outcaste since I have not gone through the thread ceremony and its associated rituals, nor the fact that I have renounced religion itself, made any difference in their perception of the ritual distance between us.[8]

---

7   Quote from the said Rina Tagore note.
8   According to 'Manu's Laws' (a foundational book on Hindu religion and society written around year 200 A.D.), a person born in a Brahmin family has to go through the 'holy' thread ceremony ideally between the age of 8 to 16 in order to become a Brahmin. That is why a Brahmin is also known as *dwija* or twice-born.

While a large number of Hindus belonging to the upper castes actively discriminate the lower castes, in India you also find many Moslems (Ahmad, 1973) and Christians (Swarup, 1987) practicing some form of discrimination based on caste (where the caste prior to conversion is known) or a caste-like hierarchy. As a result, only a minority within the Indian population is available to keep up the fight for equal human rights – on behalf of the majority of low caste people who passively accept the degrading caste hierarchy based on the twin concepts of purity and pollution. Their acceptance has unconscious repercussions. In the context of studying urban guerrilla and related phenomena, Lawrence (1979) has at some length dealt with the impact on society of such passivity among its majority. Lawrence's hypothesis is that as long as the majority of any community remains passive in the face of felt injustice meted out by the establishment, a minority will unconsciously express the anger on behalf of the majority, sometimes in very violent forms.

Nearly two decades ago in an article (Chattopadhyay, 1986), I offered four hypotheses as to how it comes about that, in India, a large number of people are treated as less than human beings by the majority of the population even after the achievement of independence and the creation of an Indian Republic that boasts of democratically elected governments both at the Centre and in the States. Theories and evidence to back up the hypotheses were recorded in that same article. All four hypotheses referred to unconscious phenomena.

The first hypothesis offered was that in every country certain very threatening negative psychological processes embedded in the society are projected onto less privileged minority communities so as to free the majority from its obligation to confront the evil within. Further, in many situations the less privileged communities introject and internalize these negatives. The punishments meted out to those who are perceived to hold the negative processes sometimes take terrible proportions. An example outside India is the Jew-Christian relationship in Europe prior to the formation of Israel.

The second hypothesis deals with my concept of 'the invader in the mind in Indian metaculture' (Chattopadhyay, 1991). I offered evidence to suggest that, as a defence against exploring the presence of an 'invader' in the mind of every Indian community, the majority 'chooses' to invade and violate all kinds of boundaries belonging to certain underprivileged communities.

The third hypothesis deals with the term 'underprivileged' in the Indian context. Historical evidence suggests that this term is used as a defence against confronting the fact that in this subcontinent the privileged elite has for ages been denying its less powerful citizens access to basic human rights.

The fourth hypothesis deals with the paradox created by a rich Indian sub-continental metaculture that has lasted for millennia. While enriching many aspects of the Indian personality, metacultural diversity has also resulted in people – whichever part of the subcontinent they may belong to – internalizing many apparently conflicting culture traits and cultural realities. The process has resulted in the creation of an Indian personality hampered by an inability to manage many internal differences. Instead of coming to terms with and dealing with uncomfortable internal realities, such parts of the personality may become experienced as bad objects and then split off and projected onto some external objects in the environment. In the age-old *varna* system, the lowest orders of the caste hierarchy presents itself as a readily available container for the most repulsive of these internal bad objects.

The Dalits of India are thus loaded with an unconscious burden. Not until comparatively recently have they, themselves, been trying to deal with this burden in an organized way – rather than passively relying on the elite to al-leviate some of the miseries of their existence. Unfortunately for India, there is no concrete structure – such as, e.g., the Berlin Wall – that as a metaphor can be seen to represent the dividing lines between the untouchable com-munity and the rest. Therefore the struggle to provide human dignity for the untouchable community of India is an extremely tough one.

The Dalits in a Group Relations Conference

One of the bolder attempts in that direction was taken by Dappu when, in 2002 – and aiming at an exploration of unarticulated and unconscious assump-tions present within their own community – it nominated two of its powerful leaders to attend a GRC directed by me in Kolkata. Events taking place after the conference show that the goals of the organization were largely fulfilled.

Soon after this first GRC, one of the Dalit members expressed the need for organizing a GRC for Dalits who carried leadership positions in several NGOs connected to Dappu. On behalf of Dappu, he agreed to sponsor the GRC jointly with the *Learning Network*, the said consulting organization based in Bangalore. Apart from having had considerable GRC staff experience in India and abroad, the director of Learning Network had also acted as a consultant to Dappu, assisting it in working through some of its major problems. During negotiations leading up to the GRC we argued that the Dalit participants' experience would in all likelihood be far richer if the GRC recruited members from non-Dalit NGOs as well as from the corporate sector, rather than restricting membership exclusively to Dalits. This logic was accepted by the Dalit executive of Dappu.

The theme chosen for this GRC was *Identity, Authority, Leadership: Resistance, Self-Empowerment & Transformation in Organizational and Social Systems,* and it took place in Hyderabad from February 17 to 22, 2003. I was authorized by Dappu to co-direct the GRC with Rosemary Viswanath, director of the Learning Network. The three other persons on the staff were Paul Divakar (Convenor, Dappu), Zahid Hussain Gangjee (CEO, Zahid Gangjee Associates) and Rina Tagore, who, after resigning from her job as Programme Officer for Human and Institutional Development of the Swiss Agency for Development and Cooperation, chose to postpone (by a month) her move to become a permanent resident of New Zealand, in order to work as a staff member.

Vignettes from the 2003 GRC

A powerful Dalit leader, who is the head of a several thousand strong Dalit NGO, entered the Opening Plenary session a quarter of an hour late, although he had registered on arrival at the venue at least a couple of hours earlier on that day. When he spoke at the opening plenary towards its close, it was to make sure that all the participants (members and staff) understood that he came late *on purpose* as a means of showing his ambivalence about agreeing to join a workshop based on the "Brahminical model and attended by corporate types". His contempt for and anger towards the staff, which included two persons with Christian names (one of whom is a Dalit leader), another person with a Moslem name, and two others with Brahminical surnames, as well as towards managers attending the conference, almost dripped from his short speech. He gave all participants to understand that he had come with the prime motive of collecting evidence showing why such GRCs should *not* be attended by Dalit 'activists' like himself and others present at the conference.

The emotional baggage of other Dalit members' consisted of mixed feelings aimed at two younger women exhibiting great excitement at the prospect of learning in new ways. However, as the GRC began to unfold, it seemed rather obvious to us that the angry Dalit leader was actually airing thoughts and feelings on behalf of most of the other Dalit leaders in the GRC. Little by little we gained a deeper understanding of the major problems besetting both Dappu and its connected Dalit NGOs in their fight for establishing human rights and ending exploitation of Dalits.

What struck me from the very beginning of this GRC was the intensity with which the Dalit leaders, who described themselves as 'activists', participated. As a group they seemed to apply themselves with far more vigour and concentration than is normally done by managers in GRCs. While a few Dalit leaders had joined the GRC in the hope of learning something that would help them carry out their duties as 'convenors' of various Dalit institutions and organizations, the majority had joined the GRC carrying in their mind a heavy dose of scepticism about the outcome of the conference. Their vigour and concentration remained alive right through the GRC despite the feeling of scepticism and associated anger that was expressed by a Dalit leader in the opening plenary – on behalf of many others who talked of mixed feelings in guarded language.

Through their GRC experiences, however, almost all the Dalit leaders began to understand the psychological processes lying behind, and being unconsciously referred to, by the two terms 'activist' and 'convenor' as these were used in Dappu. Notwithstanding the fact that the organization's activists acted in good faith and were highly motivated to assist their brother Dalits in fighting for their rights as human beings in society, these GRC members also realized how, in many ways, the said psychological processes resulted in waste of energy and other scarce resources.

As I understand the logic that became unveiled, the term 'activist' serves as a metaphor standing for minority action against a discriminating and dehumanising establishment, which is passively being supported by the majority. Partly due to the metaphorical meaning of the term, however, the management of organizational activities tends to lose touch with the tasks that must be undertaken in order for the Dalit NGOs to move towards their cherished objectives. Organizational emphasis is laid on activities that highlight the process of discrimination. This takes away the focus from designing and managing tasks that relate to the objectives of restoring human dignity to Dalits and getting them on the path of economic well-being. These back home realities began to surface in dream associations produced in the social sensing matrix event, in the small and large study group events and in the institutional event. The logic also emerged with greater clarity for the Dalit participants as, in our consultant roles within the role consultation event, we assisted them in articulating the primary task of their respective organizations and in working on specific problems.

Many of them realized and acknowledged that wastage of resources ensues when organizational processes lose their focus on the management of objective-related tasks. The process became further reinforced by their using the term 'convenor' as a means of rejecting anything having to do with 'manager' or 'management' – terms which to them represented the exploiting establishment and the passive majority. Almost inevitably, these terminological habits started a process leading to a lack of role clarity within the organizations. Dalit members of the GRC gradually gained insight into these organizational issues, as they began to realize how their anger and hatred towards the establishment – though very legitimate – had resulted in their unconsciously rejecting some of the basic tenets of managing successful organizations.

At the closing plenary, the Dalit leader who at the opening plenary six days earlier had almost spat out his rejection of a 'Brahminical model' and the presence of 'corporate types', now pointed his forefinger towards his own head and said that he had come to realize that the 'Brahminical model' had in fact been present in his own head and that he had been projecting it onto the conference staff. On the same occasion, he and several others also described how, in their anger at being denied basic human rights in a free country, they had rejected the word 'manager' as something that belonged to the 'corporate world', representing exploitation of the worst kind. Another Dalit GRC participant, who headed a seven thousand strong Dalit organization of toilet cleaners, acknowledged his earlier problem around even exploring his leadership role in the organization, due to his experience of being betrayed by many of the country's (elected political) leaders.

These are only a few examples of the multitude of insights shared by the Dalit leaders at the closing plenary. The GRC process had made them acknowledge that in rejecting the word 'manager', and using instead 'convenor' to describe their managerial organization roles, they had quite unconsciously introduced organizational processes that had resulted in mismanagement of much needed resources. They would now work towards undoing these processes.

It had been obvious to us how much pain accompanied the insights made by the Dalit leaders during the course of the GRC. The pain originated from their gradually realizing the managerial mistakes they had systematically been making while running Dalit NGOs and other Dalit organizations fighting for human rights almost year-round. It was the commitment to their chosen tasks and objectives and their deep seated motivation that helped them acknowledge their insights 'in public', i.e. during the closing plenary session.

Discussion

By way of concluding this section of the chapter I shall briefly discuss my own learning from yet another Indian reality.

In an attempt to alleviate the burden of poverty, numerous so-called lower and untouchable castes have, in more than one Schedule[9] of the Indian Constitution, been declared the beneficiaries of certain specifically reserved opportunities. It seems evident that after nearly sixty years of independence and opportunity reservations for the same amount of years, the strategy has not made any significant difference to the lot of those who are known as the Scheduled Castes and Tribes, including the so-called untouchable castes, now also known as Dalits. It is true that with the help of these benefits many of the economically better off members of Scheduled Castes and Tribes have occupied a number of important positions in political parties, in government and in the public sector enterprises. In this way, certain individuals have been allowed to form some kind of elite among the Scheduled Castes and Tribes, with access to the cream of the benefits. This fact notwithstanding, the vast majority remains little better off than it was prior to India's independence.

Yet, political parties dominating the governments at the Centre or State levels have introduced no new thinking with a potential to bring about such changes in the policy and practices as would provide *realistic* opportunities, helping the average member of the Scheduled Castes and Tribes to rise above poverty level and to challenge the hierarchy of the caste system with its dehumanising value on purity and pollution attributed by birth. The two thrusts will require very different approaches and strategies, particularly in view of the fact that many, if not a great majority, of the so-called low caste people actually accept their caste status in terms of pollution by birth. This happens largely because of the religious sanction behind the caste hierarchy and individuals' fear – based on the twin processes of projective identification and introjection – of some kind of terrible punishment both here and hereafter if the caste related taboos are broken.

This fear is so deep seated that, at a personal level, I have failed to establish my *bona fide* status as a person without religion and an outcaste by virtue of not going through the thread ceremony prescribed for those born in a *dwija* (Twice Born) family. Since the so-called second birth takes place after the thread ceremony, by not going through it I and my children and their progenies happily remain outcastes, but hardly anyone accepts this fact. Upper caste people feel threatened by this challenge of tradition and lower caste people do not seem to be able to accept that one can actually renounce one's religion and birth-based caste.

---

9   The Indian Constitution (which has been in force since 1950) consists of 395 articles
     and 12 Schedules, hence the concept Scheduled Castes and Tribes.

Building on the evidence of an elite having emerged among the Scheduled Castes and Tribes and the fear harboured by the so-called upper castes of losing their 'superior' position through organized challenge by the majority of the so-called lower castes, I hypothesize that both groups, by using their political and economic power, create a climate where new ideas for the alleviation of poverty and exploitation are scotched from the very start. Unfortunately, numerous groups of *Sannyasins*[10] have joined hands with the Hindu upper castes and the *Hindutva* movement to fuel the fires of keeping alive the elitism of the upper castes (and also that of the rather small groups of lower caste elite). I mention this as unfortunate because on the Indian sub-continent ancient socio-spiritual conventions dictate that a *Sannyasin* has no business to uphold religious beliefs of any kind. This is because – unlike the Christian monks and nuns – people of either sex, who resolve to become *Sannyasin* and are accepted as having the potential to do so, go through a series of rituals and training that include performing one's funeral. This signifies – once one becomes a full (*poorna*) *Sannyasin* – the death of all the person's social and societal roles. If one is 'dead' to the society and has no traditional societal role, it is an anachronism to support any particular religious view or religious philosophy.

The brand of Dalit leaders who came to attend the Group Relations Conference as participants seem to belong to a class by themselves. Defying the economic, political and religious guns aimed at Dalits in order to keep them as untouchables doomed to burn in the millennia old flames of the dehumanising fire of the caste (*jati*) and the *varna* systems, like Phoenix they have burned and risen from the ashes to organize and inspire their downtrodden brothers and sisters to challenge the system. Hence they have the guts and the ability to accept the pain accompanying transformation from within. Their motivation and intense engagement lie with the task. Beyond the GRC they have to get organized for the really tough task of putting the projections from the upper castes back to where they belong.

References

Ahmad, Imtiaz (ed.) (1973). *Caste and Social Stratification among the Muslims*. Delhi: Manohar Books.

Bain, Alastair (1999). On socio-analysis. *Socio-Analysis*, 1(1), 1-17.

Chattopadhyay, Gouranga P. (1991). Omnipotence and impotence – two faces of immature dependency. *Organisational Culture*. New Delhi: Discovery Publishing House, 67-88.

---

10   *Sannyasin* denotes a person who in the context of Hindu society gives up material possessions and follows a path of spirituality.

Chattopadhyay, Gouranga P. (1991), 'Invader in the mind' in Indian metaculture. *Organisational Culture*, 111-125.

Chattopadhyay, Gouranga P. (1986). An Interpretation of the Indian unconscious *vis a vis* the underprivileged communities in India. *Journal of the Anthropological Society*, 21, Calcutta,129-156 (Later published in *Organisational Culture*, 345-380).

Dasgupta, Birendramohan (ed.) (1989). *Samsad Bengali-English Dictionary*. Calcutta: Shishu Sahitya Samsad Private Ltd., 11th Impression, 426.

Lawrence, W.G. (1979). Today's concept for managers – managing one self in role. In *Exploring Individual and Organisational Boundaries*. London: Wiley.

Swarup, Ram (1987). Purity and pollution. *Times of India Sunday Review*, March 15, New Delhi Edition.

Viswanath, Rosemary & Chattopadhyay, Gouranga P. (forthcoming). Whose globe is it, anyway! In Klein, Edward B. (ed.), *Relatedness in Global Economy*. Madison: Psychological Press.

Max Pagès met Gunnar Hjelholt in the small group of EIT-founders during the 1960s. Later, he co-trained a laboratory in Denmark with Hjelholt. On his part, Hjelholt held high regards for Max and was inspired by his early writings, cf. Chapters 2 and 14. In his introduction to Chapter 9, Pagès recalls how contact with Hjelholt proved to be nourishing for him in a personal sense. The chapter is a chronological presentation of important themes and topics from his own life as a researcher and consultant, presented in the way he *would* have structured an account intended as an opening statement in a conversation with his now deceased friend.

During the time when he first became acquainted with Hjelholt, well over thirty years ago, he was driven by an ambition to build bridges between psycho-/sociodynamic and phenomenological approaches. Chapter 9 describes how, later in his career, it became increasingly important for him to refine the very concept of synthesis. In its traditional Hegelian sense, synthesis is understood as a movement whereby apparent contradictions are transcended and somehow swallowed up in a new unitary conceptual gestalt. This implies a hierarchical view of intellectual production. Concepts or theoretical models higher up the 'dialectical ladder' are by definition carrying a higher truth value than concepts and models in a lower position. The chase for the *ultimate* concept or model – the one that may be hoped to *beat all the others* – is thus legitimized. Pagès offers the concept of 'polyphony' as an antidote. When working polyphonically, you are *not* chasing the one single voice that 'says it all' thereby making all other voices superfluous. Rather you strive to let individual 'voices', i.e. concepts, models, theoretical disciplines and traditions, be heard as singular, discernible intellectual tools which, by their peculiar ways of interacting, each gives its unique contribution to a harmonic whole.

Pagès also reflects on political violence, fostered by states of collective unconscious insecurity, and he addresses 'the deadly triangle' between paranoid regression, all-or-nothing ideologies and political violence as such, as well as processes of mutual response strengthening, corresponding to positive feedback loops.

Professor Emeritus Max Pagès (b.1926) retired in 1992 as a professor in clinical psychology at University Paris-VII. In 1958, he founded ARIP, Association pour la Researche et l'Intervention psychologique, which played a role in developing psychosociology – or social psychology? – in France. In 1968, he founded Laboratoire de Changement Social (LCS). Now located at the University Paris VII under the leadership of Vincent de Gaulejac, LCS is still a very active institution. Max is a member of Le Syndicate National des Practiciens en Psychothérapie (SNPPSY) in France, and he is an Honorary President of the French federation of integrative and multireferential psychotherapy. Nowadays, Pagès works as a psychotherapist and supervisor. He recently took an interest in large-scale political events, something that is indicated by his latest books.

9   TOWARDS POLYPHONY IN THE HUMAN SCIENCES

Facing complexity

By Max Pagès, France

I have known Gunnar Hjelholt for more than thirty years, since the days when, together with a group of European colleagues, we founded the EIT, the European Institute for Trans-National Studies in Group and Organizational Development. During that period, we did not see each other very often, we were not intimate, and we were very different persons altogether. Still, I observed one curious thing about our relationship. Almost every time I had contact with Gunnar, it somehow turned out to be beneficial to me. The most important occasion was after the death by accident of my elder son aged 21. "Why don't you come with your wife to visit us at our place?" said Gunnar. Together with my first wife, I spent a few days in Vust with Gunnar and Berit. When arriving, we were in a very bad shape. Only a few words were exchanged during that visit, and no unnecessary ones, but we left the place better off than when we had arrived. Gunnar's main quality was presence.

Gunnar was a creative person. I never participated in a mini-society,[1] but what I heard about these events interested me. In the seventies I was engaged in a parallel kind of work, experimenting with 'flexible structure laboratories' aimed at exploring the boundary zone between sociological (class, money, power) and psychological dimensions in group formation, and the way these dimensions may mix or interact (Pagès, 1975).

Intellectually and professionally speaking, I see Gunnar and I as brothers. But we have both been busy working in our own areas, each with our own affiliations and traditions. I was working mainly in France, Southern Europe and Latin America. My books were published in French, translated into several languages, but never into English. I now regret that the two of us, together with the rest of our EIT-colleagues, did not find time for more exchanges on our similarities and differences, i.e. on the boundaries separating us and linking us at the same time. Gunnar's death makes it impossible to bridge that

---

1   Cf. Chapters 2, 6 and 13.

gap now. In the following pages, all by myself, I shall try to move a few steps in such a direction.

The emotional life of groups

Like many others from our group, I had a varied background. I was first trained in philosophy, then in experimental psychology. During a one-year scholarship in the US (1950-51), I became enthusiastic about Carl Rogers and spent a few months studying with him at the University of Chicago. In 1955, I went back to the US and was trained in group dynamics at Bethel and other places. In France, in between the two visits, I had my first practical and theoretical contacts with psychoanalysis.

I was trying to use this background in my first job as an industrial psychologist, working in a large consulting firm, experimenting with training, research, and change methodology within organizations, what we then called *interventions psychosociologiques* (psychosociological interventions). In parallel fashion, I was working on my main doctoral thesis named *La vie affective des groupes* (The Emotional Life of Groups, Pagès, 1968) also carrying the subtitle (a very modest one!): Outline of a Theory of Human Relationship. My ambition was to build a *synthesis* between, on the one hand psychoanalysis, on the other hand phenomenological approaches like the Rogerian, including also – on a more practical side – group dynamics.

My central hypothesis was that men are related to each other by a common anguish of separation basically rooted in their anxiety about confronting death – death being the ultimate separation. Paradoxically, this anxiety is the basis of relationship, mutual respect and authentic love, all terms which presuppose acceptance of the other as different, separated from oneself. According to my hypothesis, there is a conceptual link between separation and relationship. Group members experience these existential paradoxes unconsciously, but they disown their experience by means of various collectively organized defenses, mainly in the form of aggression and dependency.

From syntheses to interactions: socio-mental systems

I have never really abandoned this conception, but I have moved towards a more dialectical position, leaving aside the quest for overall syntheses in favour of an emphasis on *relating* diverse approaches.

In the late seventies, I directed a group of young colleagues in a research project on power within organizations (*L'Emprise de l'Organisation*, Pagès et al., 1979). The research took place within a large multinational firm. Using the more 'classical' industrial enterprises as our comparative baseline, we wanted to understand the changes in power structure that occurred in large multinational firms. The latter we baptized 'hypermodern' organizations. The explanatory model we finally developed, and which best fitted our observational data, pointed to a link between organization members' collective means of defense against anxiety and the kind of sociological and political power exercised in the organization.

Compared to the 'classical' organization or enterprise, the hypermodern organization experiences a basic change in its power structure. It changes from an obedience-disobedience structure involving dependency on individual authority, i.e. on the boss, towards a more impersonal kind of power. Implied in this change is a movement from *orders* to *rules*, from subservience to the boss to an identification with the organization and its philosophy. An order you have to obey after which you are rewarded; or you disobey it and are duly punished. A rule has to be interpreted and internalized. Hypermodern organizational power rests on a philosophy, or a 'culture' as management jargon has it, which is the core of the organization itself and with which all members of the organization are called to identify themselves.

According to our model, the described way of functioning is based on and also leading to organization members' regression to an archaic dependency on the organization as a mother figure in the Kleinian sense of the term, i.e. an all-powerful, protecting and threatening figure, an object of a love-hate relationship. The organization becomes the central investment of individuals, instead of the boss. Contrariwise, the traditional organization, or should we say enterprise, rests psychologically on an oedipal structure where the father role, as well as the customary rivalries for its power, are predominant issues.

I described this way of linking a psychological, unconscious and collective structure with the social-economic-political power structure as the theoretical establishment of a *socio-mental system*. Of course, the concept is of a general nature. Socio-mental systems other than the hypermodern do exist, among them the abovementioned variety governing the modern (rather than hypermodern), classical or traditional enterprise.

As already stated, in this research my colleagues and I endeavoured to bring about a fundamental shift in scientific orientation, away from the attempt to *synthesize* various approaches, thereby also trying to *unify* them. Instead, we let ourselves be guided by a methodology aimed at *relating* two or more *independent* approaches, at the same time allowing us to discover and to study their *interactions*.

Complexity

This methodological approach is a road to *complexity*, in the sense Edgar Morin (1990) and others use the word.

Following that direction, we hypothesize that reality responds to more than one system of interpretation and action at a time and that these systems are interacting with one another, thereby giving shape to real world affairs as they can be observed. We further hypothesize that such systems of interpretation and action refer to, or are embedded in various theoretical disciplines and schools of thought, such as, e.g., Psychoanalysis, Phenomenology, Sociology, Political Science, Ethology, Theory of emotion. It is important to note that no given list of theoretical traditions or approaches can be considered exhaustive, nor should any particular list item be considered obligatory across research contexts. It belongs to the individual researcher-practitioner to choose a particular angle and on that basis to pick the relevant selection of theoretical ideas or hypotheses to guide his observation, interpretation and action.

Each major school of thought in the Human Sciences has tended to become a *scientific religion*, mixing authentic scientific work with irrational faith often centered around a revered Master figure, e.g. Freud, Marx, Reich, thereby transforming hypotheses into doctrine and dogma, articles of faith, prohibitions, etc.

We have moved towards a more pragmatic stance. When using a theoretical system, our emphasis is not on finding and applying all-embracing, all-explaining *Principles*, such as libido, death-instinct, class struggle, sexual energy. Instead we move our analysis to the intermediate level of *processes*. We focus on the interaction of processes of a heterogeneous nature, for instance the interaction between economic-political domination, psychological processes of regression, repression, identification, projection, emotional processes of suppression, expression, etc. Each scientific object is defined as a complex object in which various lines of interpretation and action interact.

We tend to move away from *contradictions*, mutually exclusive scientific propositions, to simple *contraries* that oppose without contradicting one another. In our work we strive for *creative conflictuality* – between theories, between methods, between people and groups of people.

This leads us to combined strategies of action, combining individual and group levels, psychological, sociological, and emotional methods of analysis and action.

Political violence

I am now coming to my most recent research. It originated as a process of joint reflection on political violence in which I engaged with a few colleagues[2] (Pagès et al., 2003). Please accept my apologies for the necessarily schematic character of my presentation.

The late XXth century was full of political violence: two World Wars, the genocides of Armenians, Jews, Gypsies, Tutsis, Kosovars. The present century confronts us with the symmetrical threats of terrorism and counter-terrorism.

One can define political violence as a violence which affects the whole social body. It is exerted in the name of the state or against it. It aims at changing or defending political institutions.

In our book we have tried to generalize psychosocial hypotheses, previously tested at the organizational level, to the level of macrosocial phenomena. I was greatly helped by the work of Franco Fornari (1964), an Italian psychoanalyst who expanded the Kleinian hypotheses to cover also the relationship of individuals to the state and other large-scale institutions at the time of atomic risk. Basically speaking, Fornari's hypotheses claim that grown-up individuals, when psychologically relating to large scale institutions such as Kings, States, Religion, Law, tend at an unconscious level to regress partially to the state of infants being in an archaic dependency relationhip to a mother figure. The rest of the world, i.e. society at large, is sensed as chaos, the absence of the mother figure is felt as abandonment and the individuals, particularly when acting in groups, are likely to respond to this felt desertion with rage, aggression, or depression. They become potential paranoiacs.

---

2   Jacqueline Barus-Michel, Edgar Morin, Charles Rojzman, Dan Bar On, Fethi Ben Slama, André Sirota, Patrick Schmoll.

Continuing this line of thinking, the present-day situation of generalized and important institutional changes in both the political, religious, moral and other domains can be said to result in states of *collective unconscious insecurity* which creates a favourable ground for political violence. In the absence of solid institutions as a defense against such feelings, the institutional instability tends to induce a collective regression to the paranoid position – rage, fear, hatred. We then enter into the deadly triangle: psychological paranoid regression, ideological Manichaeism (all-or-nothing ideologies in terms of absolute Good and Evil), and political violence as such ('law of retaliation', revenge and destruction as the only solution to conflicts). Each of these terms interacts with the others. At each level of interaction a change takes place away from ternary structures, i.e. structures consisting of three terms thereby allowing for mediation and compromise, into binary, all-or-nothing structures.

What can be observed within the described social climate are *processes of mutual response strengthening,* equivalent to the cybernetic concept of positive feedback loops. A positive feedback loop establishes itself when a change in some given direction in one part of the system induces change in the *same* direction in some other part of the system. The reciprocity of influences produces a cumulative effect. Contrariwise, a negative feedback loop occurs when system changes in one part and in one direction induce changes in the *opposite* direction in other parts. Negative feedback loops thus tend to *regulate* change. In the present world situation positive feedback loops leading to mutual response strengthening can be observed, e.g.

- between collective psychological insecurity and the choice of leaders advocating politics of violence. Adolf Hitler is one good example of this. In 1923, when he failed in his putsch at the Feldernhalle in München, Hitler was ignored or considered a fool by a large majority of the German people. Ten years later, elections of an almost democratic nature made him Chancellor of the Reich. Once in power, such leaders arouse and strengthen the people's impulse towards psychological and ideological violence, they channel it into action, and it is very difficult to get rid of them.

- between adversaries, as for example we observe nowadays between Israelis and Palestinians. Extremist positions on each side mutually strengthen one another. Likewise at the international level, we find mutual response strengthening between terrorism and counter-terrorism or rather (to put it more bluntly) imperialism. Terrorism strengthens imperialism, imperialism strengthens terrorism, it goes both ways.

At all the levels mentioned, moderate parties feeling sympathy for both sides and thereby carrying a mediating potential are weakened or may simply not exist. Good examples at the international level are Europe and UN.

In the present-day world at large, we thus find ourselves in a very dangerous situation of generalized mutual response strengthening (positive fedback loops) between various sets of factors with a potential for triggering political violence: between the level of the psychological unconscious and the ideological and political levels; between a population and its leaders; between political adversaries; between local events and international events. This is apt to lead to what may be called a state of *paroxystic violence*. Paroxystic violence differs from 'normal' violence, i.e. violence maintaining links with realistic economic or political goals like defending or augmenting one's territory, augmenting one's wealth or power. Paroxystic violence refers to a state of crisis where violence goes beyond or even becomes contrary to the goals it proclaims. Its real meaning is expressing anguish, impotency and despair. It could be interpreted as an alarm signal from Society as a whole directed towards itself and elicited by its own impotency in dealing with the changes that it is producing itself.

The point of view presented here should not be interpreted as an overall pessimistic prophecy. The changes induced by hypermodernity have many positive aspects, such as worldwide communication, mixing of cultures, economic growth (in the long-term perspective), scientific creativity – aspects that are consciously supported and actively lived out and enjoyed by large segments of the population. But at the same time, living in the present, changing World environment induces a state of both conscious and unconscious anxiety leading to the dangerous, potentially damaging consequences which have been delineated.

Some hope resides in the fact that the generalized feedback patterns characteristic of hypermodernity may be reversed. At any one point in the global system network, positive feedback loops may be turned into negative feedback loops. In order for this to happen we must show courage and responsibility when confronting the situation as it is, the suffering and dangers it creates, and we must show creativity when searching for solutions based on compromise and mediation.

Some sort of grief labor is probably a key prerequisite for putting an end to certain situational states governed by paroxystic violence. Former enemies may thereby come to realize and recognize the enormous amount of suffering they have themselves endured as well as inflicted upon their counterpart. Sincere grief may then be experienced and, through this, a true concern for oneself and for the other. Both parties may resolve to restructure their relationship anchoring it in a new set of values. An example has been the Committees for Truth and Reconciliation initiated by the Reverend Desmond Tutu in South Africa. Another example is the French-German reconciliation after World War II. Taken to the scale of Europe as a whole, the latter example constitutes, much more than the economic union, the real core of the 'European Project'. In the context of world history where, consistently, creation of new political entities has been based on nation-, federation or empire-building by way of conquest and assimilation, such a project of building a political entity on an intent towards reconciliation and union of *different* peoples, prior enemies, is radically new. The European project can be conceived as the ideal-type of a world governed by peace.

Conclusion

I shall conclude with a few remarks of a methodological or epistemological nature.

The approach I have described is *non-essentialist* and *non-fundamentalist*. It does not try to explain the world from above, once and for all, from Great Principles, supposedly operating alike in all circumstances, Death instinct, for example, closely resembling the concept of Sin in a religious framework; or Class Struggle; or other like examples.

The approach is *relativist, plurideterminist* and *interactive*. It cuts across frameworks, theories and methods – in short, boundaries. It focuses on interactions of psychological, sociological, political and historical perspectives.

It is *situational*. It relates analysis and action to single situations, localized in time and space.

Lastly it is *dialectical*. It aims at revitalizing living contraries: antagonism and cooperation; positive and negative aspects. At one and the same time, it seeks to conceive of such contraries as mutually opposed *and* linked to each other. It studies dialectics at work within each dimension, e.g. the psychological, the sociological dimension, and between them.

The word complex best summarizes the ideas presented here. The ideas are intended only as a pointer for the future. It is my optimistic conviction that we are in no more than a prehistoric stage of doing human sciences. It is my hope that, in the future, we may develop a much stronger emphasis on *polyphonic work* in the human sciences, thereby making these sciences our tool in building a polyphonic world.

References

Fornari, F. (1964). *Psicanalisi della guerra atomica.* Milano: Edizioni di Comunità. (French translation from 1969: *Psychanalyse de la situation atomique*, Gallimard, Paris.)

Morin, E. (1990). *Introduction à la pensée complexe.* Paris: ESF.

Pagès, M. (1975). The laboratory with flexible structures. In Benne, K.D. et al., *The laboratory Method of Changing and Learning.* Palo Alto: Science and Behaviour Books.

Pagès, M. (1968/1990). *La vie affective des groupes, esquisse d'une théorie de la relation humaine.* Paris: Dunod. (Translated into German and other languages).

Pagès, M., Bonetti, M., de Gaulejac, V. & Descendre, D. (1979/1998). *L'Emprise de l'organisation.* Paris: Presses Universitaires Francaises.

Pagès, M. et al. (2003). *La violence politique, pour une clinique de la complexité.* Erès.

PART THREE

PUBLICATIONS BY
GUNNAR HJELHOLT

Chapter 10 reports on results from a number of applied experiments, or group training programmes, from which data were gathered. Some of the experiments took place in the U.S., others in Denmark. In most of them, Gunnar Hjelholt served as group trainer. The aim of the experiments was to increase self-insight and to encourage group members to test their grounds by means of more appropriate behaviour, including increased productivity, increased efficiency in problem solving and improved leader-capability to predict the reactions of his group members.

The title emphasises *attitude* changes (in Danish: indstillingsændringer), but Gunnar focuses as much, if not more, on behavioural change. As for attitudes, he mostly concentrates on attitudes toward one self and toward other group members and fellow human beings. In order to achieve change, particularly behavioural change, mere talk does not suffice. Gunnar's line of reasoning is that any training situation should include the possibility for action in order to observe the efficiency of each participant's behaviour and the way in which others would interpret this behaviour. Only then will we have a tool for adjusting our behaviour. In addition, group training must incorporate a feedback system that will provide participants with information on appropriateness and consequences of their behaviour.

In all the reported experiments, a built-in element was small feedback groups; Gunnar calls them mirror groups. In some experiments, he designed role playing, enabling participants from different company departments to exchange roles, hence facilitating the act of putting oneself in the place of the other.

Chapter 10 is a slightly abbreviated translation of Gunnar Hjelholt's original version in Danish: Den lille gruppe som faktor ved indstillingsændringer, *Nordisk Psykologi*, 1960, 12, 122-128.

10 THE SMALL GROUP AS A FACTOR IN ATTITUDE CHANGES[*]

By Gunnar Hjelholt

Our behaviour and our attitudes are influenced by the groups we belonged to in the past and the ones to which we presently belong. Our group membership influences and characterizes our degree of aggressiveness or cooperation (Lewin, Lippitt & White, 1939), our self-respect and confidence in ourselves (Cartwright 1951), our work productivity (Coch & French, 1948), as well as our concepts of what is true and right (Morrow & French, 1945). These characteristics may be viewed as the 'qualities' of groups and interpersonal relationships. In plain English we refer to the 'good work group', the 'snobbish' family etc., that is, we attribute certain qualities to the group.

If we want to change the individual's attitude and behaviour, it would seem reasonable to work with the variables that brought about his attitudes and behaviour in the first place. A comparison: when treating individuals – in particular if children are involved – we seek to influence the family group of which the child is a member. Or we introduce the individual to new groups that have certain qualities, e.g. an accepting climate, in order to bring about changes in the individual.

A short description follows below of some experiments on leadership training in various populations as well as concluding remarks concerning demands on training programmes that aim at bringing about changes in participants.

During the past ten years or so, Scandinavian commercial life has attempted to influence its leaders by means of so-called human relations training carried out in small groups. Originally inspired from the USA, this method is meant to increase a leader's self-insight as well as his capability to predict the reactions of his group members. A number of studies have documented a relation between self-insight, sensitivity and group productivity (Chowdry & Newcomb, 1952; Fiedller, 1958; Nagle, 1954; Taylor & Faust, 1952). Indeed, there has been a strong demand for increased productivity during the long after-war period.

---

[*]   Written in 1960

The mirror group

In the spring of 1958, while I was a research fellow at Fels Group Dynamic Center, an American East-coast company asked me to organize a human relations training course for leaders at the second level from the bottom. The company's consultant was Dr. S.S. Kight from Fels. The course lasted for five whole days with 12 participants and two trainers. It focused on the specific difficulties related to the job as foreman-in-chief. To a large degree, it was based on role playing, group discussions and a few, brief informal lectures. A built-in element of the programme was small feedback groups, or mirror groups as we named them, each group having three or four members. ('Feedback' is a loanword from the natural sciences; the general meaning is, however, applicable for all kinds of processes that involve change. For instance, feedback may be a report to a group or an individual, rendering them/it capable of clearly understanding and overcoming obstacles *that need to be addressed*).

Throughout the course, these small groups would meet at the end of the day. Each individual had to describe how he had experienced his own behaviour and why he had acted the way he did. Subsequently, the other group members were asked to compare their experience of his behaviour with his description. Furthermore, they were asked to inform the individual of how his behaviour, in their opinion, had influenced the leadership problems of the large training group, just to mention one example. In these mirror groups an attempt was made to introduce a norm of mutual feedback, thereby increasing the self-insight of the group members. In addition, members of the large group were encouraged to test their ground by means of more appropriate behaviour.

My co-trainer and I had the impression that these mirror groups were influential in bringing about changes in participants' behaviour and attitudes towards themselves. As a matter of fact, the participants actually gave credit to the groups in this regard.

Based upon these experiences, the company initiated an experiment to be conducted by Dr Kight. The result of the hypothesis testing is now available (Smith & Kight, 1960): feedback will in fact increase self-insight and productivity. At a course for foremen at the bottom level, the participants were organized in groups that were to meet for 30 minutes twice a day. In the control situation, the participants were organized in groups and were merely asked to talk about the events of the day. In some instances, the participants were not organized in groups until the last day, where the effects of group participation were tested. On the fifth day all groups were given a test involving some 20 questions concerning problem-solving. In other studies (Goldman et a., 1958;

Smith, 1957; Taylor & Faust, 1952) these questions had turned out to be effective in discriminating between groups whose efficiency was measured in other ways. Furthermore, each individual was asked to state which leadership roles out of ten he had assumed during the week. Self-insight was defined as the difference between the number of roles stated by himself and the average number of roles stated by the two trainers.

Table 1 presents the number of problems solved by the groups under feedback conditions and in control situations. The difference is significant (p=.002). (The two control situations were not significantly different; consequently, we may conclude that the change was not brought about by better knowledge of each other).

TABLE 1. NUMBER OF GROUPS THAT SOLVED PROBLEMS UNDER CERTAIN CONDITIONS COMPARED TO GROUPS WITH NO PROBLEMS SOLVED

	Feedback	Control
One or several problems	10	9
No problem solving	0	12

As regards self-insight, there was no significant difference between control groups and mirror groups. However, as the experiments proceeded, it turned out that the trainers had allowed less time for the mirror groups. Table 2 shows the average figures (M) and the standard deviation (SD) regarding self-insight under experiment and control conditions.

This investigation indicates that small groups with a feedback norm will increase the efficiency of problem-solving and, given the proper time, this circumstance may also increase the self-insight of participants.

TABLE 2. SELF-INSIGHT SCORE UNDER FEEDBACK AND CONTROL CONDITIONS

	Feedback			Control
	I	II	III	
Number of minutes in feedback group	230	193	165	0
M	.90	1.73	2.38	2.41
SD	1.30	0.89	1.73	2.07
N	10	1	12	69

Low score indicates self-insight. The difference between Feedback I and Control is clearly significant, and the difference between I and III is significant.

Role exchange

In 1959 I worked with role exchanges in two training groups from a Danish company. In this particular firm, one of the purposes of the training courses was to lessen the gap between the departments and to change attitudes. Each group had 16 members and was composed of the employees from the four departments in question, thus representing a miniature company.

The first training group was assembled for 3½ days, the second for 7½ days. Each training group was divided into various small groups in order to increase the contact between the company's departments. Furthermore, role-plays were designed, based on the company working procedures. During these role-play situations, the participants were to play other roles than their usual ones, i.e., participants from one department were to play the roles of another department. According to social psychological role theory (Sarbin, 1954), exchange of roles will increase sensitivity and thereby facilitate the act of putting oneself in the place of the other.

There were additional variations in the design, but these will not be reported in the present context.[1] A valid conclusion cannot be drawn however on the basis of results from this training, due to the following conditions: the two groups did not receive the same amount of training, the two programmes were not identical, and certain conditions were changed from the first to the second group. However, the anonymous course evaluations show that, in the last training group, 9 out of 16 participants spontaneously mentioned that, among other things, the training had resulted in a change of attitude towards other departments. One of the purposes of the course was in fact to change these attitudes but this had not been revealed to them.

All in all, we are convinced that the exchanging of roles will increase people's capability of putting themselves in the situation of others. In courses to come, we will attempt to incorporate reliable methods of measurement to support the thesis.

---

1   The editors of the present book have excluded approximately one page of the original paper that reported on a particular attempt to implement attitude changes.

The T-group

The last experiment to be dealt with in this article was carried out in April 1959. The eleven participants attending the one-week residential course came from eight different companies and were to become teachers or instructors at the companies in question.

The main training means was the renowned T-group method, developed in Bethel, as well as the mirror group method mentioned in connection with the first experiment. The T-group is an attempt to create a new group with particular norms, particular forms of leadership and a particular work programme. The trainer's task is to make the members of the group look at the group process.

At the end of each day's work, the mirror groups would meet for individual feedback. In the evenings, each participant would complete a questionnaire to evaluate the other participants' behaviour during the day. Each participant would, in private, get an evaluation of himself and his behaviour from each of the ten other participants in the group.

In my opinion, the T-group is the most efficient tool for providing greater self-insight and, simultaneously, sensitivity towards other people. Combined with practical tasks, T-groups will lead to changes in behaviour as well. The laboratory method (Seashore, 1957) does, however, make heavy demands on the trainer.

The participants evaluated the last training programme as highly valuable; that is, they noticed that they had changed with regard to attitude towards themselves and others as well. In addition, their behaviour changed, a fact that was indicated in the daily evaluations of each other's actions. One month later the companies they returned to noticed that the behaviour of six out of eleven participants had changed considerably.

Training requirements

Human relations training requires a clear formulation of the purpose of the training. A direct goal is to change the participants' daily work behaviour.

Behaviour, however, cannot be changed simply by means of increased knowledge or attitude changes. Therefore, a training programme would not be satisfactory, were it only based on acquiring facts or eliminating old conceptions and attitudes. It is frequently assumed that discussing a problem, analysing a matter, exchanging experiences, and introducing an oversimplistic technique will, as a matter of course, lead to changes. If used in a total training scheme along with other methods, the use of some of the techniques may be justified, but they, in themselves, will seldom lead to changes.

If one intends to introduce changes, the first step is to diagnose the need for change and the forces that stand in the way of change. Furthermore, a total training scheme must be developed, a scheme that involves several methods. Actually, the group trainer must be a 'diagnostician' and a 'designer' as well as a fully educated trainer.

Several demands can be made on training that is meant to result in behavioural change. Some of these demands are emphasized by Bradford (according to Seashore, 1957). Let me mention the individual's opportunity for engaging in an experiental situation in the group. Unless the actual behaviour of the individual is drawn in and exposed, there will not be a lot of possibility for change. Quite often we see our problems as results of the behaviour of others. We believe that if we can 'cure' or change the other person, then the problem will go away. In reality, we are usually a part of the situation that needs to be changed. Furthermore, the training must incorporate a feedback system that will provide us with information on the appropriateness and consequences of behaviour. Any training situation should include the possibility for action in order to observe the efficiency of each participant's behaviour and how others interpret this behaviour. Only then will we have a tool for adjusting our own behaviour. There will be a need for emotional support, by means of an accepting climate, for instance. We must feel accepted in order to be able to receive data concerning our own shortcomings. In most training situations we tend to defend ourselves and refuse to recognize that changes or improvements might be necessary.

By using the small group in the training, based on the above demands, we make it possible to change the participants' attitudes towards self and others and hence create a basis for behavioural changes.

References

Cartwright, D.P. (1951). Achieving change in people. *Human Relations*, 5, 281-292.
Chowdry, K. & Newcomb, T.M. (1952). The relative abilities of leaders and non-leaders to estimate opinion of their own groups. *J. Abnorm. & Soc. Psychol.* 47, 51-57.
Coch, L. & French, J.R.P., Jr. (1948). Overcoming resistance to change. *Human Relations*, 4, 512-532.

Fiedler, F.E. (1958). Interpersonal perception and group effectiveness. In Tagiuri &
Petrullo (eds.), *Person Perception and Interpersonal Behaviour*. Stanford University Press,
243-257.

Ghiselli, E.E. & Barthol, R. (1956). Role perceptions of successful and unsuccessful
supervisors. *J Appl. Psychol., 40*, 241-244.

Goldman, M., Bolen, M.E. & Martin, R.B. (1958). The effect of group structure on the
performance of groups engaged in a problem solving task. *Amer. Psychol., 13*, 353.

Lewin, K., Lippit, R. & White, R.K. (1939). Patterns of aggressive behavior in
experimentally created social climates. *J. Soc. Psychol., 10*, 271-299.

Marrow, A.J. & French, J.P.R., Jr. (1945). Changing a stereotype in industry. *J. Soc Issues,
1*, 33-37.

Nagle, B.F. (1954). Productivity, employee attitude and supervisor sensivitity. *Personnel
Psychol., 7*, 219-233.

Porter, LW. (1958). Differential self-perception of management personnel and live
workers. *J Appl.Psychol., 42*, 105-108.

Sarbin, T.R. (1954). Role theory. In Lindzey, G. (ed.). *Handbook of Social Psychology*.
Cambridge, Mass.: Addison-Wesley, *vol. 1*, 233-258.

Seashore, S.E. (1957). The training of leaders for effective human relations. In Likert, R.
& Hayes, S.P., Jr. (eds.), *Some Applications of Behavioural Research*. Unesco, 81-123.

Smith, E.E. (1957). The effects of clear and unclear role expectations on group
productivity and defensiveness. *J. Abnorm. & Soc. Psychol., 55*, 213-217.

Smith, E.E. & Kight, S.S. (1960). Effects of feedback on insight and problem solving
efficiency in training groups. *J. Appl. Psychol.*

Steinar, I.D. (1955). Interpersonal behavior as influenced by accuracy of social perception.
Psychol. Rev., 62, 268-274.

Taylor, D.W. & Faust, W.L. (1952). Twenty questions: Efficiency in problem solving as a
function of size of group. *J. Exp. Psychol., 44*, 360-368.

Preamble for Chapter 11

The following paper by Gunnar Hjelholt and his close American colleague Matthew Miles is reproduced on the basis of a mimeographed version dated January 1963. Excerpts from a supplement dated February 1963 are included as well (the omitted parts of the supplement deal with trainer comments and outline of contents). Small language adjustments have been made by the publisher. According to the mimeograph, both parts were to be published in the *Journal of the American Society of Training Directors.* However, it appears from later publications by Hjelholt that the journal had a slightly different title, the correct reference being: *Training Directors Journal*, 17, 1963 (3), 3-10.

The case study describes how the two authors, in a 1962 laboratory in Denmark, extended the conventional Bethel version. They settle with the notion that a lab should be run in a consecutive period of time, their extended version including four phases: two weeks of basic learning, one week of self-arranged fieldwork, a twelve-week digestion and application phase back home, and finally a follow-up week. This model ensures *reality connection*, a quality Gunnar constantly sought to enhance. In additon, he and Matt Miles explain how they transformed the standard authority and power relations between trainers and trainees, gradually granting the members added responsibility. Finally they are impressed by the possibilities inherent in the examination of the lab itself as a system made up of participants *and* staff.

In hindsight, one can see how the extension of the traditional laboratory method was a step in the direction of Gunnar's later creation, the mini-society. This unique kind of organizational experiment is treated in Chapter 13.

11 EXTENDING THE CONVENTIONAL TRAINING LABORATORY DESIGN[*]

By Gunnar Hjelholt & Matthew B. Miles

The vivid, intensive methods which fall under the general heading of 'laboratory human relations training' have by now diffused very widely through American organizational life, and are spreading rapidly in Europe. (Miles, 1962). 'T-group' is no longer a strange term to training directors in industry, government or private agencies – and the manager who has been to a 'lab', inside or outside of his own organization, is no longer a rarity.[1] The pioneering work of National Training Laboratories has developed and consolidated; work under this heading now goes on at 34 universities, eight of them with organized centres. A growing body of research is available (see Durham & Gibb, 1960; Stock, in press).

Yet, with all this ferment, thoroughgoing innovation in the design of human relations training laboratories is rarer than it should be. They usually involve about two weeks of time, isolated from 'the world', with standard activities (T-groups, theory sessions, exercises of various types), combined in a way that seems acceptable to the staff members involved.

During the winter and spring of 1962, the authors collaborated in a laboratory for Danish educational leaders. Although we did not start out deliberately to 'innovate', we found as we began to plan with the sponsoring agencies,[2] and

---

[*]   Written in 1963.
[1]   See Ferguson. (1959); Hoy (1959); Foundation for Research on Human Behavior (1960); and Argyris (1962) for accounts of the use of human relations training as a means for management development.
[2]   These were the Danish State Teachers College for Advanced Training (a national graduate school of education), and the Danish Adult Education Association. Financing was by the Danish Ministry of Education, and the lab was titled *Study-Conference for Group Psychology and Adult Education*.

the participants themselves,[3] that it was necessary to rid ourselves of the usual assumptions about laboratory design. Should a lab necessarily be concentrated within a short period of time? Should participants be excluded from its design and execution? We thought about this, and as a result, our final experience proved novel – and exciting – in a number of ways.

This paper describes the laboratory design, reviews its unusual features, and discusses some of the issues that the experience raised in our own minds about current practice in laboratory training.

Over-all design

The laboratory was planned and staffed by the authors, with the steadily increasing participation of the members. The sites for the laboratory included a country inn in Korinth, Fyn, Denmark; villages and towns near Korinth; and the work situations of participants. The design fell into four units of time:

Basic learning. The first period of two weeks (February 13-23) focused on small groups' learning processes and intergroup dynamics. It was run by both trainers, with English as the working language. Great care was taken to see that theory sessions and practice exercises closely followed the development of the two T-groups (and the lab as a whole). Theory session methods were strongly inductive (e.g. in a session on teaching-learning theory, members were asked to analyze their early and late perceptions of the trainers).

During the second week an intergroup exercise was run, the task being to plan the entire next part of the laboratory (third week) and select a steering committee with members from each T-group to administer the plans. In this way, a bridge to the next part of the lab was established.

The latter part of the second week included many exercises which the participants themselves designed for each other; careful critique followed each.

Fieldwork and planning. The third week (February 26 – March 2) was run in Danish, under the control of the steering committee, with Hjelholt as a con-

---

3 The participants were 17 key persons engaged primarily in adult educational work including management and union leadership training; the preparation and training of public school teachers, and teachers of the blind, of prisoners, of counselors, of home economics, and those working in technical institutes. The age of the participants ranged from 26 to the middle fifties.

sultant. Its aim was to test the learning process (with particular emphasis on training methods) and to make plans for further work at home.

A special feature of this phase was self-arranged fieldwork. Small groups planned actions at the lab, then went out to various institutions, schools and other nearby settings where one member carried the plans out while the others observed. They then returned to the lab and reported the experiences. The populations varied: boys at a technical training school, shop stewards, laundry owners, and old-age pensioners. The actions tried out were equally varied: observation of teacher styles, skills of handling a large meeting under attack, use of inductive-type exercises.

Application. In the third phase, occupying twelve weeks, the delegates had the opportunity to digest and apply their learning experiences at home. Many different activities were initiated. Two participants (from different organizations) ran residential courses with a modified T-group approach. Others changed existing teaching courses, and ran conferences for their own organizational personnel. Initiative was shown too with regard to participants' own personal position. Redefinition of jobs occurred, and two participants applied and were accepted for the NTL Social Science Internship programmet Bethel.

Thirteen of the 17 members actively 'did something' in this period, and two others had activities planned.

Follow-up. The last unit was the follow-up week (May 27- June 3). The participants were confronted with the task of defining goals, and planning and administering the complete program, with the help of Hjelholt and Miles as consultants. It proved a difficult task, especially since one of the staff arrived midweek and an observer from the sponsoring Teachers College came at the same time. The participants agreed on a general plan for the week, and gave authority to rotating committees of three to handle each day's program. Each committee conducted a general feedback session at the end of the day, where changes in the next day's programme could be decided.

The substance of work done in this part of the laboratory included reports on the 3-month application period, the hammering out of a final report (to the sponsors, the Ministry of Education and the participants' organizations), consultations, and the planning of further work.

Striking features

Certain aspects of this lab – in addition to its extension in time – seemed especially interesting to us.

System development problems. In this design we started with 'trainees' and 'trainers', and hoped to transform these roles into those of members in a fully functioning social system, and consultants to this system. This authority shift was managed more or less skilfully by us, and helped and hindered by participants.

The first major event in this shift was the intergroup exercise, which evoked very high interest, even excitement. The task evoked some anxiety too, however. One delegate said: 'Maybe it's too early to give authority to a steering committee'. Another expressed concern about the lack of control the main body of participants would have. Also, the lab administrator's role,[4] which had not been an issue while the trainers were securely in command, was now in the limelight and had to be tackled in both the second and fourth parts of the lab.

During the second period, difficulties naturally arose when the two T-groups – with somewhat different norms – had to work together under the guidance of the steering committee. Sub-grouping started, but a 'maintenance' meeting where feelings were freely expressed (commonly referred to as 'The big Tuesday evening smash') helped to form the lab into 'one group'; the excitement of the fieldwork and the planning for back home took hold. The task output was especially outstanding in this second period. More than two thirds of the duplicated notebook material from this week was produced by the participants themselves.

The authority shift was completed (though perhaps not fully accepted by all members) in the fourth period of the lab. It meant added responsibility for the members of the system. They were presented with the reality of a 'real-life' organization, here and now – without some of the usual protection of appointed authority, economic sanctions, and restriction of feedback. Thus the authority shift meant fight/flight, strain and stress for both staff and participants – with a good deal of learning as well.

---

4   This was filled by a participant from the Teachers College (who also supplied a secretary).

Accompanying the authority shift, a shift in closeness and intimate feelings occurred. At the end of the first period, a member wrote: "I think I'll miss old mother T-group". And at the start of the last part of the lab, perhaps during the whole week, there was a keenly felt sense of coming to miss closeness. In the intimate T-groups, feedback was often given in a characteristically pungent, poetical way; feedback in the larger social system was somehow 'greyer', less potent and intimate.

System development was not – as indicated – a smooth process. After the interim three-month period in back-home settings, a rather drastic regression occurred in participants' – and our – personal behavior during the fourth period. The midweek arrival of the second trainer and the Teachers College observer was an added stress on the system. It was as if the previous T-group development had to be worked through once more. (Some of the confusion and regression appeared to stem from ignorance of the practical requirements of a working social system – ignorance which was occasionally startling, given that participants all had long and responsible experience in their own organizations).

The Utopian expectations of the T-group, where everyone in some miraculous way will get what he wants, gave way to the reality of the external world, where one has to struggle hard to change only a little – and where one has to take responsibility for the changes. The effect was sobering.

Interest in laboratory learning methods. The need to learn about 'learning methods' was striking, even considering the participants' vocations. We found strong interest in discussing inductive learning methods, in planning exercises for each other, in criticizing the pedagogical value of particular learning experiences.

In stress situations, however, it became clear that the resistance to inductive learning methods was great. The learner's assumptions about learning are deeply rooted; attitudes toward teachers and trainers are just as deep as those towards fathers and bosses. Working in an inductive way was a strong challenge to everyday practice, a challenge to what one had been doing for years, a shift of one's teaching role at home. But as joint planning and working continued, participants seemed to get even more involved than in a usual lab – partly, we felt, because of their keen interest in laboratory methods as such.

Reality connection. In this design, care was taken to connect with the outside world. For one thing, recruiting in a small country produced a set of participants with a strong network of acquaintanceships. Nearly everyone had worked with other members before as a teacher, student or colleague. The administrator/participant and the visiting observer both had influential, responsible positions in the Danish educational system, as did a number of the participants.

During the lab, we tried to emphasize reality-connection further. In the exercises we provided involving, reality-centered tasks (e.g. "Sponsors financing labs like this one often want to know the results of their investment. Make a practical proposal for evaluating this lab"). The inter-group exercise, too, stressed the fact that the decisions would have real consequences. The second period's fieldwork engaged the outside world in a direct way. One had to initiate contacts with real people out there, make plans, and carry the plans out in the different settings. The learnings were tested in 'reality'; old-age pensioners in one Danish city now have reduced bus fares as a result of one team's fieldwork.

The success of the fieldwork, we believe, led directly to the large amount of experimentation in the interim period. Also, the application back home was courageous (e.g. one participant asked another to run a five-day residential conference for him and his whole department, where grievances, inter-personal relationships and organizational practices were discussed and changes initiated). Knowledge that the follow-up week was coming also prompted the participants to try out things in the application period.

Some issues for laboratory training

We felt that this design, as we and the participants experienced it,[5] raised some fairly crucial issues for lab training as it is now practiced, especially in the United States.

Follow-up. The experience of working with laboratory participants three months later is sobering and instructive. Forgetting, regression, despair and confusion are all present. We have the feeling that most lab trainers, lulled by the splendour of life in a fully-developed T-group, are inclined to confuse artifactual system changes with durable changes in *members*. Participant X does come out

---

5   In passing, it might be noted that we felt (and feel) the design to be essentially sound, though there are operating problems (ex: the definition of the trainer-consultant role, use of process analysis to examine system development problems, and amount of pre-structure in the fourth period) which would need attention in a replication.

of his shell, Participant Y 'learns' to inhibit his hostile attacks – but how much of this stems from the fact that T-group is an easier, more nurturant environment at the end of a lab than at the beginning? We saw some behaviour in the fourth week of our lab as 'regression' – but was it? Perhaps – is it faintly possible? – people are not really learning as much as trainers think they are. A lab without follow-up invites trainer 'blindness' to this problem.

Trainer responsibility. Most laboratory designs at present indicate that the trainer-participant 'contact' is in force only during the laboratory itself. Many trainers hardly look at the application forms of participants; labs are staff-designed, without explicit recourse to the work situations of participants; and there is no follow-up. The 'cultural island' notion itself implies a lack of connection with the surrounding world. Yet our experience suggests there is great profit in trainers' knowing the work situations of participants before the lab begins. And the presence of a follow-up in the design means that trainers must *care*. They cannot emotionally detach themselves from the engagements of the lab as soon as it is over. Life goes on; it is quite impossible to dismiss Participant Z as having 'learned little'. One is going to work with Participant Z again. Are we prepared to extend the duration of the trainer-participant contract in this way?

Reality connection. Our experience suggests the importance of lab designs which require participants – as well as trainers – to engage the outside world *while they are still in the lab setting.* The fieldwork in our third week proved enormously useful to participants; the experience of hammering out a final report to real outside organizations in the fourth week was a painful reminder of the world of vested interests, power struggles, and interorganizational misunderstandings. It may be argued that labs operated in larger, more mobile, impersonal social systems (the USA, as compared to a country the size of Denmark) need this connection less, but we doubt it. Experience with labs within single organizations and with intact work groups (Argyris, 1962; Buchanan, 1962; Blansfield, 1962) tends to support our view that there should be far more experimentation with labs in a narrowly-limited geographical/professional area than at present.

Participant autonomy. Most labs proceed under the assumption that design matters are to be left to the staff. Participants have little or nothing to say about the content or procedures of learning experiences they go through (with the exception of T-group). Yet our experience suggests that learning is greatly enhanced when responsibility for planning is increasingly shifted to the participant. A number of the exercises, and the fieldwork experiences planned by participants, were among the most ingenious and interesting designs we have ever seen. Participant autonomy also led, we thought, to clearer and more direct internalization of inductive, laboratory-type learning methods than in any lab we had ever participated in before. Can trainers afford to continue controlling as much of laboratory design as they do now?

Design flexibility and lab size. Part of the success of our design lay, we felt, in the ease with which content and procedures could be readily shifted to meet emerging needs. The preliminary design for the first two weeks bore little resemblance to what finally emerged, particularly on the content side. As the day-to-day planning proceeded it was clear that the initial participant plan for the fourth period was being changed considerably. With a participant group of 17 and a training staff of two, such flexibility was very easy; rescheduling was a simple matter, and maintenance problems within the staff were at a minimum. One had the sense of an organic development in the lab; it *flowed*, rather than being 'staged' or 'presented'. We believe a good deal more experimentation with small labs is desirable. (Follow-up, too, tends to require very small labs for success.)

The laboratory as a social system. Finally, we were much impressed by the possibilities inherent in examination of the lab itself as a system that is larger than a face-to-face group. Up to now, most lab staff have preferred to ignore the fact (as far as participants are concerned) that operation of the lab requires real people (trainers, administrative staff, participants) to function in a real organization, having real conflicts, satisfaction, emotions (etc.) in the process. Conflicts among lab staff form part of trainer folklore, yet participants are carefully shielded from such phenomena as if they did not exist.

System analysis is classically encouraged in the miniature system of the T-group, of course, and there have been a few brief attempts to analyze the 'lab community' at NTL Bethel labs. However, part of the problem is that T-group system analysis works because it is supported by a surrounding, stable, unquestioned 'platform' – the lab. What is the 'platform' on which to stand while analyzing the *lab* as a system? We found that it is difficult and unnerving to have one's 'real' role questioned and analyzed, as contrasted with one's role as a 'T-group trainer'.[6] Our design also required the confrontation and working-through of trainer style differences to something like interdependence – and it wasn't easy.

---

6   One participant wrote: "- we are caught in the lab situation, and have to recognize this as a fact when we analyze the lab-system process ... and the analyzing itself is a disturbing fact".

To us, the opportunities in lab system analysis are quite exciting – both from the standpoint of participant learning, and for the research possibilities involved. (For example, a participant pointed out to us the strong analogue between events in this lab and the phenomena of a departmental merger through which he had been going; problems of managerial succession, communication restriction, and organizational adaptation to the environment could equally well be studied systematically, using the lab as a setting). The question is: are we prepared to examine lab system phenomena directly with participants?

Supplement

This supplement to our article contains added comments on the use of language in the laboratory. It describes immediate reactions of participants; gives sample comments made by participants and several trainers from Europe and the USA, who saw an early draft of the article; outlines content covered during the lab, and suggests "How we would do it differently". This supplementary material is presented as a way of encouraging further communication and comment on the issues raised in the article itself.

Some comments on language. The first and fourth periods of this design were conducted in English. Language difficulties were reduced after a short while, though participants reported a good deal of fatigue in expressing themselves in a foreign language under conditions of high involvement. (One struggling T-group member, however, when urged to revert to Danish by the others, said, "the feelings are the same in Danish"). We did invite members to use Danish whereever the activity {for example, sub-group work) permitted, and during the fourth period, the final problem-solving work on the preparation of the report to the sponsoring agencies (itself in Danish) was also conducted in Danish, with occasional simultaneous interpretation for Miles.

Several participants reported that using English enhanced the cultural-island effect, freeing them to be more spontaneous ("I'm not *really* saying it, because it's in English"). We also noticed much closer listening and checking of communication than is ordinarily the case in indigenous-language labs.

Another comment by Miles after watching an extended problem-solving session in Danish was that participants, as might be expected, had an enormously greater economy of expression when using their native tongue. (Minor gestures could indicate strong rejection, but while using English, very strong gestures were needed to express the same emotion.) Miles also felt he saw sharper discontinuities between the 'English' and 'Danish' personal styles of participants who had spent extended periods of time in English-speaking countries, and had thus become more fully socialized.

Some of the members who were most fluent in English did dominate to some extent, and the T-group with Miles (which had some of the more fluent speakers of English) felt superior to the other. Fluency of speech could also be used, of course, as a flight mechanism, and it was. In Hjelholt's T-group English was (by agreement) abandoned when feelings were very high. In the second part of the lab, when Danish was the working language, members from this group lapsed into English on several occasions when they really wanted to express emotions!

Reactions of participants. A large amount of data was collected during the course of the lab, primarily to aid participants in clarifying their generalizations, and to steer the planning. For example, after each exercise, statements of learnings, together with critiques of the exercise, were collected from each participant, (who retained a carbon copy). Rating data were also collected all through the inter-group exercise, as in current American practice; the results were highly comparable to the usual American findings.

The reader may be interested in seeing a sample of comments made after the first period (two weeks), and at the end of the entire lab (after the follow- up period).

Learnings after two weeks. Some samples here will indicate the range of output at this point in the lab.

- Not to take anything for granted. Things are not always as you think them to be.
- What communication means between people. I met myself.
- Not to make good-bad judgments about suggestions or behavior.
- The ability to understand other people in a better way. Not to let my own defenses block the contact.
- To listen – my ears are growing up, I feel them, like a hare.
- To allow myself to have feelings and to accept them in others.
- That you can have a conference without having a fixed and detailed programme in the agenda sense, and that it can be very constructive and 'giving' to have a conference arranged that way.
- That there is a reality behind books about social psychology; it has given me an opportunity to be a more effective member of a group.
- A lot of good ideas which I shall want to try to adopt in my work at home.

Negative feelings after two weeks. Members were also asked to respond to this question "Not all of the feelings at this point in a lab are positive. What concerns, doubts, puzzlement, or negative feelings do you have at this point?" Sample responses are shown below.

- The pressure to change (directed) sometimes at the member, especially in the T-group.
- None, except being very tired.
- Too little time to study all the impressions, handouts, and so on.
- In a way I feel a bit undressed. I still have not got a new suit as an exchange for my old one, which was taken from me in the T-group. But I hope I will be able to make a new suit myself.
- Perhaps we were not really mature enough to plan the third week for ourselves, but on the other hand, I am excited to see how it will go.
- It is a very fine *experiment*, but I must have much more time to see the problems and their connection to my daily work.
- Still a little *en garde* not to be overrun or trapped.

Learnings after the lab. A similar question to that above was asked following the end of the follow-up period. Samples below.

- To speak less and think more, to listen.
- A number of teaching-learning devices. The purposity of being open to new things. Useful knowledge about other people's reaction to my behavior. How difficult intergroup cooperation is. And a lot of other things.
- That the application of the lab method is possible also in fields where I did not think it could be applied.
- To clarify. To take it easy. To see the situation. To consider feelings as real things.
- Much more about inductive learning. Something about problem-solving. Very much about what is going on in a group. That it isn't easy to rate or evaluate the results of educational methods.
- Better tools for the evaluating process. As a teacher: don't go hunting for 'the perfect human being'.
- The necessity of using lab methods outside the lab situation in order to test learning. If you are not able to do it, it implies that the use of lab methods is a sectarian amusement without relation to the life of human beings.
- How important sensitivity and imagination is for the success of the learning situation.

Perceived changes in own behavior after the lab. Members were asked in what ways they thought they were acting differently than before. Some samples are:

- More willing to be contented, although full consensus in the group can't be reached. It is a regretful fact that most of my faults still exist, but I hope that the way my attention has been directed to them may in time cause some desirable changes.
- Allow myself to show feelings (more participant – less an outside controlling onlooker). Trying to control my tendency to direct others.
- Less self-defense. Less hostility.
- It isn't possible for me to answer this question.
- I speak more directly, and I am not so afraid of giving and receiving critique and praise.
- I think that, to a small extent, I am now working a little more in the interest of the group and less in the interest of myself.
- Much more aware of which methods I have to use to produce a theory out of a specific situation (lectures don't always work well).

Changes in perceived behavior of others after the lab. An analagous question was asked ("Example of ways I have seen others act differently"). Samples follow.

- Some members have broadened their views, their range of tolerance; their flexibility seems to have grown considerably. With regard to other members, I have felt things going the opposite way. To some of them their new, not yet digested pedagogical knowledge seems to have become a rather dogmatic religion.
- More tendency to try to understand others.
- Better expressing themselves. More free towards each other.
- Shift in one person from ego-defending manipulation with other people to a rather non-defending work in the interest of the group.
- Some regard well-known methods as new. Some have become more tolerant. Some have become more intolerant. Some have come to fear analytic and effective procedures and group discussions. Some seem to have forgotten to compromise.
- Greater ability to clarify a problem. Greater ability to clarify feedback.
- It isn't possible for me to answer this question.
- Greater tendency to try to understand others.

Suggestions for design improvement. How should we do it differently next time? It was felt that the first three weeks should, substantially, be as before, except that rather more attention should be given to direct interpretation of events in the social system of the lab (for example, the hard work centering around the authority shift taking place at the time of the intergroup exercise, and the role of the steering committee). Theory sessions could also be helpful here.

The fourth week of the lab was most difficult, and perhaps most challenging, from the design point of view. How could the problems of 'greyness', lowered work level and regression be solved more effectively? The most obvious answer lies in avoiding unnecessary stress on the lab system (for example, having all trainers present the entire week rather than arriving at different times).

Secondly, it is possible that slightly more structure might be built into the design from the start (for example, indicating that daily theory sessions would be held, with the group itself responsible for content). Thus, the area of freedom for planning might be restricted somewhat, and more cognitive support supplied to aid system development.

A more extensive library might also be of help (although one participant commented that this might turn out to serve as a flight mechanism).

Finally, even more time than the substantial amount we used might have been devoted to skill practice in some depth (on matters such as consulting behavior, how to operate role playing, and the design of exercises and longer programmes). Where this time could come from, we are not sure.

Generally speaking, we feel that more attention should have been paid to the nature and problems of the consultant role, as the trainers exhibited it. This could have helped progress in the immediate situation, and supplied aid in clarifying the participants' role problems as consultants when they returned to their own jobs.

Nearly all of our improvement suggestions for the fourth week do, in fact, depend on clearer and more skillful definition of the trainer-consultant role in relation to the group. We erred in believing that our roles could be defined for the group with reasonable directness, and the struggles involved in shedding the T-group – trainer role and building a consulting role were substantial.

(One participant commented that an underlying problem may have been the unspoken fear of the trainers that participants would in fact 'take over' T-group trainer functions). At any rate, more conceptual clarity on our part about desired role shifts, prior to the fourth week, would have been desirable.

Concluding comment

Perhaps we have said enough to indicate our feeling that this design was an innovative and productive one. The possibility has occurred to us that some present lab practices may be unnecessarily limited by American cultural assumptions and values, as well as by the growing body of lab 'traditions'. At any rate we warmly commend to others the experience of similar collaboration.

References

Argyris, C. (1962). *Interpersonal Competence and Organizational Effectiveness*. Homewood, Illinois: Dorsey-Irwin.

Blansfield, M.G. (1962). Depth analysis of organizational life. *California Management Review, 2* (2), 29-42.

Buchanan, P.C. A strategy for organization development. *Social Science Research Reports, Vol. V*, Report no. 106. New York: Standard Oil Company (New Jersey).

Durham, L.E. & Gibb, J.R. (1969). *An Annotated Bibliography of Research*, National Training Laboratories, 1947-60. Washington: NTL.

Ferguson, C.K. (1959). Management development in 'unstructured' groups. *California Management Review, 1*, 66-72.

Foundation for Research on Human Behavior (1969). *An Action Research Program for Organizational Improvement*. Ann Arbor, Michigan: The Foundation.

Hoy, G.A. (1959). A brand-new breakthrough in management development. *Factory*, (July), 74-79.

Miles, M.B. (1962). Human relations training: Current status. In E.H. Schein & I.R. Weschler (eds.), *Issues in Human Relations Training*. Washington: National Training Laboratories, 3-13.

Stock, D. A summary of research on training groups. In L.P. Bradford & J.R. Gibb (eds.), *Theories of T-Group Training*. New York: Wiley.

Preamble for Chapter 12

In Chapter 12, Gunnar Hjelholt describes the ways in which he conducted group training and the results that were achieved when he worked with a tanker crew in the early
1960s. The difficulties were many. Still, the failures and the recurrent process analyses
helped the group to develop into a high-spirited team and to reach important consensus
decisions. One of the significant tools used was the allocation of a great deal of autonomy
and responsibility to the crew as a whole. At the end of the training period the captain
who had only one term left with the company before retirement declared: "It's the best
ship I ever had – and I mean the crew. It was a pleasure to sail this last year". Gunnar's
own conclusion goes like this: "Due to participative planning and the resulting changes
in the organizational system, this experiment with reduced crew size was a success. It
produced better-than-expected results, both in economic costs and in further innovation,
as well as in personal growth".

Chapter 12 is reproduced (with minor typing corrections) from *Working Paper no. 5*, 1968,
The University of Leeds, Department of Management Studies. The text was read at the
Third Informal Conference on Human Relations Training, held at Royaumont, France,
in December 1963 and was first issued as a Working Paper in April 1964. Small language
adjustments have been made by the publisher of the present book. The 1968-version
includes a supplement with data concerning crew training that is not included in the
present chapter; the conclusion may, however, be cited: "The four tankers that started
with the crews who had been working together and involved in the planning of the ship's
operation, differ clearly in a positive direction from the company's remaining ships".

The original editorial note introduces the 1968-paper as follows: "Gunnar Hjelholt's work
in Denmark has excited a great deal of interest among those concerned with T-group
training, both in Europe and in the United States. We are delighted that this should have
been the first Working Paper to be contributed by someone not working at Leeds. It is
a characteristic report of a highly skilled piece of consulting".

12 TRAINING FOR REALITY[*]

By Gunnar Hjelholt

This report describes the social context of the experiment, the training which took place, and the results which were achieved.

The social context

There was a critical economic-political situation in the Danish merchant fleet in 1962. Since 1957 the freight market had been low. The old organizational structure was still in existence; seven unions were involved in the manning of one ship; and automation of the technical machinery had not yet been used to any great extent. The owners complained that they were not able to compete in the international market with the high wages they had to pay, and they pointed out that other nations' ships were manned by fewer men. The Danish state has certain laws relating to the number of people required to man ships of different sizes and tonnage. The relationship between unions and shipowners was rather strained.

Many years ago (1956) a conflict between the Deckhands Union and the Engine Room Assistants' Union on one side, and the Ship Owners' Association on the other, resulted in a law suit where the unions were heavily fined, and it is an understatement to say that the unions and the owners were not on speaking terms. The ship owners put pressure on both Government and Unions to change the crew regulations because profits were low. As regards the political situation (1962), the Government was made up of Social Democrats and a minor party, and the Social Democrats obtained their major support from the unions.

Other forces in the social context were crew regulations in other European countries, and the experiments taking place at that time in Norway, where ship owners and unions had agreed to run experiments with ships organized and manned unconventionally. These experiments started in the spring of 1962.

---

[*] Written in 1964/68.

Also, at the same time, discussions concerning the manning of ships with less men were taking place in Sweden.

The company which started this experiment is one of the more progressive shipping companies of Denmark. It has for some time been interested in the training of employees, e.g. they have conducted training programmes for officers, which since the autumn of 1959 have been of the laboratory type based on T-groups. The company has also been concerned with the technical development and operation of its ships.

The company had ordered a new tanker for delivery in the autumn of 1962 with more automated equipment than in any previously built Danish ship. As the company competes on the international market it felt that it should attempt to have the new ship manned with fewer men than usual. A ship of that size in the Danish tanker fleet usually had sixty men on board, and they hoped to cut this by approximately one-third.

They therefore approached the Ministry with a plan, explaining that they had invested in the new equipment, and requested that the crew regulation rules should be waived for this ship. This was granted for one year. The number on board was fixed at 42 by the Ministry of Shipping and Commerce. In the dispensation it was agreed that the Ministry of Shipping and Commerce should have regular reports from the ship during the first year, and that these reports would be distributed to the interested parties, including the unions. The granted waiver was violently opposed by the Deckhands' Union, by the advisory representative board to the Minister, and by the press – including the trade union newsletter. It was also silently opposed by other shipowners, who said that the company, by investing in new equipment, had betrayed the other owners' viewpoint. (Owners had claimed that without any innovation it was possible for ships to be manned with fewer men than the regulations stipulated).

The 'actors'

The persons in charge of the vessel, the captain, the chief engineer, the chief mate and the first assistant engineer, had been participants in the company's training laboratories conducted by myself. The chief steward had also taken part in a supervisory training course.

The captain was one of the oldest captains of the company and had only one and a half years left before retirement. He felt frustrated in his life-job of sailing, and regarded experiments with people and machinery with scepticism. However, he was capable and highly intelligent. The chief engineer was eager to try new methods but was very status-conscious; he thought his position ought to be on the same level as the captain's. The two supervisors, the chief mate and the first assistant engineer, were rather authoritarian in personality structure and, efficient as they might be, they felt that this new ship, which only had one officers' mess and one mess for the hands, was rather too democratic. (Usually there are six to seven rooms on board the ships.) They agreed, however, to try the new procedures for one year. In my opinion the most co-operative of the officers was the chief steward, who suddenly realized that a great deal had been done technically to help his department in its work. He felt that his department, which was usually neglected and considered the lowest on the status ladder, had now been moved upwards. (Usually it is true to say that there is a constant fight going on between deck and engine room, and that engineering officers wish to obtain the same status as officers on deck).

Involved in this training were the two directors from the head office, the technicians who were responsible for the design of the ship, and the managing director, who dealt with external policy in relation to the owners' association, Government, and the union. Also involved were the heads of the departments for ships' officers and crews.

I was given a free hand in designing the training, but I also knew that the directors and department heads had it in mind that these sessions should be used, for the most part, to pass necessary information on to officers and hands, as well as to bring them together in a training type conference in order to help them to meet the expectations of the company. The directors believed that psychological help might be needed to get agreement on the reports, but that if officers and hands worked together this would help to make a success of the experiment.

The plan

The following rough plan was approved: a five-day conference at the end of September 1962, to be followed by the training of conference members in the technical aspects so that they would be in a better position to handle the new mechanical problems they would encounter. Finally, another conference would be held in the middle of November just before the ship was delivered from the shipyard. This second conference was to be held near the shipyard so we could visit the almost-completed ship.

The programme ran as planned, the first part taking place from the 25th to the 29th September. The participants were the captain, the chief mate, the chief engineer, the first assistant engineer, the chief steward, the cook and two hands from the engine room. Participants from the company office included one of the directors, the heads of the crew and deck-officer departments and two technical officers who had been in charge of the supervision of the building of the ship. At an evening session, one of the owners participated. It had been intended that the boatswain and the pump head (another deckhand) should take part, but on their arrival the Seaman's Union, who were trying to block the waiver, stopped these people from coming so they did not participate in the first conference.

This incident had to be brought before an Arbitrator, who ruled against the Union, and consequently the two men did attend the November conference. During the period between the two conferences some of the officers and the hands took part in practical training to handle new technical equipment, and some of the officers (the captain and the chief engineer) went to the shipyard where they followed the finishing of the ship.

I was in charge of the conference and had an assistant, a female psychologist (she had never before taken part in conferences of this type). The participants from the company's head office did not take part in all of the conference, e.g. in November they only took part in the last two of the five days.

The first conference was held in a conference house owned by the company, while the November conference took place at an inn near the shipyard.

The September conference

The aim, as stated by the company at the beginning, was to present information about the new ship and about new technical matters which officers and hands would have to manage. This was to be followed by a discussion of the problems which might arise, and in this way prepare for the difficulties the new system would bring. In his opening speech the technical director stated that it was also of value that the people involved became acquainted so that the ship could be – as he said – a 'happy ship'.

The pre-planned presentation of the new technical equipment and drawings of the ship took place and were discussed. I did not take the leadership until the following day when the group was alone.

When, as consultant in charge of the conference, I stated the aims as I saw them, I declared that we were going to work together and make decisions. The responsibility of the group was to make plans and take decisions which primarily fulfilled the needs of those on board. Naturally we had to take into consideration the fact that decisions made for this ship should not be contrary to the company's main policy, but primarily we should consider the ship's own needs and then we could have the company, represented by the department heads, come in and approve our decisions and help us make them work. I stated too that all decisions had to be unanimous. If this was not possible, it was up to the captain alone to make the decisions.

I emphasized that the head office departments were staff departments, and that they should not make decisions or put pressure on the group to make decisions that pleased head office; I would see that the department heads were effectively used. I also stressed that we should not make any final decisions at this conference because we did not have representatives from the ordinary deckhands with us and that it would be wise to have a month or so to think about the proposals coming up in September. At the next conference in November, the proposals could be assessed in a proper perspective, and the final decisions taken.

The group listed what they wanted to discuss and plan, and the planning sessions progressed. The planning concerned the cafeteria system and meals; regulations for the use of alcohol; the location of quarters on the ship; the use of the washroom; use of leisure time; the content of reports to the Ministry of Shipping and Commerce and how it should be produced; the introduction of a safety committee; and maintenance of the ship.

At the start of the conference everybody felt anxious, most especially the new members of the engine room who felt uneasy; hardly anyone spoke to them and the officers' remarks were derogatory. On the second day the two engine crew members came to me and said that they were leaving. During the analysis of group processes which was introduced by me, their feelings were discussed and it was decided that they should telephone their Union Head. This resulted in a letter from the Union Head to the members asking them to stay on, but later in the conference they nearly packed their bags again. Until the fourth day the group was alone and worked with the problems.

It was difficult in the large group to handle much planning, so small sub-groups were formed and reported back in plenary sessions. The captain attached himself to the 'deck-group' as the natural thing to do. The impression based on his remarks was that he felt himself to be the head of the deck.

One session handled problems about alcohol. Next, they started with a rough plan for the division of labour between deck, engine room and catering. The deck and engine room groups had difficulties and took refuge in such statements as "We already know all about ..." or "It must be the same as we are used to".

The catering group which consisted only of the cook and the chief steward made some sort of division of labour, but as the plan was discussed in the plenary session and I started to ask questions, almost every sort of plan was torn up. They had not taken the number of people into account, had no estimate of the work load, and so on.

The process analysis was based on questionnaires and some aggression was evident, as well as remarks like: "We are unsure how far to venture into the unknown".

The large group was conducted or chaired by me as consultant, and it was chaired rather firmly. On the fourth day, when the 'fight/flight' atmosphere changed, the whole group finished work on two major plans in the morning. These were, how the report to the Ministry should be produced and what it was to contain. The group succeeded in reaching a consensus in this area. When these decisions had been reached the group, by itself, started working on process analysis and the original behaviour changed. The captain served coffee for the engine hands.

In the afternoon one of the two owners of the company arrived, together with department heads from the office. The owner contributed, not by giving orders, but by asking a few sensible questions. However, the pressure on the group from the department heads was such that the group felt like schoolboys. The captain did not participate. It was a very difficult meeting and it continued in the evening. A very firm hand was needed to conduct it. I had to regulate, support and take a lot of needed leadership roles.

On the last day my assistant tried to summarize some of the preliminary planning that had been done, and a decision was reached to go over these plans at the next conference and take up some other subjects. Suddenly the group decided to tackle the question "How can we feel responsible?" A previously dormant question was now on paper.

The conference was evaluated by the group members. They said that the information given had been valuable and they were pleased that they had been able to handle the report and make a preliminary decision regarding the handling of alcohol. The meeting had given them more respect for the work done by other departments. In the questionnaires it was answered that there was great value in participating with other people. However, the deckhands, by their absence, had hampered their decision-making. One participant stated: "If we are able to transfer the positive climate we have created at this conference to the ship, handling of the ship will be very much easier." There were fears though that the rest of the crew might create difficulties, and effectively destroy all the efforts that had gone into the experiment.

My assistant (not being involved in this experiment) had made her own evaluation. It was her impression, she said, that the engine room assistants were the two most positive in their attitude to the rationalization of the ship. The chief mate and the first assistant engineer, she felt, were trying to prove that the number of crew had been reduced too drastically and also that both the captain and the chief engineer would silently support this viewpoint. The two engine room assistants were accepted by the other group members. The failure of the group at first proved to be a helping factor in the betterment of the training later on. However, the captain's attitude of not being involved in any of the problems made this difficult. She concluded: "It will be very difficult to get the captain to take any standpoint at all as he does not seem to be interested in shipping".

Summarizing this first conference: as consultant, I went further than anybody had intended. The authority which I had was such that the statement about unanimous decisions, planning for the whole crew, and the use of office heads only as resource-persons with very little influence, was accepted. The uneasiness was rather natural and the difficulties starting the planning were many. It was the failures and the process analysis which helped the group, kept it together, and produced results. The firm running of plenary sessions helped in reaching two consensus decisions: 1) about liquor and 2) the report to the Ministry – which established the ground work for a second and final conference.

The November conference

The November conference near the shipyard had three additional participants: two deckhands and the wireless officer. This conference was conducted in a different way. It was felt that more help should be given to the officers who would have to conduct meetings on board and that they should be helped to stand on their own feet. Therefore it was proposed in the first meeting that the plenary sessions should be chaired by the different heads of the ship's departments. The start was rather reluctant. At first the group reviewed what had been done at the first conference and went through prepared summaries. On the first day nothing really happened, no decisions were made, and the group drifted from one subject to another; once in a while I asked: "Well, how are things going"? Two or three of the officers retorted that they really hadn't time to sit there, they ought to be on board the ship supervising the installation of the equipment.

The morale of the group on the first and second days was pretty low. It was clear to everybody that no progress was being made, and that the group was not being punished. They just had to face the fact that their own behaviour might have consequences when they started on board the ship. On the second evening of the conference the officers started drinking whisky and an hour later the hands started drinking beer. Next morning the group verbally attacked the chairman of the previous day, the chief engineer. Then they attacked me: "Why had I not helped the group and steered the thing?" My comment was "Who is responsible for this ship?" (It must be said that the pressure was rather hard during the first two days. My assistant had difficulties sleeping, got angry with me for not helping the group and took refuge in the officers' group).

The chief steward, the lowest in status of the officers conducted the meeting and did so in a quite unexpected way. Till then he had spoken in a low voice, withdrew when opposition occurred, and seemed afraid of conflicts. But as chairman he was humorous, firm, allowed feelings to be expressed, listened to the deckhands, drew them into the process analysis, and directed the pattern for the later part of the conference. In the evening of the third day the head-office staff came and received their share of aggression. They tried to defend themselves and it was openly discussed.

During the last two days of the conference the group produced good results. Weekly planning meetings on board in each department, with participation of hands and officers, were proposed.

The last day's plenary meeting was chaired by the captain. Thirteen decisions were reached, and in conclusion the captain said that the only regret he had was that not all 42 crew members had been participants and were sitting around the table.

The second phase of the training had been different from the first phase, in that an expectation of decision-making by consensus had been established.

Now the sole responsibility had been put on the group and they had been obliged to chair the decision-making plenary meetings. They even took the initiative in starting process analysis. The function of secretary had been taken at the first meeting by my assistant, but rested now with the wireless officer.

The shift of responsibility was difficult but had been carried out and the captain had taken over his new role as 'Managing Director' of an enterprise with three departments.

Among the decisions made, two were rather radical and went further than anybody had imagined at the start:

1. Weekly planning meetings in each department on board where all sorts of problems could be brought up and where main crew members and officers were equally represented. Decisions taken and subjects discussed at these meetings should be communicated to all on board.

2. The decision taken in regard to the regular reports to the Ministry of Shipping and Commerce. It was decided that each department should produce its own report and have it accepted by all members of that department, and that the captain's main report should be discussed in a final meeting of representatives after having been circulated on board. (The waiver condition was that only regular reports from the ship, i.e. the captain, should be sent to the Ministry).

The main theme of these decisions had been founded with the decision concerning alcohol, where it was decided that no hard spirits should be permitted on board, but that everybody over 18 years, regardless of rank, should be entitled to three bottles of beer a day.

The evaluation of the training was positive and I felt a great step forward had been taken. My main concern at this stage was: will the decisions be carried out in reality and as intended?

The critical year

Due to delays and faults at the shipyard the new tanker first started on its maiden voyage on December 18th, 1962. It has now completed the test year, and four reports have been submitted to the Ministry. A proposal for new crew-regulations will be submitted to Parliament by the Minister next year. The company has ordered two further new tankers from Japan to be delivered in March and October, 1964. The new tankers will be equipped with more automated machinery than the first ship so the crews will be gathered before the start for a conference of approximately 10 days duration – with the object of training them in cooperation and planning for the running of the ships.

The tanker has shown less overtime (30% less) than any of the other three tankers owned by the company – and these tankers are manned in accordance with ordinary regulations. There has only been one disciplinary case all year, less than in any other ship in the whole fleet of approximately 40 ships. A detailed inspection at the beginning of December showed perfect maintenance of engine and deck. The results seem to be spectacular; so good that one gets suspicious. Is this due to 'training' and 'more industrial democracy' or have other influences come into existence?

On a trip from Japan to the Persian Gulf from the end of January 1963 to the middle of February, I followed the daily work on board the ship. As an observer I took part in the meetings in the departments, including one big meeting with the representatives and the captain when the first report to the Minister was discussed. During this trip I talked and interviewed every man on board and inspected, but tried not to interfere with, any decisions. Nevertheless I think this visit was of major importance for the carrying out of the decisions taken earlier and resulted in some new actions being taken on board.

My presence provided the opportunity for grievances to be brought into the open and handled in a constructive way, e.g. the catering department had complaints about the washing room and the dishwashing system, complaints which might have been minimized but now resulted in changes. Complaints in all departments resulted in changes, job-enlargements etc. – and most important of all, the group in the middle – second and third mate and second and third assistant engineer – were brought into the participating team. They complained about the new mess arrangement where they had to eat with the captain and apprentices, and about the democratic arrangements whereby the hands had a say in the planning of the work. By getting this out in the open it was possible to alter the representation on the planning committees. (*Catering*: chief steward, cook and one messman; *Engine room*: chief engineer, lst assistant engineer and two engine hands; *Deck*: chief mate, second or third mate, boatswain and one deck hand.) 'Middle management' took part and this resulted in their taking more responsibility. The third mate started giving lessons in arithmetic to the hands in their leisure time.

My visit reinforced both the tackling of problems on board and the pioneering spirit which produced new technical innovations, job enlargements and breaking down of barriers between departments. (One of the deckhands calls the first assistant engineer 'My boss'). This process continued for almost the whole period. The planning meetings in the departments resulted not only in less supervision of daily work but also in the fulfilment of the goals set in the planning meetings. The increase in the value of the goals was obvious. In one instance a conflict between chief mate and hands regarding the proper number of men used for tank-cleaning arose. An experiment was agreed upon and it showed that the men had calculated better than the mate. Their calculation was followed and this helped considerably. Everyone knew after this test that the planning done had been fair. Overtime was a delicate point. Due to the planning, overtime-pay decreased. As far as officers and men are concerned overtime is a big part of the payroll and on tankers people usually sign on to get overtime. Here it dropped. More work was done and pay was less. The company was not allowed to give any extra pay, as it was a member of the Ship Owners' Association, and the grumble on board was usually directed at the Association. A complaint was written and sent to the unions, but a copy of the complaint was given to the chief mate and the captain, which is a most uncommon procedure.

Outside influences

As the Deckhands' Union had failed to influence the Minister's decision about the waiver and had lost their case before the arbitrator, they tried to sabotage the recruitment of people for this ship and saw to it that the company did not get first-rate men on deck. (One of the decisions of the November Conference was that the crew's department should take great care in selecting first-rate men. In January one union official privately said to me: "Well, we have made sure that this trial is not going to succeed with that bunch of people on board".) When I came on board a few weeks later the officer said: "Well, the main reason it's working is naturally that we got first-rate men". They thought that the decision had been carried out and had behaved in this conviction; and the men had lived up to their expectations.

When the first report was sent to the Minister and was distributed to the Union heads, a meeting was held and the parties involved discussed the report. Some of the officials could not believe their own eyes or the report. Two of the Union heads wrote to their members on board implying in their letters that they were not satisfied with reports of this kind. Pressure was put on the hands to make unfavourable reports. The group cohesiveness on board, however, had already been built so strongly that this pressure did not have the desired effect at all. The reports were so factual (work done, hours used, etc.) that no great change occurred in later reports.

Closer contact between the unions and the shipping company has resulted in a training programme for machine hands so that they could take on some of the jobs previously done by the engine assistants. To some extent distrust seems to have given way to more co-operative problem solving between this company and the unions but, for the company, it has resulted in difficulties with other ship owners.

Changes in 'actors'

In December 1963, the captain, who was on leave and had only one term left with the company before retirement said "It's the best ship I ever had – and I mean the crew. It was a pleasure to sail this last year".

Four of the officers (chief mate, first assistant engineer, chief steward, wireless officer) have asked to join the next new ship which will be even more automated with a further reduction in crew size. "We would like to have a go at it and show that it can be done", they say.

The cook has been appointed chief steward on the ship and some hands have gone ashore to start an education at the deck officers' school.

Conclusion

Due to participative planning and the resulting changes in the organizational system, this experiment with reduced crew size was a success. It produced better-than-expected results, both in economic costs and in further innovation, as well as in personal growth.

Preamble for Chapter 13

Many of the preceding texts have referred to Gunnar Hjelholt's innovation, the mini-society. In Chapter 13, this unusual design is presented by the inventor himself. When compared to the ordinary laboratories five differences are worth mentioning: there was greater variation in the background of participants; participants decided how much they would pay; groups were homogeneously composed; explorations were mainly kept on an inter-group level; and a great many decisions were left to the participants rather than the staff.

The chapter summarizes the experiences from the first three mini-societies held 1968-70 in Sweden in an old isolated manor house with surrounding cottages. Gunnar documents the experiments and gives special attention to the way the emerging groups were composed and changed and how they identified and named themselves. Age and generation is another theme; he reflects on the situation of young people and observes a peculiar tendency for 'generation robbery' on the part of the middle-aged middle-class participants. One of the important features of a mini-society is the research function. The staff is responsible for collecting and analysing data and feeding them back to members of the temporary society. Gunnar notes that focusing on research has the potential of minimizing the fantasies people have about other social groups. The roles and role conflicts of the staff are touched upon, particularly Gunnar's own role as a boundary keeper.

On the last page of Gunnar's own copy of the original publication he has marked a deletion of the following sentence: "I made the unfortunate mistake of allowing myself this 'middle man' role when I should have left it for the community to solve". We do not know why, so we have chosen to maintain the sentence.

The article was originally published in *Interpersonal Development*, 1973 (3), 140-151. In a footnote that is not reproduced in the present version, Gunnar thanks Gurth Higgin from the Tavistock Institute for Human Relations for his advice and assistance in preparation of the article. In 1990 the two friends published a joint article: Higgin, G. & Hjelholt, G. (1990), Action research in mini-societies, in Trist, E. & Murray, H. (eds.), *The Social Engagement of the Social Science*, vol. I, 246-258. London: Free Association Books.

13 GROUP TRAINING IN UNDERSTANDING SOCIETY

The Mini-Society*

By Gunnar Hjelholt

In 1968 I started an experiment which I called the mini-society and which continued into 1969 and 1970. The experiment grew out of my work with sensitivity training, but I suppose for myself it was chiefly an attempt to find a better understanding of the psychological and sociological motivating forces that lie beneath the problems of our present life in society.

In the following I will try to describe briefly the distinctive features of this laboratory experiment, the mini-societies of each year, and sum up some of the impressions I have culled from these very engaging and chaotic experiments.

Each mini-society lasted 12 days. During this time, the 40-60 participants lived together on a peninsula in a large lake in southern Sweden. Surrounded by the lake and the Swedish forests, they were rather isolated and could be active in shaping their two-week stay. An old manor-house with two residential wings and five or six smaller houses nearby, along with an old barn as a meeting place, comprised our territory. The houses were at various distances from the main building with the furthest a full kilometer away in the forest.

The participants were chosen from the information given on their enrolment applications or they were recruited from interested organizations, for example, trade unions. On the application form, there was information about sex, age, employment, income, educational background, motivation for wanting to participate, together with how much the applicant would like to pay for participating. In addition, there was a declaration that 'research' was to be carried out during the laboratory.

An attempt was made to select participants so as to ensure a representative sample of society at large, particularly in terms of socio-economic status, age,

---

*   Written in 1972

and sex. In addition, I worked on the principle that for each group there should be other 'relevant' groups present in the temporary society. In table I, you can see the membership of the groups for each of the three different years.

Upon arrival at the laboratory, the participants were assigned to homogeneous groups on the basis of their age, sex, and socio-economic status. Initially, the groups were located geographically so that we had an urban area, a middle-class area and some poorer districts. Each group had in a way its own territory, and then there were common areas such as the barn and the main building where amusements, a sauna, billiards, etc., were to be found. For the first 2½ to 3½ days there was an orientation programme. First, the participants were encouraged to get to know their own group. Second, to explore the whole society with all the different groups. And lastly, to participate in community meetings and research meetings to be held in the barn.

There was no programme for the remaining time, as it was announced that after the first few days the participants had to lay their own framework and decide what was to happen. After the first few days, people could also move from one group or house to another. In this way, they had a basis for knowing where they felt that they belonged.

Although there was a staff – composed of my colleagues and co-workers – they were to participate as everyone else in the mini-society, facilitating in any way they felt was meaningful.

This laboratory had many similarities to the usual classical sensitivity training or human-relations laboratories. It was held at (1) an isolated place (a cultural island); (2) it was limited in time; (3) there was a staff; (4) the participants were divided into groups by the staff in advance; (5) it cost money to participate; and (6) it was expected that people could experiment with actions, explore relationships, and to a great extent the individual was dependent on himself for what he got out of the experience.

It differed from usual laboratories because there was (1) a greater variation in the backgrounds of the participating groups, both with regard to age and social status; (2) the participants themselves had decided how much they would pay (varying from 200 to 2,800 Danish crowns); (3) the groups were homogeneously composed and not as mixed as possible; and (4) the exploration essentially dealt with the relationship of an individual group to other groups. In addition, a great many decisions which are usually decided by the staff were left up to the participants.

The 1968 Experience

The first mini-society was launched from the 4th to the 15th June, 1968. In the advance notice, the word 'society' was emphasized. It read:

> In the beginning of this two-week laboratory each participant is placed in one of five groups in the society. Here we shall try to create a small society which partially reflects the outer world with its groupings and problems. We will have opportunities to learn about ourselves in our group and our relationships with other groups, since this is our purpose. With others, our group and the whole system, we shall explore the boundaries and distances in our society. Our exploration need not exist solely to collect knowledge about things, but here we have the conditions and a chance to affect the system and to change it.

There were five groups. The first group was composed of five male and five female students from the same teacher's training college. Then there was a teacher group of four men and three women, who came from the University of Copenhagen, where they had been very active in the recent student demonstrations. From their composition, these two groups could be characterized as closed groups. The next two groups were more loosely put together and more closely resembled neighbourhood groupings in the outer society. The participants did not know each other beforehand, age varied somewhat, and there was a large status differential. One of these groups had in common that they had completed enough schooling to qualify for university admission; there was a touch of internationalism with two Dutch and two Americans participating, and they all held professional jobs (teachers, psychologists, etc.). The second group was a bit older, and there was a strong element of trade unionism in the form of active shop stewards. Economically, they were certainly as well off as the others, but because of their age and education, they had no great ambitions for rising social status.

The fifth group, the staff group, consisted of eight people divided in two age groups: psychologists/psychiatrists who served as helpers, and two younger people, a secretary and a research assistant.

After each group established themselves in their respective houses, everyone gathered for the first community meeting with an introduction, which corresponded to a brief run-down on the purposes of the society (at the same time, they were given a loose schedule for the first three days). On the programme, time was set aside for 'home groups', so they had some undisturbed time for exploration (where they could visit each other) and for community meetings where research and presentation of the results could take place. The first activity of the groups was for each group to choose a name, which it would be known by, and which characterized the group. The professional neighbourhood group called themselves *Babel*, the second neighbourhood group *1968*, the young students *4th June*, and the teacher training college students *Theodorians* after the name of the founder of their college. The staff group chose the name *Wanderers* in order to suggest that they would be moving around.

Since there was a bit of a framework, the first days were orderly and had in fact the character of a somewhat structured sensitivity-training laboratory, where the older *Wanderers* had the role of consultants for the four groups. But when 'moving day' came and the whole society had to make up their minds as to how they should use their time and capital, the drama really began.

The *Wanderers* split up into a *Consultation Centre* and *Lonesome Wanderers*. The *Theodorians* announced that they had changed their name to *No Name* and moved out on a little island from which the others had to retrieve them. The *4th June* who had stayed abreast of the times, had changed their name with each changing day, i.e. *5th June*, *6th June*, etc. This group was very active at the community meetings and lived up to its calling as 'revolutionaries'. They sought contact with *1968*, but without getting any particularly warm reception. As in the story, *Babel* disintegrated. There was no chance for growth and development here.

A document from *1968*, which they wanted the others to respond to at a community meeting, reflects the problems people were working with and, at the same time, it indicates the group used as a support in the society:

(1) What characterizes this society?
(2) How can this society be integrated?
(3) What are the groups' attitudes toward the 'mini-society' at various stages in the development?
(4) How can we put groups together according to individuals' desires and needs?
(5) How can we co-operate across the existing groups?
(6) Is it possible for group *1968* to solve a concrete problem together with the group *4th June*?
(7) How do you establish a leadership which assures that development possibilities are not frustrated?
(8) How do we find a problem we would like to solve?
(9) Do the groups here want to have anything to do with each other?
(10) Can we form new home groups?

One theme that cropped up again and again was the question of responsibility for concrete events. At a community meeting, I reported that damage had been done to furniture and fixtures and asked for guidelines as to how this should be paid. Some groups expressed surprise, others almost anger, that I had not obtained insurance so they could experiment 'without consequences'. *1968* was the group that handled the practical problems most straightforwardly and also suggested the solution that settled the problem of damages: equal joint liability. But this meant that the poorest ended up paying for what the middle class had destroyed.

After this first summer, there was a general impression that the geographical layout of groups was good. The distances between them, which encouraged them to make contact, made it possible for us to bring central problems of the society to the surface. At the same time, I had a feeling that just as individuals act on unconscious levels, our behaviour here reflected unconscious social desires and anxieties. Within the staff group, the development of the society was characterized as a change from an 'incendiary' to a 'building' attitude. After initially encouraging the exploration of differences and confrontation between groups, the staff tried to help them find a common ground for cooperation.

The 1969 Experience

The main recruiting in 1969 aimed at getting younger people with other than academic tendencies. We were looking for those who were getting a practical education or had dropped out of the educational system. The other groups were collected around this basic group. Characteristically enough, the ten young people took the name of *X*, and they kept this name throughout their entire life in the mini-society. The mixed middle-class group was also younger than the year before (See Table I). There was a difference of almost ten years and here we had our first married couple. This group was called *Duodenum*. The academic, internationally arrayed group had the same age distribution as the year before. They called themselves *Will*, which certainly sounded more promising than *Babel*. There was an institution group of six people from Denmark's Radio. At the beginning, they called themselves *Krrerr*, after the static sound on radio, but later changed to the *Beagle Band*, characters well known to readers of Donald Duck.[1] Wiser through bitter experience, the professional staff was reduced to five people who, at the beginning, called themselves the *Vikings*, which later became the *Reluctant Vikings*.

---

1   A group of cartoon Beagle dogs who lived in a prison-like room and who from time to time went marauding into the community, to eventually return to the safety of their secluded room.

The launching of this second mini-society was shorter and less reminiscent of sensitivity training, as the *Vikings* themselves tried to avoid the role of trainers. But this was not so easy, since from time to time they sought refuge in it.

If 1968 had been characterized by problems having to do with (1) the building of a society, (2) the contact between students, teachers, and workers, and (3) the young teachers' insecurity in their profession, 1969 was characterized by 'letting go'. It included 'happenings', a strange marriage and divorce ceremony, an exhibition of the absurd, and many inter-group social events. At the same time, the groups were more flexible. Two persons left *Duodenum*, one of whom sought admission to the *Beagle Boys*. X went out into the woods and began to build a hut which they intended to move into, but it remained incomplete at the end of the experience. A work group was formed across the groups to serve the useful function of repairing things that were destroyed, and immediately another group was formed to destroy things so the first would have something to do. In the last part of life in the society, a sort of bureaucratic group was formed. It registered people and published a newspaper. An attempt to put a little order into a chaotic, normless society.

TABLE I. MINI-SOCIETY PARTICIPANTS OVER THREE YEARS

1968			1969			1970		
Participants	Mean age	N	Participants	Mean age	N	Participants	Mean age	N
Activist students	23	7	Elementary education	19	10	Drug addicts	19	8
Teacher students	25	10				American students	19	9
Neighbourhood group, lower middle class	40	11	neighbourhood group	31	12	neighbourhood group	25	7
			neighbourhood group	32	9	neighbourhood group	41	9
Neighbourhood group, academic background	31	10	Neighbourhood group			neighbourhood group	41	10
			institution group	33	6			
Staff group	35	8	Staff group	41	5	Staff group	43	6
Others, wife and children		4				children's group	8	7
Whole population	50			42			56	

There was great insecurity and dependence on authority throughout the whole experience as a counterpart to the 'letting-go' happenings. The night before the society was supposed to take over full responsibility (after the first loosely structured period), a feeling of impending disaster was prevalent. The groups sat in their respective houses almost all night, without making any contact with the outside. The next morning when the community came together, the fear of the unstructured future had dissipated. The ambivalence of desire for freedom and resentment toward authority for not providing structure resulted in a spontaneous circle dance through the main building and out onto the lawn with loud cries, a choir of voices shouting at me: Ho-Ho-Ho Chi Minh.

The basic theme throughout this experience seemed to be 'generation robbery'. The older members and groups in the society were attempting to relive their adolescence and youth while challenging the younger ones to try and keep pace. For instance, *Will* (the professional group) tried to get *X* (non-academic youth) to dance with them during a session of pop music and to get them to be less inhibited in their bodily movements. This group was also destructive with property in a way they would never have been at home. Even within the staff group, this theme was evident as the *Vikings* split with the two young members who withdrew into their own group contacts and established some links with *X*. The 'generation gap' was most dramatically symbolized in the mixed young and old group, *Duodenum*. They united their two age factions symbolically by a 'happening' marriage ceremony conducted in full view of the community between their oldest and youngest members. It included an elaborate caricature of the role of ecclesiastical authority.

The middle-aged middle class, without the normative restrictions of conventional society, were intoxicated by the chance to get out of a straightjacket, to give expression to their feelings by taking over the standards of the young. The young people were suddenly robbed of their distinctiveness, their youth. They were at a complete loss because now they had nothing for themselves. They said they felt numb and empty. In the middle of the second week, they renewed their stock of pop records – those they brought with them having become common property. And in the middle of the intoxication was insecurity, a general feeling of anxiety: "Have we gone too far? Who's going to take care of us?" At a community meeting, one of the young people called on me to take the lead. "We need someone who will say: everyone goes to bed this evening at ten. We would obey."

The 1970 Experience

From the 23rd August to the 4th September, the last experiment on this model took place. As in 1969, the selection placed emphasis on the young. There was a group of children that put their initials together and called themselves *Anpekedochmeka*; a group from the Copenhagen Youth Clinic who were being cured of taking drugs that took the name *Hallucinations*. With the same average age we had a group from America consisting of poor black-white students who were sent by their university but who had worked to pay for the journey. They called themselves *Dilemma*. There were three neighbourhood groups: *The Green Rags* and *Tatters* and *The Radishes* (both non-professional) and the professional group, who at first called themselves *Association*, later *Establishment*. Under the influence of the children, the staff took the Greek-sounding name *Hyheph*. At the end of a week, a number of break-away individuals (from the *Radishes*) formed a family group called the *Pearl Divers*, while *Anpekedochmeka* was swallowed up by *Rags and Tatters*. One person left *Rags* and joined the *Establishment*.

In earlier years, the participants, after having paid admission according to their circumstances, were not required to concern themselves with the society's finance. This was dealt with by the staff group. However, in the previous year, the groups had made comments about wanting 'a real problem' to work with, and at the same time discussions about money, damages, and their attitudes toward these topics brought feelings out into the open which indicated real differences in conceptions about the structure of society. When money had been mentioned, I had an impression that there were stronger feelings of taboo here than about sex. In 1970, one group, the American students, paid the maximum amount (through their institution) and so did most of the members of the *Establishment*. There was a possibility that income and expenses might be able to balance. The manor-house declared itself willing to suffice with 26 full-paying participants.

So, after the first introductory days, I introduced the budget at a community meeting and asked for guidelines as to how the money should be used. Twenty-six could eat at the manor-house. Which? And the others had to keep house for themselves. How much money should they have? After that, it was my task to manage the money and payout by authorization from the community meeting. The groups' attitudes toward each other and what they considered each group deserved was expressed in concrete figures. Applications for allotments were addressed to the community meeting; among other things, the question of who was or should be privileged was raised. Were the privileged those who ate in the main building at set times, or were they the ones who could decide for themselves when and what they would eat? Pressure was applied to groups. The *Establishment* (professional group), who had their meals prepared and had their beds made, were forced out to the most distant house in the woods where they had to prepare their own food. Later they insisted that this house had to be the main building.

The *Pearl Divers* (family group) and the *Hallucinations* (young, cured drug-takers) made it through the upheavals in the society and developed as distinct groups. The *Pearl Divers* stuck together at the community meetings and gradually assumed a great deal of influence on decisions, while the *Hallucinations* lived their own life-style in their house, where the door was always open. Only toward the end of the mini-society did they attempt to make contact with the community.

The polarization between the two cultures, the *Establishment*, with their 'social' parties and alcohol culture, and the *Hallucinations*, with their hippy, drug culture, and spontaneous and uninhibited behaviour, left their mark on the other groups. The other groups were tugged first in one direction and then in the other. *Dilemma* (poor, black-white American university students), who came from a socio-economic and age group resembling the *Hallucinations*, but by virtue of their presence at university were about to enter the culture of the *Establishment*, felt the tensions so strongly that they found it difficult to move between groups. The *Green Rags and Tatters* (neighbourhood group) were almost torn apart by the fight, which never blossomed out as a confrontation between the two poles. The *Establishment* considered the *Hyheph* (staff group) who, at the beginning declined the usual staff leadership role, as traitors to the established culture. It was only the daily pursuits and the common economic problems that kept the society functioning.

The different groups in the various mini-society experiences

How did the institutional and professional groups fare? Are there any conclusions that can be drawn?

The *Theodorians*, studying to be teachers, were both an institutional and a professional group. This group tried to isolate itself, to retreat, and it was the society that said to them: "We don't trust you and won't send our children to your schools if you persist in isolating yourself from us." The institution was powerfully confronted with its mission in the outside world. The older *Beagle Band* (Denmark's Radio), who were an institution with a professional background, had defined their role through their choice of name.

Dilemma (poor, black-white American students) was also a closed group on account of its culture and its common university. Here the pressure was strengthened by culture shock, and even if the other groups did not have difficulties with them, they were aware of their cultural isolation. This was reflected in the fact that they never wandered too far away from their house, certainly not far away from 'ear-shot' of their pop music!

The next closed group was the staff group, which had a personal and professional role in common. In 1968, the *Wanderers* split into *Lonely Wanderers* and *Consultation Centre*; that is, the professionals isolated themselves from those who were not professionals and closed in around their profession – which they felt they had to emphasize. In 1969, the *Vikings* became the *Reluctant Vikings*, and the 1970s *Hyheph* hid behind a seemingly Greek word which they never explained.

The neighbourhood groups? What were the various forms of association and attraction toward each other?

It was felt that the more or less decent middle class (dentists, teachers, doctors, etc.) brought up in an academic tradition as individual decision-makers. could meet and form some kind of common work effort (these were *Babel*, *Will*, and *Establishment*). With age it became more obvious that they drew together around the things they had in common: their good jobs; their intellectual culture so they could discuss books, films, and wines; and their role as guardians of the 'system'.

The lower middle-class groups, which were not comprised of professionals (*1968, Duodenum* and *Radishes*), did not live so visibly in the society. The stronger the labour representation in the groups, the more it grew into the backbone of the society and raised the practical questions for solution at the community meetings. In addition, they demonstrated a surprising tolerance for the less conventional groups.

One middle-class group, *The Green Rags and Tatters*, however, had a hard time. Whether it was the individual member's loneliness – and their desperate attempts to get away from this – that did it, I cannot say now. They moved most restlessly about in the society. They drove cars in spite of a distance of only one kilometre, had the children on the roof of the car, and paid frequent visits to other groups in the community. As the community meeting had decided that children should have the same amount of money as the adults, the group hurriedly adopted as many children as possible, but then ignored them.

Investigations of families have played a small part in this society experiment. The first year, we had a family with a baby and a mother with a daughter, but they belonged to the staff group. In the second society, there was a married couple in one of the neighbourhood groups. The wife broke out of the group and applied to another group, while the husband wandered about bewildered, until he later applied for a good solid job in the administration group. In 1970, there were more children and families, both broken and intact. One family formed its own group, the *Pearl Divers*, and tried to collect other children around them. A rebellious daughter joined another group, however.

The children were pretty much left up to themselves, and even though many talked about them, as we do in this 'children's century', all the groups forgot them when it was time to make a decision. The children had to draw the other's attention to their existence from time to time. It has been mentioned that *Rags and Tatters* used the children to gain economic advantages, but otherwise they let the children look after themselves. One group, *Dilemma*, arranged a children's party. The children seemed to thrive in spite of the grown-ups. They could move from one place to another and here they had a much greater chance to be a part of everything that happened; they were not restricted to just one part of existence. Is it the children who get the most out of collectives and compound families, while the pressure is greatest among the adults? On successive investigations of the effects of the mini-society, there is much evidence that family situations are altered in this respect, that the children take a more active part in the upbringing of their parents.

Special interest has been dedicated to youth. How does a young person fare in society, what has an influence on him/her, what becomes of him/her?

The *4th June*, the closed action group with school-leaving certificates, dissatisfied with the state of things held their own through crises and resistance. They guarded their standards and their norms jealously, while others, both the *Theodorians* of the same age and the older members of *Babel*, tried their hands at being emancipated. It did not go as well, however, for the younger people in *X*, who had no common goal or any education. They tried to influence the society, but were simply knocked down by the overwhelming interest and takeover of their life style by *Will* and the *Beagle Band*. Depressed, they closed themselves in, sought other groups, or went to pieces.

With age, *X* might become *Green Rags and Tatters*; or they could pull out of society and live with their own culture, isolated in a semi-fantasy world as did the *Hallucinations*; or the *Establishment* could patronizingly help them to come in and take up establishment standards; or else they could become the slightly rootless, artistic candidates for the middle class.

Conclusions

Reflecting on the outcomes of the experiment in group training for understanding the social roles and forces in society, a number of points come to mind with respect to the role of the staff and my own role. Although the staff group participated on an equal basis with the rest of the participants – they did not get any form of compensation and they involved themselves in the research activities of the society – they found themselves in dual-membership roles. On the one hand, they were to gather information and impressions from the groups in the society and to help and facilitate development and, on the other hand, they were encouraged to participate in those activities that they felt met their own needs as individuals. It is extremely difficult to do both of these things simultaneously; one can either become involved and absorbed in an ongoing group or one can cling to observations and impressions and the protection of the trainer role. This was particularly noticeable with the staff and the professional groups; the staff identified with the groups of professionals and yet they tried to dissociate themselves from the professional role.

I had the role of 'boundary keeper' taking care of the relationships between the participants and the cleaning staff, and coping with the issues involving the outside world. The battle to test the limits of the community and the outside was fought symbolically 'on me'. I made the unfortunate mistake of allowing myself this 'middle man' role when I should have left it to the community to solve. In addition, I had the role of initiator of research and feeding back the results to the community. In this way, I intervened in the life of the society and forced the groups to examine certain issues and behaviour.

It may be that these two roles, boundary keeper and active research intervener are necessary and have to be personified. The lack of clearly defined boundaries seemed to allow freedom within the society, and hence exploration and movement. The research focus, in addition, provided the participants with a means of discovering 'where they are at' inside the community, which minimized the fantasies people have about other social groups.

This last discovery has the greatest effect on individuals participating in the mini-societies, together with a heightened disinclination to accept social role patterns as being stable. Social actions are reported by participants and they have to cope with attempts at changing institutions, as well as shift in work roles.

As far as I am concerned, the special problem of the role of youth in our society has led me to clarify my own thinking, as I discovered in the mini-society how complex these problems are. My belief is that the mini-society reflects developments in society that we do not ordinarily see because movements in society are much slower. This is the real value of the mini-society, as a diagnostic instrument for society. In addition, those who take part in it can experience the effect of experimenting with other social roles and the difficulties of crossing social boundaries.

The Danish poet, *Piet Hein*, said: "Man is that animal who himself draws the lines he himself stumbles over". The mini-society provides possibilities for moving these lines.

Preamble for Chapter 14

"Europe is different: Boundary and identity as key concepts", originally from 1976, is the title of Chapter 14. In Europe we are brought up with notions of borders and boundaries and we know that moving or being moved means crossing lines and paying for the crossing in one way or the other, Gunnar observes. Our history is an account of struggles over national boundaries and class boundaries. Boundaries are vital because if we fall outside them we become stateless and lose our passport and identity. There will always be a need for identity, for self-identification.

Gunnar draws on three illustrations from his experiences as a trainer and as a consultant: his work on the tanker fleet (see Chapter 12), the mini-society (see Chapter 13) and the Hammerfest case (see Chapter 15). As for the crews aboard the big ships, Gunnar states his conviction that the members of this organization should be allowed full authority to plan within their territory and to handle boundary problems themselves. Relating to the mini-society, he notices that in the unstructured setting of this experiment, emotional issues around boundaries are acted out. He gives credit to his old friend Max Pagès (see Chapter 9) for having shown the different ways the emotional life of groups manifests itself. As for the Hammefest case, Gunnar identifies three systems: the trawler fleet, the fishing plant and the town; he concludes that the factory's problems with the trawler fleet were due to the crumbling identities of the fishermen. The interventions resulted in a re-establishment of these identities.

Looking back at his work, Gunnar sees two major influences on his thinking about organizations and his way of analysing facts: Marx and Freud. The reason he gives is somewhat surprising: both scholars took their point of departure in studying the single case and warned against generalizations. Unlike most Marxists in those days, Gunnar insisted on looking into the whole complexity of society, not merely the economic sphere and people's place of work.

The paper was first published in a book edited by Geert Hofstede and M. Sami Kassem, *European Contributions to Organization Theory*, Assen/Amsterdam: Van Gorcum, 1976, 232-243.

14 EUROPE IS DIFFERENT

Boundary and identity as key concepts*

By Gunnar Hjelholt

Characteristic of Europe is the presence of many borders and boundaries between groups of people. These boundaries form the central concept of this chapter – it is about how groups of people live with and perceive their boundaries in the organizations they belong to. The illustrations are drawn from the author's practice as a trainer and as a consultant. Three kinds of illustrations are given:

1. Experimental organizations and mini-societies. These have been developed from the more individual-oriented sensitivity-training groups. In mini-societies, people from various walks of life live together for two weeks in an isolated place in groups which are internally homogeneous but very different from each other. Group images and group behaviour are studied and discussed with the members. Ancient and modern class conflicts can be seen repeating themselves in these mini-societies.
2. Closed systems. This refers specifically to ships where the author has worked with the crews of tankers and drilling ships to design the social and productive systems for a new technology.
3. Organization and society. An example is given from fishermen in the North-Norwegian town of Hammerfest. What first appeared to be a productivity problem was later defined as an identity crisis of the group of fishermen which had to be resolved at both the productive and the societal level.

These ideas reflect the heritage of Marx, Freud, Trist and Pagès. They imply a critique of modern organization theories advocating matrix organization or temporary systems, because these try to blur the essential group identities. Real solutions are those in which groups are allowed their identity but can extend their boundaries to influence the organization as a whole – to share

---

* Written in 1976.

in the power. This has implications for the role of the social scientist as a 'searcher.'

The importance of boundaries

I am a Dane, living on a farm in North-Jutland and by training I am a social psychologist. My old father is a historian who for the past half century has written about the border-wars and conflicts between Germany and Denmark.

When I travel I have to cross borders, show my passport, and subject myself to custom inspection. I shall have to change my money to the new valid currency and try to pick up the new habits, learn a new language, so I will not seem too 'foreign'. And I may have to discard some of my old practices. Maybe they will not fit into the new environment or if I stick to them they may make me too conspicuous.

In Europe we are brought up with notions about borders or boundaries and we know that moving or being moved means crossing lines and paying for the crossing in one way or the other. Our history is an account of struggles and revolutions, opposing nations and classes over boundaries. Boundaries are vital because if we fall outside them we become stateless and lose our passport, our identity which is connected with our social life, history, occupation, culture. Our social existence determines our consciousness.

For the past twenty years I have been active in two fields: education or training and consultation with organizations. In this paper I shall report on the special outlook I have acquired in these activities, an outlook which has to do with boundaries.

Organization laboratories and mini-societies

The small group as a vehicle for change – as well as an object for study – has as its father Kurt Lewin, the German-American social psychologist. The organization in the USA which took over his ideas and developed them into a sort of 'training movement' as well as a consulting style was the National Training Laboratories, now NTL-Institute for Applied Behavioral Science (Back, 1972; Bradford, 1974). In Europe the Tavistock Institute of Human Relations acted on the base of Bion's work on phases in group development.

The interesting and new aspect of this leadership or human relations training is the 'unstructured' small group of eight to twelve strangers who meet regularly with a consultant or trainer. They have no agenda and the consultant refuses to take ordinary leadership functions, but he declares that his job is to help the group look at the process, at what is 'happening here and now.' In this way three fundamental group-issues – goal-setting, leadership functions, and group norms – are brought into focus. Ordinarily, groups have tasks or agendas, appointed or elected leaders, and norms. Here all three items are lacking and therefore become very visible. At Tavistock, this small group is called the 'study group', as the learning comes from the self-study of the process. Otherwise the word Training group (T-group) or sensitivity group is being used.

Working with mainly union shop stewards using the group-centered laboratory training, I felt that the whole setting in which the training took place could usefully be analysed, so that the group *in the organization* would become the subject (Hjelholt & Miles, 1963). In the middle of the sixties, when a humble counterpart to NTL was formed in Europe – EIT, European Institute for Trans-National Studies in Group and Organizational Development – the laboratories they staged or organized took a much more comprehensive view of the 'here and now'. The whole temporary training system, the 'organization laboratory' as it is called, with power struggles and intergroup conflicts is up for analysis. In Europe the move has been to look at the group in its setting, the organization, while in the USA the individually oriented encounter movement took over in the late sixties. Kurt Back, in his study of sensitivity training (1972:64), has recognized the differences in approach, while Traugott Lindner (1972) has described the special EIT-training model. I should add, however, that much of the leadership training done in Europe is following the US individual-centered model.

The gain in knowledge about the organization's influence on its subparts, the groups, which resulted from the organization laboratories on the one hand and from consulting with organizations on the other, has led to further explorations, the mini-societies (Higgin, 1972; Hjelholt, 1972). In 1968 I started some experiments which in their set-up resemble the training laboratories. They have a temporary life span, two weeks, and are being conducted at an isolated place: last year in Sweden in a partly abandoned village. The number of participants has been from 40 to 140, and participants are chosen or recruited from organizations so as to ensure a representative sample of society at large, particularly in terms of socio-economic status, age, and sex. The participants are then grouped according to their 'role' in society; I try to get groups which have relevance for each other, so that other groups confirm the members of a group in their identity. Each group gets its own territory, its house.

Let me quote from the invitation: "Here we shall try to create a small society which partially reflects the outer world with its groupings and problems. We will have opportunities to learn about ourselves in our group and about our relationships with other groups, since this is our purpose. With others, our group and the whole system, we shall explore the boundaries and distances in our society. Our exploration need not solely consist of collecting knowledge about things, but here we have the conditions and a chance to affect the system and to change it."

Some colleagues and I form one group which only differs from the other groups in one respect: we bring with us the special task of doing research and of feeding back the research results to the community. The research has more and more taken the direction partly of projective instruments which can be fed back at once, and partly of 'hard data'. An example of a projective device is the requirement that each group name itself. Examples of hard data are the number of empty beer and wine bottles found outside each house, the registration of how the groups use their time, how people move, whom they visit, etc. These data can be reported back to the community immediately and give everybody a picture of where one is at the moment.

I have come to the conviction that research, when it is reported back, should not be vacuum cleaned of the emotions which were in the data when they were given. In a mini-society a group of middle class, middle age, partly academic people first called themselves *The Association*, a week later they renamed themselves *The Establishment*, and in its last stage they took the name *The Saints*. Through these names the group gives away a lot about its self-image in the society. And the names can also be seen as signs of wishes or desired moves.

The name giving – identity – can not only come from the group itself and its appreciation of its role in the society. The name can also be invented by another group. Recently in Austria one group defined themselves – feeling abandoned – as *The Peasants*. Having acquired an identity they promptly went on and named the three other estates: *Citizens*, *Nobility*, and *Church* – and then started producing proposals and documents in the spirit of the peasant revolution of 1530, seeking help from the Citizens against the Nobility and the Church. First the other groups took the identities assigned to them and did their best to conquer the rebellious Peasants and to isolate them, and strip them of their influence. But you cannot live with an identity which has been given to you, especially if it is contrary to your needs. There will always be a need for self-identification. After a number of days, the Nobility, having gone through internal struggles, defined themselves as *The United Worker Parties* and issued 'Das proletarische Manifest'. Suddenly the temporary community jumped to 1917 and a 'Volksfront' between peasants and workers was tried. People moved. Most spectacular was the dwindling of the Church group and the fact that some of the Citizens left the laboratory. Others formed an Institute for Political Research and tried to analyse the happenings.

Identity is influenced by many social factors. In last year's mini-society in Sweden roughly 40 of the 140 participants were Danes, a minority among the Swedes. Some of them, middle aged, were housed in a barracks and took to working in the field. To everyone they became the *Gastarbeitern* (migrant workers) and the proletariat, with their own spokesman at community meetings, etc. Here their minority position, the housing, their work – and the foreign labour problems in the outside society – all contributed to their identity and reactions. Swedish children started talking about the ill-smelling Danes.

In the mini-society laboratory the groups have to come to grips with some fundamental issues of society: how to handle and organize money and time. During this they have to look at their reactions to other existing, present groups. They cannot live only on phantasies about the others. They are too close, and they share a common existence with the other groups. In this process they detect and disclose their identity and the value system which is connected with this identity.

For me, personally, my knowledge about the influences of society on groups has been increased in these situations. I see these mini-societies as a most powerful diagnostic instrument for processes going on in the larger society. In the unstructured setting of the experiment, the emotional issues around boundaries are acted out and can be inspected.

It seems as if the mini-society gives the groups on the outskirts the greatest possibilities for moving their boundaries and for becoming aware of Society as a whole. The poor, the drug addicts, the children, and the like here show an active interest and participate or try to contribute to the running of society. But when such a group starts identifying itself publicly, other groups, especially its counterpart, e.g., 'professional helpers' feel threatened and do their best to push them back in their 'proper place'. The groups primarily defined by their relation to other groups (professionals) seem to be most vulnerable when threatened in their self-image and often become quite destructive. The more the 'majority in the middle' is characterized by professional service functions, the more difficult it becomes for the mini-society to evolve a common consciousness.

Ships as closed systems

Since 1962, when technology made it possible to enlarge tankers and changed old routines through automation, I have been working as a consultant to a progressive Danish shipping company, J. Lauritzen. A ship is the dream of a social scientist, as inside a visible boundary on restricted territory we have different groups who have to live their daily social and productive life together. There is little interference from the outside, so one's control over the situation is almost complete.

The company ordered a new tanker to be delivered in the autumn of 1962. It was to be bigger than any previous tanker and to have more automated equipment than in any previously built Danish ship. As the company competes in the international market, it felt it had to try to get the new ship manned with less than the regular crew of sixty then prescribed by Danish law. The ministry granted the company a waiver for one year.

I worked with the ship's groups – officers and men, deck and engine and catering – planning for the life inside the new ship being built. Due to the new technology, automation, and the uncertainty it caused, the groups were motivated to look at planning with a more open mind. And subjects which nobody otherwise would have thought of touching were brought into the discussion in a natural way.

The crew was given the full authority to plan inside their boundary, the ship, and one of my roles was to be the boundary keeper and see to it that the company's directors did not interfere in the process. The planning and decision making had three steps: First a conference for preliminary decisions, followed by a period during which the crew members had an opportunity to get more information or training so they could handle technical equipment; Second, a conference at the shipyard, just before the ship was to be launched. At this conference the last plans and final decisions were to be made. The third step came after some months aboard, when I visited the ship and we made a review of how the plans and decisions had worked out.

The first decisions to be taken had to do with the ship's relations to the outside: the company, the ministry and the unions. When the outside boundary relations were agreed upon, the relations between the different inside groupings – men and officers, deck, engine and catering – could be tackled. The decisions had to do with both social relations and technical work. For instance, it was decided that rules about liquor should be the same for officers and men, which until then had not been the case. A deck hand, the pump man, should report to the first engineer. Weekly planning meetings should take place inside departments and between departments, and should include representatives of all the groups on the hierarchical ladder.

Planning and training of crews for subsequent tankers and other new ships have been going in inside this company since then due to rather spectacularly good results (Hjelholt, 1968; Clark, 1972). I can mention that partly due to prompting from Einar Thorsrud, who also is fascinated by ships as systems, future officers now are involved as early as when a ship is on the drawing board in the office. They now take a hand drawing the lines themselves – the lines they have to live inside.

The main issue of the consultation is – as you clearly can see – that the responsibility for the system and the handling of boundary problems was placed inside the system, with the members. Also, social and technical relations were handled simultaneously, and it became possible to express value systems.

I would like to give another recent example of work with closed systems, which will show that the problems can be most difficult and can play havoc with some groups. A new sort of ship is being constructed: a drilling ship. This means a ship with an oil-rig in the middle. And now we find two different cultures on board; the oil-drilling people with the drilling superintendent's safety norms, *oil, rig and men*, and the seamen with the captain's safety norms, *men, ship and cargo*. How should that organization find a satisfying way of living when the value systems are so different.

The group which can extend its boundaries most easily is the engine-group, which by training can expand its occupational skills to the drilling, thus perhaps raising the level of performance of the entire system. They can see a connection with their occupation and an enlargement of their area. But how can the seamen, the navigators relate to the new situation? First ships were stripped of sails and now this ship is not supposed to move! What sort of identity will they have in the future?

Organization and society: the Hammerfest fishermen

The last example I am going to present has to do with visible boundaries, too. In 1967 EIT undertook to investigate the reasons for high production costs at Findus' deep-frozen fish plant in Hammerfest, a small town north of the polar circle in Norway. Findus is a subsidiary of the multinational company Nestle. The situation had become so serious that at Nestle's headquarters in Switzerland some people suggested building a new fishing town elsewhere.

A Norwegian psychologist, Trygve Johnstad, carried out the initial explorations of the situation and the following picture emerged. In the small town with approximately 700 inhabitants, the fish-processing plant with 1400 employees was the main economic factor in the life of the town. If the company should stop, the town would die. The plant was dependent on the supply of fish from the trawler fleet of twenty ships. The supply was not regular and because of this, twelve percent of the landed fish was spoilt before it could be used. This was the main reason for the high costs. There was also a high turnover among the trawler crews; 800 percent per year was mentioned in a report to headquarters. The plant had a young, ambitious management group, the town looked down on the fishermen, a drunken lot of bums, and the fishermen themselves saw no future in being fishermen. They regarded themselves as being the lowest on the status ladder, even if in terms of income they were at the top.

However, when we looked at life on board the fishing trawler, when the group was at work under pretty rough working conditions, we found a smooth, well-functioning crew where no boundaries hindered the work.

Going back in time to before the war, we see that the situation of the fishermen was quite different. Then the fisherman was respected by the community and respected himself; he was a member of the community, a free man. The war, however, destroyed Hammerfest as it was hurt when the Germans retreated. By this the visible links to the past, houses and lay-out of the town, were wiped out and with the rebuilding, shifts in the population occurred. Apart from this, the new modern factory's insistence on fixed delivery restricted the freedom of the fishermen's planning.

The analysis of the situation showed that three systems existed inside the boundary we had to look at: the trawler fleet whose personnel had lost their former identity, the factory which put restrictions on the ships but was also dependent on them, and the town which was dependent on the plant and the fleet but did not give the fishermen the possibility to live an ordinary social life outside the working environment of the boat. The change in the fishermen's self-image had to do with the increase in distance to other groups and with the lack of recognition from outside. It was due to 'society' that the identity was crumbling; only production still kept the group functioning.

We installed two sorts of forums. One was a weekly meeting between the management group of the plant and those fishermen who were that day in harbour. Here feelings, grievances, complaints, proposals regarding production, and relations between the plant and the ships could be handled. The other forum was a meeting on the same day between the influential fathers of the town, the mayor, bank president, labour-union leader, and the fishermen. It was held in the town Council meeting room, and here the fishermen as important citizens discussed housing, welfare and other matters pertaining to the social life of the town and themselves.

A year later the spoilage percentage of fish landed was below one percent and the turnover of men twenty-five percent. Two years later money had been given for investment in new, modern trawlers, and a new wage system was tried out. The fishermen, who had mostly been single, started acquiring property and settled for good in Hammerfest. To be a trawler fisher was to be somebody.

Intellectual debts and consequences for theory

Looking back at my work, I see two old, big debts, to Marx and to Freud, for having influenced my thinking about organizations and my way of analysing. Common to both of them was that they worked from the study of the single case and warned against generalizations. A quotation from Karl Marx (1904:269) is enough, I think: "The general or common features discovered by comparison constitute something very complex, whose constituent elements have different destinations ... What is characteristic of their development are the points of departure from the general and common. The conditions which generally govern production must be differentiated in order that the essential points of difference should not be lost sight of in view of the general uniformity which is due to the fact that the subject, mankind, and the object, nature, remain the same."

Quoting Marx, it is natural to bring in the Tavistock socio-technical way of looking at organizations or systems. My contact with Eric Trist especially has inspired me. He and his colleagues, in the studies of coal production and of changes in the production methods, took hold of Marx's thesis about the mode of production in material life determining the general character of the social, political, and spiritual processes of life. Trist and Bamforth's first presentation in 1951 included more about the life of the miners outside the work-situation. In this respect I must confess that I feel that the socio-technical view or organizations has been dangerously narrowed. If our study of the trawler fleet had been restricted to the work place, we would have found a well functioning autonomous group and – as others did – we would have prescribed technical measures for control of the meeting point between ships and plant. But by looking at the whole life, free life included, we were able to come up with a diagnosis which meant a more comprehensive view of socio-technical systems than most present socio-technical approaches include, at least in Scandinavia.

Emery and Trist, in the sub-title to their last book (1973) on social ecology, have said what they aim at, "Contextual Appreciations of the Future in the Present" and their former colleague at Tavistock, Gurth Higgin, has called his last book *Symptoms of Tomorrow* (Higgin, 1973). I think that my experiments with the mini-societies spring from the same roots: an attempt at understanding the complexities of society with its different groupings and ways of organizing, trying to see the processes taking place and pointing to those which might be models for the future.

In the detection of the processes I owe a lot to Max Pages. Building on psychoanalytical theories, he – to my mind – is the one who most convincingly has shown the different ways the emotional life of the group manifests itself. His interpretations on the group level and his experimentation with flexible structures has given me the courage to interpret the movements and symbols of the group as collective phenomena and to experiment with ways in which I could give the groups an opportunity to express their positions in the system. By always working with situations which are as close to the 'daily life' as possible (or setting a stage which brings out the affective side of the daily life, as in the mini-society) or with situations which are real (the ships) and keeping the actual groups together as working units, I think that we make the affective manifestations of the groups more visible. The group members have to do with the real system in which they live and which affects them.

In this respect – by working with several homogeneous groups – my work differs from Pagès'. I am out to detect the boundary-problems through the affective manifestations of the groups and to investigate along with these groups whether something can be done about it. I think this last issue is a common concern for social scientists helping organizations.

There is, however, a catch to this. I think the identity of groups and systems is important. Without identity the system or the group is neither productive nor satisfying as a place to live. And if we have to get our identity from other systems and just be a prisoner in the working organization, we create a society which certainly is asking for trouble.

From this outburst you can guess my attitude toward the predominantly American organization theories advocating the organization structure as matrix-organizations or temporary systems. I think that the theories – which try to get away with or loosen boundaries, are attacking the group identities, and in this way, while temporarily ensuring flexibility inside the organization, they export problems to the outside, where we get a society of alienated, rootless individuals. I feel much more in accordance with the moves of groups to extend or redefine their boundaries, trying to let their values influence the organization as a whole. I refer to the unions' demand for a better work environment, their demand to be included in decision-making for the whole organization, and the like.

Here we come to one of the most fundamental boundaries between groups: on one side those who have, on the other side those who have not; those with power and those without.

In history many groups have experienced a reduction of their territories, and the meaningful life which at one time could be fulfilled inside one boundary had to be repressed, or the gratifications had to be sought somewhere else. Freedom of choice became restricted and, more and more, groups saw themselves as powerless. For many, the only power left is the power of sabotaging the complex society.

European social scientists are, or have been, inside the crumbling walls of universities. By staying there we certainly will experience a reduction in our free area and perhaps defensively cling to the identity of 'researchers'. If, on the other hand, we try to move to the land of business or managers and become organization specialists, as some or our American colleagues, I'm afraid the custom duties we will have to pay will be too costly.

If we recognize our identity as 'searchers' trying to formulate important questions to be answered with other groups also concerned with the common fate of our European society, I think we ourselves can experience something different from the frustration we too often live with, and we can contribute to the many-faceted systems of which Europe is composed.

References

Back, K. (1972). *Beyond Words*. New York: Russell Sage Foundation.
Bradford, L.P. (1974). *National Training Laboratories. Its History 1947-1970*. Washington D.C.: National Training Laboratories.
Clark, P.A. (1972). *Action Research & Organizational Change*. London: Harper & Row.
Emery, F.E. & Trist, E.L. (1973). *Towards a Social Ecology*. London: Plenum Press.

Higgin, G. (1972). The Scandinavians rehearse the liberation. *Journal of Applied Behavioral Science*, *8*, 643-663.

Higgin, G. (1973). *Symptoms of Tomorrow*. London: Plume Press.

Hjelholt, G. & Miles, M.B. (1963). Extending the conventional training laboratory design. *Training Directors Journal*, *17* no.3, 3-10. Reprinted by National Training Laboratories, Washington D.C., 1963.

Hjelholt. G. (1968). *Training for Reality*. Working Papers 5 & 5A, Department of Management Studies, University of Leeds.

Hjelholt, G. (1972). Group training in understanding society: The mini-society. *Interpersonal Development*, *3*, 140-151. Also in C. L. Cooper (ed.), *Group Training for Individual and Organizational Development*. Basel: S. Karger. 1972.

Hjelholt, G. (1975). North of the Polar Circle: Consulting with a fishing company. In: D.P. Sinha (ed.), *Consultants and Consulting Styles*. New Delhi: India Book Co. In Press.

Lindner, T. (1972). Organisations-Laboratorien nach dem EIT-Modell. *Gruppendynamik*, *3*: 391-399.

Marx, K. (1904). *A Contribution to the Critique of Political Economy*. New York: International Library.

Pages, M. (1968). *La Vie Affective des Groupes*. Paris: Dunod.

Pages, M. (1974). Neue Bemerkingen über das affektive Leben der Gruppen. *Gruppendynamik*, *5*: 104-125.

Trist, E. L. & Bamforth, K.W. (1951). Some social and psychological consequences of the Longwall method of coal-getting. *Human Relations, 4*, 3-38.

Trist, E.L., Higgin, G. H., Murray, H. & Pollock, A. B. (1963). *Organizational Choice*. London: Tavistock Publications.

Preamble for Chapter 15

Due to his earlier work with the Lauritzen shipping company, cf. Chapter 2, 12 and 14, Gunnar Hjelholt was approached by an international company owning a fishing plant in Hammerfest in Northern Norway. They felt that he might be able to help them save the plant from being laid down. The contract was made with EIT, the European Institute for Transnational Studies and Organizational Development. By channelling his project into the EIT, Gunnar added volume to this new organization that had been established a few years earlier. He asked the Norwegian social psychologist Trygve Johnstad to be the programme director. Johnstad, who was active in EIT, did the actual fieldwork. In Chapter 2 above, Gunnar conveys his appreciation for Johnstad.

Chapter 15 reports on the fieldwork, the analyses, the interventions, the results and Gunnar's ways of explaining the spectacular success. It also illustrates his creativity as a change agent. The main purpose of the Hammerfest project was to lower the cost of the fish delivered to the factory in town. The factory was, indeed, saved from being laid down. Other remarkable changes took place as well. The turnover rate at the fleet and the considerable spoilage percentage dropped dramatically. More fishermen were settling down in the vicinity. And all parties were happy. Moreover, the consultative intervention was relatively modest and cheap. See also chapter 14.

The text was first published in a book edited by Dharni P. Sinha, *Consultants and Consulting Styles*, New Delhi, Vision Books, 1979, 118-128.

15 NORTH OF THE POLAR CIRCLE[*]

By Gunnar Hjelholt

In Norway, 300 miles north of the polar circle, there is a small town of 7,000 people living in barren cliff terrain. Out beyond the town, however, on the Norwegian Sea, are some of the finest fishing grounds in the world. A large plant for processing these fish dominates the town, where approximately 1,000 of its inhabitants are employed. The plant is owned by an international company with main headquarters 2,000 miles away in Central Europe, and national headquarters 600 miles away in Oslo, the capital of Norway. The town with its processing plant and fishing fleet with 400 men is the target for the consultation undertaken and described in this paper.

The contract

In 1966 I was approached by the international company who owns the factory in Norway. In a few conversations the situation was described as seen from the international headquarters. The company in Norway was not showing the profit desired, and the international company was uneasy about putting more capital into the Norwegian branch. They felt that they should stay in the frozen fish business, but were debating if it might not be wiser to give up this plant completely and move to another part of the world where there were not so many government restrictions as in Norway. Even if they had to build an entire town and train a fishing crew, they thought this might be the best solution. They did not see how things could be improved in Norway.

I was called in because their staff expert on fishing had once read a paper of mine[1] at a management course describing work on board ships. He and the Norwegian managers agreed that improvements in the situation were to be sought in the trawler fleet which provided fish to the company. They told me that in recent years they had improved the factory considerably with the help of work study consultants, and that consultants had also considered improvement

---

[*]   Written in 1979.
[1]   Gunnar Hjelholt (1964). Training for Reality. Working Papers, No. 5. University of Leeds, Department of Management Studies.

of the trawler fleet. The consultants, however, felt their suggestions would not be accepted and sensed great resistance on the trawlers towards changes in working conditions or manning of the ships. It was through my earlier work with ships that they felt I might be able to help them.

Through our conversations a sort of agreement was made that I should undertake an investigation of the situation, but there was friction between the main headquarters and the Norwegian headquarters, because requests for capital from Norway had been denied. The Norwegian office said they had to have money to improve the situation. But the main headquarters refused more money until Norway had proven that the situation could be solved, and were inclined to move out if nothing happened in Norway. Due to the conflicting views of the national and international headquarters, I met with the national directors in Oslo and signed the actual contract for consultation with them. However, there was quite a lot of communication going on between Oslo and the international headquarters, as the latter were rather uncertain about the possibility of help from consultancy, as other consultants had not succeeded.

The contract was made between the Norwegian company and the European Institute for Trans-National Studies in Group and Organizational Development (EIT), a European organization consisting of social scientists from various countries, somewhat parallel to the American NTL-Institute of Behavioural Science. At that time I was the General Secretary of EIT and by making it an Institute contract, I had the opportunity to draw on members of the Institute for their experience and also for practical work.

The main points of the contract were as follows: EIT was to work with social conditions related to the trawler fleet. The main purpose was to lower the cost of the fish delivered to the factory in the town. We were to make an investigation of the situation and come up with a proposal on how prospective problems could be solved. The proposal was to include a time-schedule, an evaluation of costs, and an assessment of the results we thought could be achieved. In four months this work was to be completed. Also, naturally, there was a clause in the contract about EIT's rights for publication of the investigation. The time-plan involved two visits to the town in northern Norway, one in December, 1966, and another one in February, 1967, and the writing of a report for March, 1967. Included in the time-plan were internal discussions between the programme director, Trygve Johnstad, who did the actual fieldwork, and myself as responsible for the contract.

Translating the contract

Trygve Johnstad, a member of EIT and a Norwegian social psychologist, was well-equipped for doing the investigation. Not only did he know the local dialect of northern Norway, but he was at ease on the sea, had an easygoing manner, and had a talent for making contact with people. He and I, looking at the contract and considering the stories told by the company, decided that what we wanted first of all was to try to get a picture or a map of the whole community up there in Norway, where the sun always shines in summer and never shows itself in winter. Trygve was not only to take stock of the trawler fleet and its operations, but also to observe the factory and the town, and to get as complete a map of the whole of life in this small town as possible.

Unfortunately, at the beginning of 1967 I had to go to hospital, so Trygve Johnstad visited me there after having made his visits to the town. It was through our conversations in the hospital that we did the actual consulting by mapping out the situation and translating the task into a meaningful social-psychological question.

At the end of January I had the first exciting meeting with Trygve Johnstad, who had been up to the community, had talked with all types of people, and had been out on two fishing boats in the middle of winter. He showed slides of the town and the fishing, had all his interviews with him, and for two days in the hospital we tried to get a picture of what was involved. The town in the slides lay in a sort of valley with high cliffs overlooking it, and was quite deeply snowed in. It was a remarkably new town, according to Trygve Johnstad. All of northern Norway had been burned out during the war when the Germans retired. So there was not a building older than twenty years. The factory was very modern and automated. Then came the slides from the fishing boats, which looked rough. Water froze as soon as it came in over the deck and the ten-day trips certainly seemed brutal. How could men work under those conditions? A turnover of 800% had been mentioned in one of the reports submitted to the main office. But Trygve's impression was that there really were no frictions on board once work began. Under extremely difficult conditions, when sober, the groups performed their work with interchangeable roles and a lot of autonomy. Really there were no special status difficulties and, as the picture unfolded, they looked a lot like the autonomous groups in coal mines described by Eric Trist and Bamford.[2] Where was the catch? In conversations with the mayor of the town, the chief of the police,

---

2   E.L. Trist, and K.W. Bamforth (1951). Some social and psychological consequences of the Longwall method of coal-getting. *Human Relations*, 4.

the owner of the bank, the manager of the factory and other employees, the following circumstances were disclosed: the town recognized that it was dependent on the fisherman. The town could not live unless fish came in to the plant, though the fishermen themselves were looked upon as a bunch of tramps that compared with lost seamen in the great harbours of the world. They were people whom nobody wanted to know and if you happened to sit beside them in the cinema you would want to move, because they smelled of fish. That such a group should have the high income they had was regretted. Also some felt that it was awful that the town was dependent on them, such an irresponsible group. However, not all the reactions were of this negative nature. For instance, both the mayor and the head of the welfare council for the town said that the fishermen never got the recognition they deserved. They, however, did not know what to do about it.

The big central unit, the factory, looked upon the group with a sort of despair and expressed its feelings as follows: the fishermen have very low morals; they drink too much; they have no feeling of responsibility; they are thieves; sometimes they even go to another town with the ships and sell their fish to get liquor. The group of young executives in the plant saw the fishermen as the main obstacle to obtaining better economic results.

The fishermen themselves expressed: we are the lowest on the social ladder; we don't think it means anything to be a fisherman; for instance the girls in town won't have anything to do with us. They excused their drinking as necessary after ten days of working in turbulent hard weather on board the trawlers. Coming in they had to get drunk; nobody wanted their company, and they had to drink to forget all of this. They excused their lack of responsibility by saying they did not need to feel responsible because they were not going to be fishermen all their lives. Only a few percent of them were members of the union.

This status situation was quite new. Earlier, for many hundreds of years, the fishermen of the North were at the top of the social ladder. The towns in the Arctic made their living from the sea, and to be a fisherman was to be 'somebody'. The towns were dependent on the catching of fish. The income, just as now, was good. And there was even a sort of heroism involved. A captain of the Arctic was really admired. Somehow, after the war, this changed. And the map we have now is one of a trawler fleet, bringing in fish to be processed by a large modern plant, on which a whole town is dependent for its livelihood. The town, however, as well as the plant, sees the group of fishermen as irresponsible and wants little to do with them. They do, however, recognize that if they do not get the fish, the plant and the town will suffer.

Trygve Johnstad went up to the community again in February, interviewed more people, went out with one of the trawlers again, and gathered a few statistics. We had a renewed long talk at the beginning of March 1967 and, for our own satisfaction, formulated the problem as we saw it. The key problem for the town, the plant, and the group was the fishermen's lack of identity in the group – and this key problem was kept alive by forces both in the community and in the company. However, the working process on board the trawlers had a high degree of autonomy and it seemed important not do destroy the values imbedded in that system.

By perceiving the key problem as one of identity, it was possible to understand some of the reactions as symptoms. From the fishermen: there's no sense in getting organized, since I'm not going to remain a fisherman anyway; I don't care about the trawler costs, since I'm not going to remain a fisherman anyway; I'm not interested in settling down here in Hammerfest, since I'm not going to remain a fisherman anyway; I can behave like a pig now, since I'm not going to remain a fisherman anyway.

And the forces nourishing this identity failure can be localized as follows: that in the triangle where we have company, ship and community, the lines to the ship from the company and community were not only loose but sometimes negative. There were many indications of the fishermen's low status in the talk of the community, such as: they are not the best people you can find; it means nothing to be a fisherman; they are a bunch of bums; I don't normally talk with fishermen; they are people you don't know; they know too little about trawling; if I happen to sit beside one of them in the cinema, I move; they smell. And it was difficult for them to develop a feeling of belonging to the community, as their working schedule with one day off every tenth day or so offered very little contact possibility. The distribution within the total group of age, marital status, chance of reaching home on the day off, and duration of engagement with the company clearly showed the likelihood that the fishermen felt themselves uncommitted to a situation characterized by shallow and short-lived contracts. The fishermen were badly informed on local and municipal affairs, and the company seemed to follow a kind of minimal information theory in its handling of communication between the land and the sea. This resulted in all sorts of guesses and suspicions on board the ships that something was wrong with the company. Granted, some efforts had been made, but with very little success. A trawler course, which used to be offered, was not held any longer due to lack of attendance, and ongoing training was limited to casual instructions given on board.

The report to the company

At the end of March we submitted a report of our findings to the company. In this report we outlined the key problem as being the problem of identity within the fishermen's group. We gave our reasons and stated the principles that actions taken to deal with the problem should have the impact of (a) facilitating the identification process; (b) integrating the fishermen into the community; (c) offering stabilizing factors for the men; and (d) activating the fishermen's planning on a long-term basis. We said that the idea was not to reform men of the sea into men of the land, teaching them to behave like decent citizens, but to make possible a way of living for the fishermen by which they could experience themselves as members of the society they serve. We went further to say that this process of integration could only be accomplished by activating all parties involved, namely the fishermen, the company, and the town, a development necessitating a definite feeling of responsibility in all three groups. So far it seemed that the fishermen constituted the group where this attitude was least developed. This was not surprising; it was a part of the problem. The fishermen had to take part.

The practical proposals were: (1) to shape two working groups, one for handling the ship-company problems, and another for handling the fishermen-community problems; (2) to print a small, inexpensive newspaper containing company policy, production, personnel matters – a small newspaper for all the fishermen; and (3) to have a representative of the fishermen, in a role like that of shop-steward, one whom the others trusted, who could keep contact with the company on behalf of the fishermen. There were more practical suggestions, but these three were the main proposals seeking to help with the process of identification.

Trying something new

On April 5th, 1967, a one-page mimeo was sent out from the company to all 400 fishermen in the trawler fleet. It said:

> Let us try something new! This is a letter to all of you working on board the boats. We who work on shore feel that there are many questions of common interest that we would like to talk with you about. And it is not only us working here at the company. The same thing is true of those who have responsibility for the development of the town. To make it possible to meet we have thought that we could form two working groups where you would meet with the leaders of the company: the chief of personnel, the chief of planning, and myself; and in the other group you would meet with people who represent the town, the

town where you by occupation belong. But how many of you would come? We would naturally like to talk with as many as possible, and we think this could work out if you all sort of rotated in working groups. Then a few men from the boat or boats ashore could come up at a time.

In addition we would like to have a representative on shore, a representative of you on the boats. It should be someone who could be a contact man and talk on behalf of the whole group. If this could be arranged like a shop-steward through the union, that would be fine; otherwise you could elect a representative with each man on the payrole lists having one vote. What is important is that we get a man who has the confidence of the fishermen as a group.

So that everyone can know what the working groups are doing and what sort of results they achieve, we are going to print a Boat Post, which will be sent to all the boats. In the Boat Post we can also include other things of interest, and you will all be welcome to write about what is on your mind.

We hope and believe that these innovations will give strength so we can find the best solutions to our problems and also our work together for the company can be practical, that it can pay, and so we all can thrive.

The mimeo was signed by the managing director of the plant.

In April, a contact man was elected by all the boats, and the meetings began. The reaction was immediate. The meetings uncovered a number of questions of which the plant was quite unaware. Also, they seemed to be so valuable that they were held each week, and a lot of the fishermen came. The meetings with the town were held at the town hall, where the town council usually meets, with the mayor, the managing director of the bank, and the head of the welfare council, who at the same time was the union representative. Interest grew, and things started to change. Trygve Johnstad was up there three or four times sitting in on the meetings and helping, giving them a bit of feedback on the procedures, and especially trying to help them get into a problem-solving mood, instead of putting up defences.

One year after, at the end of the contract, in April 1968, I went up to the community for the first time.

It was a strange feeling, a year after the proposals had been put into effect, to travel so far north to see with my own eyes the people and conditions I had been concerned with for more than a year. The snow was high in the town when I arrived by boat, the only means of access. At the modern hotel where I stayed they showed the latest fashions from Paris, while up in the mountains the last nomads of Europe kept watch over their reindeer. Here, snowed in, a prosperous town lived from the rich fishing grounds with Gulf Stream warmth beyond. I visited the modern plant where the loads of fish came in and were processed, mainly by women from Finland; migrant workers, who, through a semi-automated process, prepared the fish and froze them for export to southern Europe (where the Pope had just caused such a stir in the economy by declaring that Catholics no longer had to refrain from fish on Friday). There I met a group of young, enthusiastic management persons who were very happy with the results they had achieved during the last year, though they still had a lot of difficulties with handling the situation. So many things had come up, they said, and there were so many things to change, nearly at once. They saw that they had better opportunities now. The mayor, who was up for election, felt that relationships had started to change, and I saw on the following days that he was right. He had never had such well-behaved and properly dressed people in the town council room as the fishermen.

We were able to get some statistics on the changes. During one year the turnover rate had dropped to 45%. The personnel manager said: "Now we can choose and select", and one of the fishermen remarked that "there's no place for bums in our group". Regarding the landed fish, the spoilage percentage when we started was 12, that is, every eighth fish had to be rejected. Now the spoilage of fish was below 1%, dropping in effect to zero. So we had accomplished what we were supposed to accomplish under the contract, namely to lower the cost of fish landed in the factory. But the most important development was that more fishermen were settling down in the vicinity, that the town had plans for building, and that all of the groups felt that they were living in a growing town. Half a year later a long article was sent to me from one of the leading Norwegian newspapers about the wonders of this town, where the mayor, the manager, etc., told about changes taking place, due to their own efforts. There were only one or two lines mentioning that they had had the help of some social psychologists.

Reasons for success

Naturally I have been speculating about the reasons for the spectacular success of this consultancy and I must confess that I do not get results like these so often. More often perhaps I have the failures.

One reason for success is that there was eagerness in all the groups for something constructive to happen. There was no group which felt that it had anything to lose by changing. First there was the international food company, the owners in Europe, who had nothing to lose by having a consultant in. They could wait a year before making a decision. And on their staff the fishing expert was intent that they should not close down the operations in Norway. The managing director in Oslo also wanted to succeed, or else his territory would have been diminished. The group of executives in the town – those directly involved – were glad to prove themselves. The town officials and leading citizens naturally wanted the town to prosper. And the fishermen's lot could only get better. So there was not the usual antagonistic group to work with.

A second reason for the success, I think, besides the skill of the programme director, Trygve Johnstad, was that the problem was stated in the right way, and that the identity question was seen as the main cause for all the symptoms. A third factor was that the proposals for changes and action were visible, real events, which everyone could experience firsthand, not only the Boat Post with figures and summaries of meetings, etc., but also the meetings where they could go and work in person with the town's important people. This visible act of holding meetings for the fishermen with the mayor, the president of the bank and other leading citizens, in the same room as the town council held its meetings, really showed that the community considered the fishermen important. Naturally a fourth influence might be added: that the office in Oslo and the headquarters in Switzerland did not interfere by making other suggestions during this time.

In conclusion, I can add that the consultancy involved did not cost the company much. Five or six visits had been made to the town, only one by me. I suppose there were 60 man-days of work in all, including the writing of reports, etc. No training of people was involved, except the indirect help given by a consultant sitting in at a few meetings. It simply consists of a mapping out of the whole of the real situation, putting all the pieces together, hopefully finding the underlying socio-psychological cause for the symptoms, and working in a visible manner with the relationship between groups in the community.

Preamble for Chapter 16

Gunnar Hjelholt's paper, "For-underligt – kan det komplekse og dynamiske gøres enkelt uden det forsimples?" [Too Strange – can we simplify our understanding of a complex and dynamic reality, and still avoid making it simplistic?] was published in Per Krogager (ed.), *Ubevidste processer i organisation og ledelse* [Unconscious processes in organization and leadership], Copenhagen: Dansk Industri, 1995. The translation brought in Chapter 16 is slightly abbreviated by the editors of the present book.

Too often our preoccupation with methods makes us think in terms of structure before we think in terms of purpose. However, the first things one should ask are: what is the meaning? What is the task? What is the usefulness of the system? What is it supposed to produce? The next question is how we organize ourselves so that our structure can implement the function. But alas: "Frequently it seems as if the people living in the system have forgotten or ignored the very function of the system!" If one has read the former Chapter 2 it will be apparent how much Gunnar strove with such questions. In Chapter 16, he relates these fundamental points of view to the functional-structural systems theory.

The consultant comes from the outside, he is different, that's his strength, said Gunnar. Don't let yourself be swallowed up by the system, because then you will become just as helpless, said Gunnar. As an outsider you can be as curious as a child. By having a different perspective and by asking the questions that are not otherwise asked by the system, you manage to disturb the balance to such a degree that changes are bound to come about, said Gunnar. Stay and consider the fact that the people are not the drama, they are the actors. Only the system itself can find the solution, said Gunnar.

16 TOO STRANGE

Can we simplify our understanding of a complex and dynamic reality and still avoid making it simplistic?[*]

By Gunnar Hjelholt

When I was a child I very much enjoyed when my father would tell stories that he had been told when he was a child. And I have told these stories to my children and grandchildren. When I woke up the other morning, one of these stories came to mind. The story was about a farmer who ploughed his roof from one end to the other. Suddenly the horses stopped because the plough struck something. This something turned out to be an iron box. The farmer opened the box; inside he found a somewhat smaller box. This box contained another box, the last box he found was very small. So small that he could hardly open it. When he finally managed to open the box, a little calf appeared. "Moo", it said. I accepted this strange story. It was indeed too strange. In a tiny box the farmer had found the kind of genuine, living, newborn calf that I knew from the cow house.

Children wonder about, ask questions about and attempt to understand our big world. This curiosity probably disappears to some extent when one grows older. Very often I just move on in my daily grind. When I encounter this or that, my reaction will be: strange! Then I will shake my head a little. But once in a while I feel a similar pleasure that makes me stop for a moment to experience the feeling I remember from my childhood. That the world I am part of is magic; that it is enchanted. A fairy tale.

The questions
The same kind of questions that preoccupied us when we were children are posed by scientists and writers: where are the boundaries between our lives and those of others? How can matters be two things at a time? And how do we explain our complex and contradictory world so that it makes sense? The

---

[*]   Written in 1995.

strangeness of it all is that authors make use of metaphors, paint in words. Scientists will now have to do the same, make use of analogies.

Those periods of our history are over when matters were not for us to explain, but for God to explain. After the French National Assembly had abolished God by law in 1792, reasoning, focusing on natural sciences and reducing life to one of many elements that you could then use to reconstruct life in a more appropriate way, is over too.

Two decades ago, I watched a Swedish broadcast of a discussion between the Nobel Prize winners of the year in question. It struck me that both micro and macro physicists agreed that no matter how far out they got into the universe, it would remain complex. Complexity is not reduced by looking at smaller parts. No matter how far these scientists would get, it would still not get any simpler.

Our bio-psychological system and our social systems are so complex, so change-able and so contradictory that only images get close to an adequate description. To reduce love to mere changes in the hormonal balances of the two people involved is actually to leave out important details of the experience.

Gleick's book, *Chaos – Making a New Science*,[1] also made me return to my child-hood curiosity and questions. We cannot forecast the future, but on the basis of history we are able to grasp that lines are not necessarily linear and that certain patterns connect widely different worlds.

The above will suffice as introduction, but now let's get to the issue: our social systems. And to us as observers of the systems. We have created the social systems: the family, the multinational company, the state and our local communi-ty. In the words of Piet Hein: "the human being is the only animal that stumbles over lines drawn by himself". As consultants we are in fact asked to assist in moving these lines. But alas, we have created the social systems ourselves.

And just like God created man in his own image, the social constructions reflect the patterns and lines of thought of the human psyche. The difference being, however, that these psychological systems form part of the surroundings of the social systems. It is true that we participate in these social systems as actors or role players. We can, however, leave the systems and look at them from the outside, reflect on them.

---

1   Gleick, J. (1987). *Chaos: Making a New Science*. Viking Penguin.

Systems are entities, associations that exist in a world. They have a life of their own.

The system model

The simplest form of life we know of is the amoeba. I have chosen the amoeba as a model for social systems. That is what I can manage for now. The complexity of the amoeba will suffice to ask the questions I have hitherto come up with in relation to organizations.

The ordinary, almost account-like questions are: What does it feed on? What do the surroundings provide for its living? What does it provide? Does it have a positive effect on the environment or does it pollute? Then there is the problem of boundaries. In the case of biological systems, the membrane or the skin separates one system from another; however, in the case of psychological and social systems boundaries are not that easily defined. As a matter of fact, boundaries must be defined by the system itself. What should be included or excluded according to the system. Inclusion and exclusion is something we know from our childhood, the emotional experiences are easily activated. An important matter in any group and in a large-scale context concerns refugees and immigrants. Then there is the question of defining which elements belong to the outside world. Where does it end? Presently this issue is discussed in the boardrooms of many organizations.

A social system is interesting because, based on its history and its self-image, it will make decisions concerning its environment. This is called self-reflectiveness. It seems as if our constructions get a life of their own, in which we can recognize characteristic features that we thought characterized human beings only. These constructions are just as self-centered, illogical and contradictory as we, as individual beings, are – and they too work on the assumption that they are logical, reasonable and acting out of the best of motives.

Ordinary systems theory, the science that attempts to understand differentiated sciences on the basis of common frames – just like the chaos theories – started by emphasizing structure. Assuming as the point of departure that all systems must have the same type of structure, the objective then was how to make the individual parts carry out the function corresponding to the purpose of the system.

Much modern organization theory has this character: you learn about abstract models and afterwards you try to make the systems fit into the models. The pyramid, the matrix.

Seemingly not that logical, but we all recognize the tendency in ourselves. When we get a new toy, we cannot wait to play with it. Too often our preoccupation with methods makes us think in terms of structure before we think in terms of purpose. The technological development within the fields of gene technology, surgery, etc., seems to endanger the general level of our health service system. Doctors should be allowed to play with their toys, shouldn't they? Systems theory has developed into a somewhat more coherent theory that may be termed the functional-structural approach.[2]

Those of us who have watched quiz programmes on TV where children are to explain matters and concepts without revealing the name, will have noticed how often expressions like 'in order to' or 'used when' are applied in these explanations – functional descriptions, that is. This is also how consultants approach problems when they work together with a client system. What is the meaning? What is the purpose? What is the task? What is the function?

The functional-structural systems theory[3] inquires into the function of the system as such and in particular the meaning of the system in relation to its environment. The question "What is the meaning?" is so fundamental and simple that we tend to forget it. A common experience is that only when there is no meaning will we discover that there ought to be one.

I suppose that function and meaning are some of the consultant's most essential questions. In actual life, a number of actions will not be oriented towards the function that the system is claimed to have. Frequently it seems as if the people living in the system have forgotten or ignored the very function of the system.

Social systems in which some of the original functions have disappeared are problematic. The family is one example: washing machines, etc., have emptied the home for a number of work functions that used to be there, just as nursery schools, youth club activities have removed some of the functions from the family system.

However, if we manage to catch hold of the fundamental question concerning meaning, structure will be subordinated to function and this will result in a functional-structural systems theory. The matter is radicalized and turned into a question of how the system is related to its environment. For the meaning of a system can only be found if the criteria for evaluation are externally defined.

---

2   Luhmann, N. (1991). *Soziale Systeme* [Social Systems]. Suhrkamp.
3   Wilke, H. (1991). *Systemtheorie* [Systems Theory]. 3rd edn. G. Fischer.

Now we are about to approach the question concerning structure. The large system is the earth. All other systems are defined as parts. Structure turns into systems that are somehow connected in order to work for and carry out the function of the suprasystem.

Above all, the functional systems theory deals with the question: what is the system supposed to produce? What is the usefulness of the system? What is the meaning? The next question is how we organize ourselves so that our structure can implement the function. So, there is no divinely defined way of handling all the tasks as is how we might have felt in connection with the organizational pyramid. Apart from function and structure there is a third question: how do we handle the fluctuation that may be caused by external influence, be a result of the interaction between the structural parts, or be developed in the tension field between function and structure?

No matter which part of the world we consider, the same peculiar regularities will unfold. Let's turn to an example that is well-known to all of us: the small group. In the beginning it spends time investigating several matters: where do we go from here, who are the members of the group, where are the boundaries, and with regard to belonging: what can and what cannot be allowed for.

This is what Bion calls a nursing period, a period that is followed by a work period filled with energy, and then by a stage of relaxation or reflection, and eventually you concentrate on the next task. These phases may be compared to the life cycle: childhood, adulthood, retirement. Very often they include the ups and downs that are experienced in the small group. Periods of conflict: phases of dependence and counter-dependence, fight-flight, pairing and splitting which are included in Bion's theory, as well as periods of analogizing, 'as if', that may open up to further understanding.

The complex world

In our existence we have become overwhelmed by the big world that has come so close that the complexity and the speed of events frighten us. We tend to seek a bygone age in which it was easy to get an overall picture of the world. Personally I have moved as far out into the country as is possible in Denmark, a life that includes sheep, dog, cats – and a wife.

Looking back a bit, a couple of million years or so, it seems – from a genetic point of view – that all living systems grow more complex. From amoeba to a human being with a cerebrum that clashes with the surroundings and gives rise to either conflict or dynamism. In the interaction between the human being and its surroundings we have developed remedies that have necessitated specialization, hence our social systems have become complex too, causing similar dynamic processes. Still a steady reciprocal process exists between the human being and its creations. Tavistock representatives[4] speak of socio-technical systems, meaning that the technique applied by a company influences human interactions just as the need for human coexistence influences the utilization of the technical remedies.

Again, I need to present a bit of theory that will be useful to us when we act as consultants, namely the theory concerning functional and genetic aspects. I have been inspired by theories concerning biological systems; taking history into account, they fit well with social systems. The theory in brief: with the passage of time complexity increases.

Given the fact that all structures consist of systems that strive to be autonomous, matters must become complex. Just think of how hospitals were organized in the past and of how they are organized nowadays. This genetic part of systems theory also describes how social systems arise, and this brings us to the group theories. You draw a circle round some of the people involved in the system, then they are caught inside that circle and need to organize themselves, to find ways of communicating and acting.

Those of you who have participated in group training will know what I am talking about. In group training we often get the feeling that in that small world we will find all kinds of complexity and dynamism that we would sometimes rather be without.

The inherent diversity and increasing complexity of the systems in our industrial society – or, perhaps, information society – seems to make it rather impossible to manage society and will at the same time, so it seems, result in it falling apart. Since any system has a wish for autonomy, self-guidance and self-reflectiveness, meaning that it interprets the world from its own perspective, it is no wonder that we shake our heads and say strange or foolish things. On the other hand, system consultants can look forward to permanent employment.

---

4   Tavistock is a British research centre for social and psychological interaction. Well-known provider of socio-technical analyses of organizations based on a psychoanalytic approach.

The complexity of a system is linked with the number of relations between structural parts, having different functions. And dynamics are the result of the changing environmental conditions, requiring new decisions and adaptations. The meeting between the system and a changed environment provides the choices of action. Within philosophy and systems theory this is termed Contingency (according to the dictionary, corresponding words are arbitrariness, unpredictability). We have several possibilities, a freedom of choice from our point of view – but this freedom is subdued by our uncertainty, by the unpredictability of the social environment's freedom of choice. What will they do? The dilemma: "Perhaps I could – but what will she do then?"

The social system and the individual

For many years I worked as group trainer or consultant and spent a lot of time in the so-called T-groups where people would have an opportunity to test their possibilities for action in a small group and to get feedback as to how they were perceived by others. Satisfactory work, but results on the organizational level were meagre. This kind of training would be much more rewarding on a personal level and from a family perspective. The larger social systems would more or less remain the same. I have seen individuals change, however, if the social context was changed.

The human being is so complex and is involved in so many relations that in the very same conversation you may get a chance of speaking with Jens Jensen, with the managing director, with the member of the confederation of employers, with the Dane, as well as with the member of a religious community. It is a question of figuring out which kind of relation you are in, in order for your conversation to be relevant in any of the relations.

The complexity of our world has increased due to the fact that individuals stand outside the social systems and hold roles in many systems at the same time. The systems interfere with each other, that is, they disturb the balance of each system. Within each small structure the role enactors experience a conflict as to where to place their loyalty. It is vital that you, as a consultant, include any system-relevant environment when you suggest changes and how they are to be carried out – for instance, by inviting trade union representatives to attend conferences, etc.[5]

---

5   Cf. Marvin R. Weissbord (1987). *Productive Workplaces*, Jossey-Bass. And the more theoretical: F.E. Emery & E. Trist (1973), *Towards a Social Ecology*. Plenum Press.

Before we have a look at practical matters, let us sum up some of the basic conditions for social systems – as I see them:

- Social systems are human constructions
- The boundary is important. It is defined by the system itself.
- Systems exist in a world, the relevant environment as we say. Systems are autonomous and self-organizing
- They are self-reflective, meaning that their experience and interpretations determine their actions
- Systems tend to become more complex
- They are determined by function
- Their inherent structure consists of sub-systems, just as they are sub-systems themselves, structures in suprasystems.
- The actions of systems are unpredictable
- Human beings exist in the environment of the systems. As human beings, however, we hold roles in many social systems.
- The small group implies the same phenomena as the larger social system.

The consultant and the organization

Whether we as consultants see ourselves as missionaries, as specialists within a certain area, as guides, fifth columnists or whatever image, we will probably agree on the indeterminateness of our task: to make things happen, to make things function, or function differently.

The consultant comes from the outside, he is different. That is his strength. The encounter may make things happen. Stay there, don't let yourself be swallowed by the system, because then you will become just as helpless. To a consultant it is a matter of figuring out whether he is on the right path, whether he deals with the right system and what kind of system it is.

Sometimes we need to construct a system, to draw a new circle around the problem area we agree upon in cooperation with organization representatives. During this phase you are very much like an explorer. Not the blasé type who has already been all the places that are worthwhile exploring, but the type who is as curious as a child who can tell snowflakes apart as they are all different. During this phase I will often ask actors to draw pictures of their organization and to tell me by means of metaphors about the country I am visiting. An outsider has a right to learn something about the magic country that he or she has come to visit.

After this it is a matter of making things happen. And no matter which problems have to be solved in this connection, the solution can only be found by the system itself. The consultant participates, but is still an outsider. You can, of course, contribute with specific knowledge, and by staying close you can ask the questions that are relevant in relation to the system's function. The purpose of being there is for the mission, the purpose, of the organization to be accomplished in a better way.

The questions will frequently be like a wonder that initiates the self-reflectiveness of the system: why do we do things the way we do? It is a matter of the processes between function, structure and fluctuation. By having a different perspective and by asking the questions that are not otherwise asked by the system, the consultant manages to disturb the balance to such a degree that changes are bound to come about. (I recently observed a consultant at work. She had acted as observer in a work group. At the end of the session the group asked her what she had observed. She said that she would like to tell them what they had not talked about.) The consultant must be the difference that makes a difference (to quote Bateson).[6]

When a system starts reflecting on itself and its processes, it will result in dynamism. Ghosts will appear, enemies made up, fears arise, and dramas will unfold. This may be frightening to the observer. But stay and consider the fact that the people are not the drama, they are the actors.

Quite a lot can be learned from the training of small groups. This kind of training focuses on the group and interprets actions on the basis of the whole. What is the function of this person in relation to that particular group, or which aspects of the group are expressed by that person? Bear the totality in mind and judge the drama on the basis of how subsystems fit into the message of the play.

When the system has been at work and has changed function and/or structure and found a way of handling fluctuations efficiently, time has come for the consultant to exit. Three simple steps in the process of consultancy work: get in, make things happen and leave.

---

6   Bateson, G. (1973). *Steps to an Ecology of Mind*. Paladin.

Preamble for the Epilogue

In 2005, on April 29th (the day of Hjelholt's birth), *The Gunnar Hjelholt Prize* was awarded to Steen Visholm. A translation of his speech on that occasion is brought as an epilogue in the present book. In the epilogue, Visholm sees group work as a mixed blessing, but he acknowledges at the same time Hjelholt's unique contributions to the area. The epilogue includes critical remarks regarding the Lewinian notion of democracy, and Visholm also points to the fact that 'authority' and 'authoritarian' are two entirely different matters. Finally, he addresses issues related to our social and political engagement in a globalized world.

Steen Visholm was born in 1955 and has a PhD degree in psychology from the University of Copenhagen. Before his PhD, and before being appointed Associate Professor at RUC (Roskilde University in Denmark), he worked as a clinical psychologist. At present he is head of an RUC-based Master's course in organizational psychology.

Visholm's areas of interest encompass psychoanalysis, projective identification, group analysis and psychodynamic systems theory. His latest book is Torben Heinskou & Steen Visholm (eds.), *Psykodynamisk organisationspsykologi – på arbejde under overfladen* [Psychodynamic theory of organizations – working below the surface], Copenhagen: Reitzel, 2004.

EPILOGUE

Why on earth always group work?

By Steen Visholm, Denmark

Until around 1968, my childhood was quite ordinary. I lived with my father, mother and big brother in an apartment at Lersø Parkallé in Copenhagen. I knew nothing whatsoever about groups or group dynamics. I enjoyed being a boy scout, I had a hate-love relation to school, I was curious to learn about the world and preoccupied with friendships, competition, inventions, girls and my big brother.

From 1968 and onwards, my interests changed to politics, music, revolution and groups: Pupils' council, rock groups like the Doors and the Rolling Stones, going to high school, undergoing existential crisis, questioning everything, and being attracted (motivation unclear) to studying psychology.

From their very first day at university, psychology students were divided into groups and asked to give their opinions concerning study content as well as process. We were expected to have opinions on all kinds of subjects, even though we knew next to nothing about them. We were expected to 'be ourselves', understanding at the same time that certain ways of being oneself were definitely more acceptable than others. I believe four years passed by before I experienced myself listening to a lecturer talking to me in a lecture format. Most teaching was structured as group discussions on articles that nobody had had the time to read because everybody, or at least the majority, were engaged in political projects deemed by us to have far more importance.

On the other hand, lots of exciting theory stuff circulated and extremely engaged teachers were there, inspiring us to such a degree that we actually found it worthwhile to spell our way through intellectually stimulating German books dealing with Freud as well as Marx. Working in groups with term papers was hard work. Not only did we feel obliged to do a critical re-examination of psychology as an academic discipline. We also had to deal with the interpersonal conflicts evolving from the process. Some lifelong friendships were formed, while other group members were not missed a lot afterwards.

During my practicum at the Student Counselling Office I met psychologists who thought – like I did myself – that groups were the solution to all sorts of problems, some kind of rudimentary socialism. I got involved in group-analysis and, later, I discovered the group theories of the Tavistock tradition and the Leicester concept. During the first 12 years of my professional career, I worked in the psychiatric field, where group and community therapy were central ingredients in the treatment programmes.

In 1995, I was invited to become an OPU staff member, OPU being a two-year training programme in organizational psychology within the Danish Institute for Group Analysis. Here the Leicester concept was combined with the psychoanalytic training model involving theory, supervision and personal therapy – but transferred from a therapeutic setting to management and consultancy. This gave me opportunities to do group work at an even more intensive level. In 2001 a fusion was made between the OPU concept and the group-oriented teaching style cultivated at Roskilde University, the result being a master's course in organizational psychology – MOP. Till now, roughly 300 managers and consultants have been trained in psycho- and group dynamics using these two educational programmes.

Generally speaking I experience group work as a mixed blessing. Particularly mixed in so-called democratic groups where you spend hours and hours talking about what should be done rather than doing it. In spite of my ambivalence, for more than 20 years I have been working as a group therapist, group consultant, or supervisor for groups several times a week.

Portraying Gunnar Hjelholt

During a trip to England I looked up central figures who knew the history of group analysis, group movement and group dynamics. I wanted to know whether all these group people had any particular political ideas as the driving force behind their untiring group work. I visited Malcolm Pines who told me the history of group therapy, and when I touched upon the political aspect he immediately mentioned Gunnar Hjelholt. This was the first time I heard his name. In times gone by, Pines and Gunnar Hjelholt had arranged a mini-society where all the participants, upon arrival, had deposited their pocket money in one large heap. Later they would be placed in different social classes: some were provided with money, others had nothing except their work power. "Very powerful dynamics", Pines said.

Later I got interested in the question: Why on earth must everything always take place in groups? I did some research on 'The Group Movement after World War II' – and realized that Gunnar Hjelholt had been one of the founding fathers behind the professional ways of thinking that had dominated my youth, my years of study, and even my first job in the psychiatric field.

When becoming a permanent staff member at Roskilde University in 1996, it was the same old story once again. The structure and identity-forming methods of that particular university could only be understood as a reflection of the fact that *Gunnar had been there too:* Big groups, small groups, groups here, there, and everywhere.

I met Gunnar Hjelholt in person only once. It was at the annual meeting for Danish occupational psychologists, most probably in the year 2000. That occasion made me realize his importance in shaping organizational psychology in Denmark. Whatever discussions and territorial fights went on among participants, however much they might belittle, scorn or despise each other, everybody would still unite in a common sense of gratitude towards Gunnar Hjelholt. Even so, the most important contributions to my picture of Gunnar Hjelholt did not come from this brief encounter, but rather from the light I had seen in the eyes of people who actually worked with him. Whenever the conversation turns to Gunnar Hjelholt, people's voices become warm and inspired.

When reading Benedicte Madsen and Søren Willert's book on Gunnar Hjelholt, *Survival in the Organisation* (1996), I was struck by the amount of undissolved ambivalences, tensions and contrasts that seemed to be part of his character. On the one hand, Gunnar describes the concentration camp as 'the perfect organization' (p. 87), on the other hand, it seems that he had to challenge the boundaries of any organization that he encountered. As a young man he had been driven by the wish to make the world a better place to live in. Towards the end of his life, this wish was softened into one of understanding the world a little bit better. He never lets go of his watchfulness concerning systems, organizations, institutions and hierarchies, seeing them as something that subdues the creativity of the individual. At no point will he tell you that organizations may actually be great inventions solving indispensable tasks for society and its individuals, bringing people together and making interesting things happen.

Perhaps his ambivalence is best expressed in the following quote: "I know that you cannot live without structure. Boundlessness is not good – what is good is to *overstep* boundaries" (p.86).[1] Gunnar Hjelholt was not a man who liked to set up boundaries, he preferred to cross them.

I believe Gunnar Hjelholt must be seen as a unique combination of leader and consultant. He exercised leadership over a professional movement, but by using the consultant role. His encounter with Nazism, combined with his personality, lay behind his ambivalence as far as organization and leadership were concerned.

The group dynamic movement

The group-dynamic movement to which Gunnar Hjelholt belonged got its drive by challenging and criticizing a rigid, outdated and at times authoritarian system.

The movement was motivated by democratic thinking and by a wish that Nazism should never be repeated. I once put forward the hypothesis that a certain vagueness attached to ways in which Lewin's democracy concept was used by the group dynamic movement formed a background factor behind the anti-authoritarian revolution in the 1960s. Recently, after having examined the matter more closely, I have realized that Lewin's democracy concept was, in fact, not concerned with democracy in a political sense, but rather with the ability of leaders or teachers to establish a democratic atmosphere. Thus, what the revolt of the 1960s actually did was to give to Lewin's concept its literal meaning. We were not content with atmosphere, with choosing the colour of the toilet paper. We wanted real power, to decide for ourselves.

The system was pushed, shaken, discussed, and a cultural revolution swept over the Western world. Lots of creative energy was mobilized. In the long run, however, the movement could not avoid getting stuck in those defensive, destructive group dynamics described by social psychology. Among left-wingers during the seventies it was considered bad form to compete for leadership or promote yourself and your ideas. Group, community, cooperation, solidarity, peace and socialism were understood as left-wing prerogatives, whereas the various right-wing groups were typecast as defenders of the individual, family, competition, market, war, imperialism and liberalism. Once again, undiluted goodness was placed in opposition to absolute evil.

---

1   Editorial note: the citation is brought in the prologue as well.

As has been convincingly shown by experimental social psychology, groups characterized by such polarized thinking will become marked by massive self-righteousness and uniformity among their members. Being different is seen as being disloyal. Criticism is understood as treason. Independent thinking is replaced by blind obedience. Fear of being excluded or annihilated becomes a guiding principle.

As one effect of the political mobilization in the 1960s and the 1970s, concepts like power, leadership, responsibility, authority, competition and skills became taboo. Among left-wingers, in large sections of the public sector, among faculty members and in the labour movement, topmost priority was given to the values of informality and solidarity. The absence, in informal systems, of *talk* about power, leadership, responsibility, competition and skills does not, however, mean that these phenomena no longer exist, it only means that they are placed beyond the reach of ordinary language – leading to a state of affairs where power and leadership cannot be openly addressed, nor challenged, nor made accountable.

Reality doubles itself. One version is the reality talked about. The other version is simply enacted. The aggression inherent in competition, critique, ambition and power is ousted from the shared world, thereby becoming part of a hidden underworld – but without losing any of its aggressive energy.

Authority or authoritarian

In 1997, at my first Leicester Conference, I was introduced to the concept of *authority* as a positive quality. The Conference theme was – as I believe it always has been – *Authority, Leadership and Organization*. That's what you were supposed to learn about. At that time my vocabulary did not differentiate between authority and authoritarian. In all probability I was not the only one who could not account for the difference given that, throughout our education, we had been guided by slogans such as: "Don't follow leaders, watch the parking meters", "Destroy the system", etc. In my opinion this differentiation between the terms 'authoritarian' and 'authority' is the key issue in Gunnar Hjelholt's way of thinking – as it is in my own professional paradigm: psychodynamic systems theory.

Like all relations, authority relations have two endpoints. At one end you find a person making decisions concerning particular subject matters, at the other end you find one or more persons bound by these decisions. The relation turns authoritarian when the person in charge gets disconnected from the task, using more power (personal power or positional power) than is legitimate and necessary, namely in order to compensate for his own weaknesses or to outlive regressive omnipotent fantasies. Using too much power scares the competences out of people and destroys their ability to think independently and express themselves freely. Instead their relation to authority becomes one of passive hatred. They are eagerly waiting for an opportunity to take over.

In this connection I find it pertinent to draw your attention to psychoanalysis, not least Melanie Klein and her followers. Among other things, psychoanalysis is about anxiety and defence – about the things that, at a personal, group, family, organizational or societal level, prevent us from assuming the adult citizen role.

It does indeed seem that psychoanalysis is acquiring new relevance with the advent of postmodern organizations where the employees' investment of emotions, commitment, personality and creativity has become part of the strategic agenda and where learning has become a key issue. In earlier times, problems concerning differences in skills, questions of authority or questions concerning group membership would be solved by referring to the organizational flow chart. Nowadays the new organizations with more flexible boundaries give priority to the exercise of psychological skills.

Social engagement

If you want social engagement to mean more than simply preferring extroverts to introverts, issues of value and vision must be added. Truth, justice and democracy would be my bid for such values, and these could also serve as a vision. When a western journalist asked Gandhi for his opinion of western civilization he got the answer: "That sounds like a great idea". To me, the term democracy is not to be understood as Lewin's democratic atmosphere but as political democracy.

Globalization is no momentary whim, but a lasting reality. Its significance has been growing steadily ever since the rise of the world market, imperialism, world wars and electronic communication media. We have all become citizens of the world. An identity not easily assumed in view of the complex and rapidly changing world we encounter every time we go shopping or watch television.

As a decent world citizen you must constantly be concerned about keeping the proper balance between your own interests and the interests related to developing and protecting the overall setting that enables individuals to realize their freedom and rights. The individual's capacity to assume his authority as a citizen of the world is threatened from within by his fear of the complex reality and inclination to use defence mechanisms: simplification, isolation, projection, etc. Other threats have external origins, namely the violent and quite harmful group dynamic processes that come into play at a political level.

In 1995, Benjamin R. Barber published a book entitled *Jihad versus McWorld*. In it he describes what may be feared to come after the East-West polarization of the cold war period. Since then it has become clear that the Western world is threatened not only by McDonaldization. A new Christian fundamentalism has become increasingly apparent, massively in the United States led by Bush, but also in Blair's Britain.

Thus, there is reason to fear that Bush and Blair, along with forces in the Islamic world, are transforming the world society into Sherif & Sherif's summer camp experiment – but, alas, without a group of experimenters who can stop the process before it turns violent. A world order may emerge where two fundamentalist religious groups oppose each other around the theme of heroes against villains, including prohibitions against thinking and telling the truth and an increased risk of violence and terror.

Campaigning for political correctness is yet another threat to thinking and democracy. In the United States, the politics of political correctness has long since assumed grotesque dimensions in areas of truth suppression, behavioural regulation and self-censorship. In Denmark we have so far limited ourselves to self-censorship. The fear of offending the Women's Lib, sexual minorities, ethnic groups, disabled people, people who are not as clever and intelligent as others, is turning language – ideally a means of contact between people – into a shared defence mechanism freeing us from sensing our fear of contact and exchange.

Finally, based on the reasoning of my colleague, Peter Koefoed, we may describe the citizen role in present society as being attacked from two sides. First, it seems that in many organizations the employee role is swallowing up the citizen role. More and more, organizations intensify their loyalty demands vis-à-vis the enterprise. Even doctors and teachers are muzzled with regard to political questions at the local community level, as if these questions were official secrets that need to be kept hidden in order to safeguard State security.

The user concept[2] points in the same direction: castrating the citizen and changing society into a sheltered workshop for people identified through their needs to be catered for, meaning that they do not have to think for themselves as long as they are willing to tick off evaluation questionnaires as requested. The political realm is no longer an arena for fights over attitudes and values, but is instead concerned with the market value of small, easy-to-grasp user services.

In the words of Storm P,[3] there's plenty to be depressed about, so if you're not depressed you have only yourself to blame. However, from a psychodynamic perspective, depression is aggression turned inward. In my opinion, there is no reason why Bush and his friends and enemies, engaged with the axis of evil, should monopolize aggression. Fight, competition and open conflicts all have a life- and contact-giving touch to them – especially when aggression and creativity go hand in hand.

---

2   Editorial note: This is a translation of the Danish concept 'bruger-begrebet'. In Danish, there is a tendency to do away with concepts like citizen, client or patient in favour of the consumption-inspired word 'user'.

3   Editorial note: Storm P, or Robert Storm Petersen (1882-1949), was a Danish actor, author, painter and poetic cartoonist.

A HJELHOLT BIBLIOGRAPHY

This bibliography is roughly identical to the one brought in Madsen & Willert, 1996 (cf. reference in the Introduction), except for the two entries from 1997. Unpublished papers and articles for daily newspapers and book reviews are not included. Most of the articles and reviews that Gunnar Hjelholt wrote for trade journals are left out. Titles in Danish are translated into English. A note is added in case the entry is published in the present book.

Hjelholt, G. (1953). Vær jer selv [Be yourselves]. In A. Fog Pedersen (ed.), *Fyraften* [Closing Time], Statsradiofoniens grundbøger. Copenhagen: Schultz, 9-19.

Hjelholt, G. (1955). Officersundersøgelse ved militærpsykologisk arbejdsgruppe. To gruppepsykologiske prøver [Examination of officers in the Military Psychology Work Group. Two group psychology tests]. *Psykologien og erhvervslivet*, 10, 120-127.

Hjelholt, G. (1957). Kammeratskabsvalg mellem 16-18 årige på tre af forsvarets skoler [Choice of friends among 16-18 year olds at three of the defense schools]. In *Nærhedens og tidens indflydelse på kammeratskabsvalg* [Proximity and the Influence of Time on the Choice of Friends], Fourth Nordiske Psykologmøde. Copenhagen: Munksgaard, 122-127.

Hjelholt, G. (1958). The neglected parent. *Nordisk Psykologi*, 10, 179-184, and *Acta Psychologica*, 13, 347-352.

Hjelholt, G. (1960). Den lille gruppe som faktor ved indstillingsændringer. *Nordisk Psykologi*, 12, 122-128.
A slightly abbreviated translation is brought as Chapter 10 in the present book under the title "The small group as a factor in attitude change".

Hjelholt, G. (1960). *Arbejdsgruppe og leder* [Work Group and Supervisor]. Copenhagen: The Danish Institute for Supervisory Training.

Hjelholt, G. (1962). *Samarbejdets psykologi* [The Psychology of Cooperation]. Danmarks Radios grundbøger [Radio Denmark Textbooks]. Copenhagen: Fremads Fokusbøger.

Hjelholt, G. & Miles, M.B. (1963). Extending the conventional training laboratory design. *Training Directors Journal*, *17*, 3-10.
An abbreviated version of the original mimeographed version is brought as Chapter 11 in the present book.

Hjelholt, G. (1964). Ansvar og stress [Responsibility and stress]. *Mentalhygiejne*, *3*, 1-4.

Hjelholt, G. (1964/1968). *Training for reality*. University of Leeds, Working Papers 5 and 5 A.
Working Paper No. 5 is brought as Chapter 12 in the present book.

Hjelholt, G. (1967). Social Science and European business. *European Business*, July 1967.

Hjelholt, G. (1968). A view from the gravel tip. *Journal of the Irish Management Association*, *15*, 34-35.

Hjelholt, G. (1969). Samarbejdets psykologi [The psychology of cooperation]. In Adstofte, F. (ed.), *Tillidsmandskursus* [Shop Steward Course], Copenhagen: Denmark's Radio, 62-66.

Hjelholt, G. (1972). Ziele des Mini-Society-Laboratoriums. *Gruppendynamik*, *3*, 371-373.

Hjelholt, G. (1972). Group training in understanding society: The mini-society. In Cooper, C.L. (ed.), *Group training for Individual and Organizational Development*. Basel: Karger, 140-151. (Reprint from the journal *International Development*, Vol.3, No.1-4, 1972).
Hjelholt's contribution is brought as Chapter 13 in the present book.

Hjelholt, G. (1973). Minisamfund. Et socialpsykologisk eksperiment [Mini-societies. A social psychological experiment]. In Haslebo, G., Holbøl, P., Høyrup, S., Madsen, F.H. & Nejsum, B. (eds.), *Magt og påvirkning i systemer* [Power and Influence in Systems]. Copenhagen: Reitzel, 202-219.

Hjelholt, G. & Berg, H. (1974). *Institutionen og folket* [The Institution and the People]. Copenhagen: Fremads Fokusbøger.

Hjelholt, G. (1976). Europe is different. Boundary and identity as key concepts. In Hofstede, G. & Kassem, M.S. (eds.), *European Contributions to Organization Theory*. Amsterdam: Van Gorcum, 232-243. Brought as Chapter 14 in the present book.

Hjelholt, G. (1976). Der Schlüssel. *Gruppendynamik, 7*, 18-21.

Hjelholt, G. (1976). Fangerne [The prisoners]. In Dyhre, B. (ed.), *Patient-sygeplejerske-læge: Hvis behov?* [Patient-Nurse-Doctor: Whose Needs?] Copenhagen: Reitzel, 66-81.

Hjelholt, G. (1978). Psykolog og samfund [Psychologist and society]. *Psykolog Nyt, 32*, 116-118.

Hjelholt, G., Lindgård, L. & Nyrop, J. (1978). Supervision [Coaching]. In *Formidling af Psykologi* [The Mediation of Psychology]. Report from the Annual Meeting of Danish Psychologist Association 1978, 135-144.

Hjelholt, G. (1979). North of the polar circle. In Sinha, D.P. (ed.), *Consultants and Consulting Styles*. New Delhi: Vision Books, 118-128. Brought as Chapter 15 in the present book.

Hjelholt, G. (1979). Questions about organisational energy. *Human Futures, 2* (3). New Delhi.

Hjelholt, G. (1984). Energitab i social institution [Loss of energy in social institutions]. *Dansk Psykolog Nyt, 38*, 9-10.

Hjelholt, G. (1985). 25 år som selvstændig social-psykologisk konsulent! [25 years as an independent social psychological consultant!] *Dansk Psykolog Nyt, 39*, 313-315.

Higgin, G. & Hjelholt, G. (1990). Action research in minisocieties. In Trist, E. & Murray, H. (eds.), *The Social Engagement of Social Science. A Tavistock Anthology. Vol. I: The Socio-Psychological Perspective*. Philadelphia: University of Pennsylvania Press, 246-258.

Hjelholt, G. (1991). Fra 50'erne til 90'erne. [From the 1950s to the 1990s]. Kursus Danmark 1991, Årbog for kursusarrangører.

Hjelholt, G. (1992). Beratung im interkulturellen Kontext. In Wimmer, R. (ed.), *Organisationsberatung. Neue Wege und Konzepte*. Wiesbaden: Gabler, 269-281.

Hjelholt, G. (1993). Das Minilab – Ein spezieller Einstieg in ein längeres experimentelles Lernarrangement. In Schwarz, G., Heintel, P., Weyrer, H. & Statler, H. (eds.), *Gruppendynamik. Geschichte und Zukunft*. Wien: Universitätsverlag, 105-110.

Bridger, H., Burgess, S., Emery, F., Hjelholt, G., Qvale, T. & Van Beinum, H. (1994). Eric Trist Remembered: The European Years. *Journal of Management Inquiry, 3*. Sage Publications, 10-22.

Madsen, B., Willert, S. & Hjelholt, G. (1994). Mini-samfundet plus-minus 25 år [The Mini-society plus-minus 25 years]. *Psykolog Nyt, 3*, 90-92.

Hjelholt, G. (1995). *Case-metoden og situationsspil* [The Case Method and the Method of Role Playing]. The Municipal High School in Denmark. Copenhagen: Forlaget Kommuneinformation.

Hjelholt, G. (1995). For-underligt – kan det komplekse og dynamiske gøres enkelt, uden det forsimples? In Krogager, P. (ed.), *Ubevidste processer i organisation og ledelse* [Unconscious Process in Organization and Management]. Copenhagen: Danish Industry, 87-99.
A slightly abbreviated translation is brought as Chapter 16 in the present book under the title "Too strange – can we simplify our understanding of a complex and dynamic reality and still avoid making it simplistic?"

Hjelholt, G. (1997). Forskerne og systemerne. Nogle personlige betragtninger [The researchers and the systems. Personal reflections]. In Graversen, G. (ed.), *Et arbejdsliv* [A Working Life]. Department of Psychology, University of Aarhus, 31-35.

Hjelholt, G. (1997). *Kulturmødet. Erfaringer fra Interkulturelt Center – Århus* [The Meeting of Cultures. An Evaluation Report]. Aarhus: Forlaget Hali.

NAME INDEX

Argyris, Chris 123, 229, 235, 242
Back, Kurt 285
Bamforth, Ken 173, 283, 286, 291
Bateson, Gregory 309
Benne, Kenneth 77, 82-85, 98, 114, 173, 213
Bennis, Warren 123
Berg, Harald 28, 95, 171, 173, 322
Bertalanffy, Ludwig von 179
Bion, Wilfred 109, 173, 178, 276, 305
Bradford, Leeland 69, 74, 76-77, 82-85, 101, 106, 108, 114, 122-24, 129-30, 173-74, 224, 242, 276, 285
Bridger, Harold 110, 122-24, 152, 156, 173, 324
Brocher, Tobias 99, 106
Cartwright, Dorwin 75, 79, 82, 114-15, 219, 224
Chattopadhyay, Gouranga 29, 183, 185, 191, 195, 201-2
Christensen, Jørgen Steen 28, 31, 143, 145
Cook, Stuart 75, 254
Dalheimer, Veronika 23, 28, 133, 135
Deutsch, Morton 75
Ehrenskjöld, Gori 94
Emery, Fred 96, 110, 114-15, 284-85, 307, 324
Ernst, Hanne Sjelle 94, 107
Fornari, Franco 209, 213
Freud, Sigmund 46, 54-55, 130, 173, 208, 273, 275, 283, 313
Gibb, Jack 74, 77, 82-85, 114, 229, 242
Hein, Piet 51, 271, 302
Higgin, Gurth 94, 104-5, 107, 112, 114, 159, 257, 277, 284, 286, 323
Hitler, Adolf 14, 35, 106, 210
Hjelholt, Berit (b. Erikson) 18-19, 31, 36, 56, 69-71, 73, 95, 112, 183, 205
Horwitz, Murray 115, 257, 323
Joenstad, Trygve 69, 94, 99, 100, 106-7, 115, 282, 287, 290-97
Kight, Dr. 71-72, 74, 220, 225
Klein, Melanie 109, 173, 207, 209, 318
Köhler, Wolfgang 173
Laing, Ronald D. 129
Lanzetta, John 74
Lauritzen, Ian 28, 157, 159
Lehman, Alfred 37
Lehner, George 98, 122

Lennung, Åke 104, 115
Lewin, Kurt 13, 22, 53, 69, 75, 77-83, 85, 88-90, 109-10, 115, 143, 147, 150-51, 171, 173-74, 179-81, 219, 225, 316
Lieberman, Morton 123
Lindner, Traugott 69, 92, 99, 107, 124, 277, 286
Lippitt, Gordon 69, 77
Lippitt, Ronald 77, 80, 83-84, 115, 173, 219
Luft, Joseph 69, 85-86, 115
Madsen, Benedicte 9, 13, 14, 23, 31, 35-36, 44, 68-70, 79, 84, 115, 133, 137, 140, 159, 185, 315, 320
Markillie, Ron 173
Marrow, Alfred 79, 81, 83, 115, 225
Marx, Karl 208, 273, 275, 283, 286, 313
Miles, Mathew 29-30, 69, 101-2, 107, 114-15, 123, 227-28, 231, 237-38, 242, 277, 286, 322
Morin, Edgar 208-9, 213
Nayar, K.P. 186-88
Nylen, Donald 69, 94, 98-99, 197, 159
Outze, Børge 48, 52-55
Pagès, Max 29, 87, 94, 107-9, 122, 127, 173, 203, 205-7, 209, 213, 273, 275, 284
Perlmutter, Howard 222
Pines, Malcolm 314
Rabbie, Jaab 124
Reich, Wilhelm 208
Rogers, Carl 206
Rubin, Edgar 50-55
Seidenfaden, Erik 48
Stock, Dorothy 123
Tagore, Rina 192, 194, 197
Thorsrud, Einar 96, 107, 114-15, 281
Trist, Eric 115, 257, 285-86, 323
Vansina, Leopold 27-28, 106-8, 119, 121, 129-31, 173
Visholm, Steen 30-31, 80, 311, 313
Wertheimer, Max 173
Willert, Søren 9, 13, 14, 23, 31, 35-36, 44, 68, 70, 79, 84, 115, 133, 137, 140, 159, 315, 320
Wundt, Wilhelm 38
Yalom, Irvin 123

SUBJECT INDEX

Chaos; Chaos Theory 112-3, 113, 146, 209, 302-23

Client; client system 10-11, 20, 25, 28, 40-1, 59, 61, 65, 72, 86, 94, 98-99, 100, 109-10, 133, 136-39, 147-48, 151-52, 153, 154-56, 165, 174, 176, 179, 204, 320

Communism 14, 129, 186-90

Complexity 28-29, 92, 143, 143, 156, 205, 208-9, 273, 284, 302-7

Concentration camp; Porta Westphallica 10, 12, 15, 23-24, 27, 35-36, 44, 55, 66-67, 70-71, 84, 97, 99, 122, 126, 133, 159, 174, 159, 198, 315

Conflict; social conflict 56-57, 60, 63, 66, 70, 73, 80-84, 102-6, 123, 127, 168, 175-76, 178, 181, 209-10, 236, 245, 252, 255, 276-7, 313, 303

Class conflict; class struggle 208, 212, 275
Conflicting forces 43, 49, 124, 196, 307
Value conflict 16, 63

Consultancy; consultation work 5, 13, 17, 20, 21, 27, 29, 69, 71-2, 105, 109, 111, 113, 128, 143, 147, 150, 155, 176, 180, 185, 231, 276, 281, 289-90, 296-97, 309, 314

Consultancy methods; consultancy intervention 21, 151, 287
Consultancy profession 2
Consultancy trainee 17, 21
Consultant 11, 17, 21-22, 25, 27-28, 30, 59, 64-65, 69-111, 119, 125-7, 129-30, 133, 135-40, 143, 145-51, 171, 175, 176, 183, 185, 192, 196, 203, 220, 231-32, 241, 249-51, 273, 275, 277, 280, 189-90, 297-8, 302, 306-9, 314, 316
Consultant role 27, 59, 69-114, 125, 143, 191, 198, 234, 241, 262, 316
Group consultant 128, 314
Management consultancy 41, 62

Organizational consultancy 13, 17-8, 41, 119, 276-77
Organizational consultant 18, 77, 108, 119, 128, 130, 136, 139, 145, 148
Process consultation 69, 92
See also: Boundary/Boundary keeper; Trainer

Control 61, 111, 122, 148, 177, 220-21, 232, 280
Self control 177, 240

Cooperation 82, 84, 86, 109, 100, 109-110, 155, 157, 176, 212, 219, 239, 247, 254, 256, 262,-63, 308, 316

Cybernetics 210

Danida 91, 183

Danish Technological Institute 16-17, 40-41, 62-63, 66, 70-71, 89, 93-94, 100

Danish Welfare State 16, 38-39, 42

Decision; decision making 15, 48, 56-57, 82, 96, 137,145, 160, 162-68, 249-59, 267-69, 280, 285, 297, 303, 307, 317

Defence; defence mechanisms 43, 130, 148, 156, 175, 195, 209, 211, 224, 240, 252, 318-19

Democracy; democratic; democratization 41, 54, 74, 78, 80, 82-85, 85, 93, 96, 97-98, 110, 113, 186-90, 195, 210, 247, 254, 311, 314, 316, 318-19

Design; laboratory design 28-30, 59, 69, 73-74, 76-77, 83, 87, 90, 97-98, 101-3, 112, 123, 143, 147, 150-66, 157, 159, 169, 190, 222, 229-42, 247, 257, 275

Dialectics 203, 206, 212

Distance; social distance; observational distance 11-12, 59, 65, 81, 87, 100, 121, 194, 261, 263, 278

Dynamic; dynamics 28, 30, 78-79, 125-26, 145-56, 169, 173, 191

Group dynamics 5, 17-8, 27-28, 45, 69, 71, 75, 78, 81-84, 86, 88, 97, 99, 105-10, 113-14, 119, 123-24, 133, 139, 160, 162, 173, 176, 206, 220, 313-14, 316-17, 319
Inter-group dynamics 157, 168, 176, 230
Organizational dynamics; system dynamics 107, 146-49, 152, 159-60, 168, 176, 230, 299, 301, 303-7, 314

See also: Psychodynamic

Emmaboda Glass Factory 104

Emotion; feeling; affect 28, 46, 57, 86, 100, 102, 111, 119, 123-5, 128, 133, 136-40, 147-50, 172, 175, 178-80, 191-98, 206-10, 234, 232-42, 249, 252, 263, 265-66, 273, 278-79, 282, 284, 292-94, 301, 303, 318

EIT see: European Institute for Trans-National Studies in Group and Organizational Development

Engagement; social involvement 11, 15, 20, 72, 78, 80, 95, 100, 104, 109, 110, 113-14, 180, 201, 235, 237, 310, 317

Entropy 100

European Institute for Trans-National Studies in Group and Organizational Development (EIT) 23, 27, 69, 98-99, 101, 105-9, 120, 121-23, 127, 134, 135, 137-38, 171, 174, 203, 205, 277, 281, 288, 290

Exercise; laboratory exercise; group exercise 75, 77, 85, 90, 93, 95, 123, 126, 229-34, 230, 232, 236, 238, 240-41

Experiental; experiential learning 30, 31, 37, 50, 63, 75-6, 79, 82, 88, 93, 224

Experiment; experimentation 29, 31, 38, 43, 46, 53-54, 72, 76, 79-82, 88, 90, 103, 108, 111, 147, 150, 160, 168, 205-6, 217-23, 227, 234-36, 239, 243, 245-47, 251, 255-56, 257, 259-60, 263, 266, 269, 270-71, 273, 275-79, 284, 317, 319

Fascism 14, 41, 80

Feedback; feedback session 73-74, 77, 83, 86, 90, 103, 160-64, 203, 217, 220-24, 231-33, 240, 295, 307
Feedback loop 210-11

Fels Center for Group Dynamics 71-75, 78, 85, 90, 101, 220

Field theory 69, 88, 179

Fieldwork 227, 230, 234, 287, 290

Fight/flight; flight 232, 238, 304

Fluctuation 113, 305, 309

Gestalt psychology 53, 88

Group; small group; group process; group structure 10-11, 28-31, 58, 60, 69, 72-73, 78-92, 84-85, 88-92, 101-3, 107-8, 111, 119, 123-26, 128, 136-39, 145, 147, 151, 153-55, 159-68, 171, 175-78, 179, 191-94, 198, 203, 205, 206-9, 220, 231-32, 235-236, 238-41, 243, 249-54, 257, 274, 275-79, 280-85, 291-97, 303, 305, 308-9, 311, 313-20

Complementary groups 102, 165
Group atmosphere; social climate 57, 73, 80, 84, 104, 175, 177, 201, 210, 219, 224, 251
Group behaviour 191-92, 275, 219-24
Group cohesion 82, 255
Group consultant 128, 314
Group discussion 80, 111, 220, 240, 313

Laboratory; training laboratory;
    laboratory training, Human Relations
    Laboratory 29-30, 74-76, 78, 82-83,
    90, 92-94, 98, 101-4, 107, 111, 113,
    123, 150, 162, 173, 203, 205, 227, 229-
    42, 259-62, 276-77, 279

    Laboratory approach; laboratory
    method; laboratory design 28, 69, 74-
    76, 78, 82-83, 84-87, 90, 96, 99, 101-
    2, 157, 159, 161, 168, 183, 223, 227,
    229-56
    Laboratory movement 84-88, 99
    Laboratory staff; training staff 75-86,
    94, 98-9, 101-3, 107, 111, 119, 123-8,
    143, 149, 152, 153, 163, 175, 191-92,
    196-99, 227, 229-32, 257, 260-66,
    267-70
    T-Group 75-78, 82, 85, 90-91, 95, 101-
    2, 106, 123, 150, 178, 223, 229-41, 244,
    246, 277, 307

    See also: Group Relations
    Conference; Sensitivity training;
    Trainer; Training

Lauritzen Shipping Company 29, 95-98,
    173, 280, 287

Leadership 54-56, 90, 110-11, 217, 219,
    221, 262, 316

Learning; learning situation 16, 18, 22, 28,
    36, 37, 44-45, 47-48, 50, 63, 70, 76, 82-
    83, 84, 86, 88, 90, 92, 123, 126, 149-53,
    156, 157-69, 171, 177, 190-92, 196-99,
    227, 230-39, 277, 318

    Organizational learning 102, 171, 178

    See also: Inductive learning; Training

Lewinian tradition 5, 27-29, 69, 71, 78-81,
    109, 133, 157, 173, 183, 311

Linear; non-linear 146, 179, 302

Love 18, 44, 57, 105, 165, 167, 186, 206-7,
    302, 313

Military Psychology Work Group 5, 39-40,
    56, 58-60, 89

Mini-society 23, 30, 69-70, 98, 101-5, 107,
    127, 156, 157, 159-69, 205, 259-71,
    276-79, 267, 284, 314

    See also: Laboratory

Mission 10, 108, 113-14, 128, 267, 309

    See also: Purpose; Task

National Council for the Unmarried
    Mother and her Child 40, 55, 62, 64,
    90

National Training Laboratories (NTL) 17-
    18, 22, 74-76, 78, 83-6, 92-94, 97-98,
    101, 105-6, 122-23, 157, 159, 171, 173,
    231, 236, 276-77

Nazism 14-15, 35, 41-42, 84, 159, 316

Observation 14, 18, 41, 45, 57, 66, 74, 83,
    86, 89, 90, 92, 93, 103, 108, 129, 146-
    47, 161, 162-63, 171, 174-75, 178, 207-
    10, 217, 224, 231, 270, 291, 309

    Observer 50, 59, 73, 76, 92, 100, 146,
    175, 233-34, 254, 302, 309
    Participant observer 41, 100
    Self-observation 90, 140

Organization; organisational life;
    organizational processes 16, 21, 24,
    26, 30, 84, 94, 98, 101-2, 103, 105-9,
    119, 127, 130, 136, 138-40, 146-53, 156,
    159, 175-81, 183, 198-99, 207, 229-37,
    243, 273, 275, 281, 283-85, 303, 305,
    308-9, 315-19

    Democratic organization 93
    Good/bad organizations 49-52, 199,
    215

Network organization 94, 133
Organizational analysis; exploring organizational life 27, 35-67; 107, 307
Organizational boundary 17, 30, 275
Organizational change; organizational development 17, 27, 64, 66, 81, 82, 147, 160, 171, 197, 206, 287
Organizational consultancy 13, 17-18, 41, 119, 276-77
Organizational consultant 18, 77, 108, 119, 128, 130, 136, 139, 145, 148
Organizational disorder; organizational death 64, 100, 177-78
Organizational dynamics 107, 146, 148
Organizational experiment; experimental organization 227, 275, 276-80
Organizational learning 102, 171, 178
Organizational level 150, 209, 307
Organizational membership; organizational roles 14, 37, 63-7, 138, 147, 180, 199, 207, 273
Organizational psychology; organizational theory; organizational research 9, 10, 83, 107, 109, 122, 139, 177, 206, 275, 283-84, 311, 314-15
Organizational structure 10, 95, 113, 146, 245, 284

See also: EIT; System

Personal Growth 10, 84-85, 104, 243, 256

Phenomenology 50, 203, 206, 208

Porta Westphallica see: Concentration camp

Power; power structure; power struggle 10, 29, 50, 56, 84, 86-88, 95, 101-2, 108, 122, 124, 126-30, 161, 156, 175, 177-8, 181, 196-7, 201, 205, 207, 211, 227, 235, 276, 285, 314-18

Primary task see: Task

Process analysis; process awareness 75, 234, 250-53

Projection 29, 92, 139, 156, 183, 187-8, 194, 201, 208, 319

Projective identification 192, 200, 311

Psychiatry 40, 45, 105, 122, 261, 314-5

Psychoanalysis 54-55, 105, 109, 122, 128, 136, 173, 177-78, 183, 206, 208, 312, 318

Psychodynamic 31, 104, 203, 311, 317, 320

Psychological Laboratory, University of Copenhagen 16, 22, 37-39, 45-50, 54, 70, 88

Psychology 20, 21, 22, 37, 38, 39, 40, 41, 44, 47, 49-52, 56, 58-59, 62, 70, 73, 80, 88-89, 94, 96, 99, 103, 105, 107, 114, 119, 133, 143, 157, 166, 171, 206, 311, 313

Applied Psychology 18
Clinical psychology 40, 123, 203
Ecological psychology 41
Group psychology; group theory 73, 107, 229, 306
Humanistic psychology 84
Industrial psychology 133, 206
Occupational psychology 38, 315
Organizational psychology 83, 311, 314-15
Personality psychology 173
Psychology of society 28, 159, 169, 171, 180
Social psychology 13, 20, 26, 48, 58, 80, 83, 89, 1032, 104, 114, 119, 123, 160, 164, 171, 173-75, 177-81, 204, 238, 316-17

See also: Applied social psychology

Purpose 31, 37, 43, 49-50, 64, 75, 80, 84, 113, 137, 152, 162, 178, 180, 222-23, 261, 278, 299, 303-4, 309

See also: Mission; Task

Reality 20, 28-29, 76, 104, 107, 109, 129-31, 138, 155, 208, 227, 232-35, 238, 245-56, 299, 301, 317-19

Reality-testing 129
Inner and outer reality 138-39

Reflection 9, 11, 18-19, 25, 28, 35, 37, 46, 64, 73, 75, 83, 87-88, 92, 106, 114, 127, 137, 140, 148, 152, 155-56, 174-75, 180-82, 183, 185, 191, 203, 209, 257, 270, 302, 308-9

Self-reflectiveness (in systems) 303

Regression 80, 203, 207-10, 233-35, 241, 318

Research 10, 20-21, 22, 25, 29, 39, 45, 48-50, 54, 58, 72-74, 79-89, 93-6, 105-9, 123, 157, 161, 171, 173-79, 191, 203, 206-9, 229, 237, 257, 259-61, 270, 278, 315

Researcher 14, 21, 24, 28, 48, 53-54, 86, 94, 102, 104, 109, 113-14, 173-81, 220, 261, 285
Research methods; methodology 46, 59, 81, 104, 106, 150, 157, 159, 162, 175, 208, 212, 222
Research staff; research fellow 69-71, 74, 78
Searcher 95, 276
See also: Action research; Social science

Resistance 49, 81, 148, 150, 176, 192, 197, 233, 269, 290
Resistance movement 15, 23, 38, 52

See also: Defences

Responsibility 10-1, 22,26, 30, 52, 60, 62, 65, 67, 106, 111, 136, 140, 162, 167, 174, 211, 227, 232-33, 235, 241, 243, 249-54, 257, 263, 265, 281, 292, 294, 317

Irresponsibility 67, 292-93
Responsibility in freedom 28, 127

See also: Autonomy; Decision

Role; social role 13, 18, 22-3, 25, 28, 37-38, 41, 45, 66, 70-71, 74, 86, 91-92, 100, 143, 155, 191-92, 199, 201, 207, 217-221, 232-33, 236, 241, 250, 252, 257, 265, 267, 270-71, 276-77, 291, 294, 301, 307-8, 318-19

Organizational role 147, 199
Professional role 65, 87, 133, 174, 234, 268, 270
Role clarity 199
Role conflict 257
Role exchange 222
Role model 26, 174-75
Role performance; enactment 92, 151
Role-play 73, 77, 92-93, 95, 217, 220, 222, 242
Role shift 241
Role theory 222
Trainer role 69, 76, 92, 110. 232, 236, 241, 264, 270

See also: Consultation/Consultant role

Self-insight 215, 217, 219-23

Sensitivity training; sensi-group 75, 85, 259-60, 262-64, 275, 277

See also: Laboratory; Group Relations Conference

Skills 50, 53, 75, 93, 146, 160-62, 166-67, 190, 231, 241, 243, 281, 297, 317-18

Small Group see: Group

Socialism 14, 45, 129, 314, 316

Social psychology see: Psychology

Social science; social scientists 9, 80, 94, 104, 109, 122-23, 127, 130-31, 276, 280, 284-85, 290

Society; macro-society 10-11, 16, 18, 28, 30-31, 39-40, 43, 49, 57, 60, 64, 69, 78, 80-85, 95, 97, 101-4, 113-14, 131, 157, 159, 161, 165, 167-9, 176-77, 179-80, 195, 198, 201, 109, 211, 259, 261-62, 265-66, 270-73, 275, 277-79, 282, 284-85, 306, 315, 319-20

    Psychology of Society 28, 159-69, 171, 180
    Group training in understanding society 259-271
    Society experiment 269

    See also: Mini-society

Sociology 14, 16, 20, 48, 80, 89, 91, 94, 103, 104, 109, 203, 205, 206, 207, 208, 209, 212, 259-60

    Psychosociology 204, 206

Socio-technical approach 109, 173, 283-84, 306

Status; socio-economic status; status ladder 10, 102-3, 164, 167, 200, 247, 252, 259-60, 267, 282, 291-93

Structure; social structure 10, 30, 92, 104, 138, 143, 148-51, 161, 176, 180, 194, 196, 207, 210, 241, 165-66, 299, 303-9, 315

    Defensive structure 108
    Flexible structure 97, 108, 205, 284
    Group structure 69
    Motivational and cognitive structures 79
    Oedipal structure 207
    Organizational structure 10, 95, 113, 146, 245, 284
    Power structure 126-30, 207

Unconscious structure 175, 207
Unstructured groups 90
Structure and boundary 10, 69, 110-13, 168
Structure and function; structure and task 30, 113, 299, 304-5, 309
Structure and process 176, 180

System; social system 10, 11, 28, 30, 35-36, 59-60, 64-65, 84, 88, 91-92, 95, 100, 102-4, 208, 210-13, 130, 136, 143, 146, 159, 161, 164, 168, 171, 175, 187-188, 190, 197, 206, 207-11, 218, 224, 227, 232-37, 240-41, 243, 248, 256, 261, 268, 273, 275, 278, 283-5, 293, 299, 301-9, 315-17

    Functional-structional systems theory 299, 304-5
    Open and closed systems 179, 280-81
    Open system theory 10, 146
    Psychodynamic systems theory 311, 317
    Psychological system; psychic system 91, 93, 302
    Socio-mental system 206-7
    System development 18, 21, 232-34, 241
    System model 203-5
    System theory; systems thinking 10, 30, 91,110, 133, 136, 139, 146-7, 165, 171, 173, 179-80, 183, 185, 189, 299, 303-4, 307, 311, 317

    See also: Group; Organization

Task 10-11, 25, 49-52, 55-60, 64, 66, 72, 76, 92-3, 97, 100, 106, 108-9, 112-13, 143, 147-48, 151-56, 167-68, 188, 191, 198-9, 201, 223, 230-34, 277-78, 291, 299, 301-5, 308, 315

    Primary task 10, 49-52, 55, 57, 143, 147-8, 151-56, 188, 191, 198
    Task consciousness 59
    Unfinished task 79

    See also: Mission; Purpose

Tavistock; the Tavistock tradition 5, 49, 106, 109-12, 119, 125, 128, 159, 173, 184, 191, 277, 283-84, 306, 314

The Tavistock Institute of Human Relations 82, 104, 107, 124, 257, 276, 306

Se also: Group Relations Conference; Socio-technical approach

Temporary system; temporary community 9, 102, 257, 260, 275, 277, 279, 284-85

Tension 60, 79, 88-89, 101, 105, 111, 136, 148, 152, 267, 177, 305, 315

T-group see: Laboratory

Theory and practice 58, 79, 82, 183

Therapy 84, 85, 143, 152, 161, 314

Trainer; trainer role; group trainer 69-70, 74-78, 85-87, 90-92, 99, 102, 110-11, 114, 119, 175, 185, 217, 220-24, 227, 230-37, 241, 264, 270, 273, 275, 277, 307

Trainer education 76-77

See also: Laboratory; Training

Training; group training; training group 27-30, 74-78, 86-88, 90, 101, 104, 105-9, 112, 119, 138, 150, 160-61, 168, 206, 217, 220, 222-24, 229-42, 243, 245, 259-71, 275, 280-81, 292, 306-7, 309, 314

Leadership training; management training 95, 160, 219, 229, 277
Training methods 74, 107, 112, 156-57, 168, 231

Training for reality 28, 160, 245-50

See also: Exercise; Laboratory/ Laboratory training; Trainer

Unconscious 29, 111, 119, 125, 129-30, 139, 148-49, 151, 171, 175, 177-8, 183, 185-201, 203, 206-11, 263, 299

Unfreeze see: Change model

Union; labour union; trade union 64, 93, 230-39, 255-56, 259, 261, 277, 280, 283, 285, 292, 295, 307

University of Copenhagen 16, 37-38, 47, 70, 72, 76, 89

Unstructured; unstructured groups 90, 242, 273, 276, 279

Value, social; value system 15, 41, 49, 56, 63, 65-67, 80, 84-85, 113, 138, 159-60, 176-80, 186, 200, 212, 242, 279, 281, 285, 293, 317-18, 320

Value conflict 16, 63
Democratic values 82-84

Value system 80, 279, 281

Violence 29, 31, 60, 125, 195, 203, 208-12

Vust 18-20, 23, 26, 37, 63, 69-70, 74, 85-86, 94, 97, 112, 127, 183, 205

World War II 37-8, 40-4, 58, 78, 83-5, 96, 113-14, 212, 282, 291-92, 315